917.44 .B812

BT

50 Hik

DATE DUE

DATE DUE	
FEB 27 2002	
OCT 14 2003	
AUG 11 2005	
AUG 29 2005	
JAN 3 1 2006	
APR 2 3 2006	

GAYLORD   PRINTED IN U.S.A.

50 *Hikes*

In Massachusetts

**A Year-Round Guide to Hikes and Walks
from the Top of the Berkshires to the Tip of Cape Cod**

JOHN BRADY AND BRIAN WHITE

Third Edition

Photographs by the authors

Backcountry Guides

Woodstock, Vermont

An Invitation to the Reader

Developments, logging, and fires all take their toll on hiking trails, often from one year to the next. If you find that conditions along these 50 hikes have changed, please let the authors and publisher know, so that corrections may be made in future editions. Address all correspondence to:

Editor
50 Hikes Series™
Backcountry Guides
P.O. Box 748
Woodstock, VT 05091

Library of Congress
Cataloging-in-Publication Data

Brady, John, 1948–
    50 Hikes in Massachusetts : a year-round guide to hikes and walks from the top of the Berkshires to the tip of Cape Cod / John Brady, Brian White. –3rd ed.
        p. cm.
    Rev. ed. of: Fifty hikes in Massachusetts. 2nd ed. c1992.
    Includes index.
    ISBN 0-88150-454-8 (pbk. : alk. paper)
    1. Hiking—Massachusetts Guidebooks. 2. Massachusetts Guidebooks. I. White, Brian, 1936– . II. Brady, John, 1948– Fifty hikes in Massachusetts. III. Title. IV. Title: Fifty hikes in Massachusetts.
GV199.42.M4B73 1999
917.4404'3–dc21   99-28302
                                              CIP

Text and cover design by Glenn Suokko
Original trail maps by Richard Widhu
New maps by Mapping Specialists, Ltd.,
    Madison, Wisconsin
Cover photo by Paul Rezendes/New England
    Stock Photo

Photograph on page 193 from *A Hermit's Wild Friends* by Mason A. Walton (Dana Estes & Company, Boston, 1903). All other interior photographs by the authors.

Published by Backcountry Guides, a division of The Countryman Press, P.O. Box 748, Woodstock, VT 05091

Distributed by W. W. Norton & Company, Inc., 500 Fifth Avenue, New York, NY 10110

Printed in the United States of America

10 9 8 7 6 5 4 3 2 1

Acknowledgments

We thank the many park, reservation, and sanctuary personnel and friends whose knowledge, courteously shared, greatly assisted us in the research for this book. We thank Catherine Baker, Nils Nadeau, and Ann Kraybill, our editors, for their insight, patience, and experienced criticism of the text. J. B. thanks Nancy, Caitlin, Mairin, and Owen for their companionship, aid, and understanding throughout this project, and Jean Dempsey, David Dempsey, and Don Siegel for their assistance and hospitality. B. W. thanks Connie Soja for her help and loving patience and Al Curran and Mark Wilson for their tolerance as he detoured from joint endeavors to complete this project.

50 Hikes at a Glance

HIKE	REGION
1. Alander Mountain	Western
2. Mount Race and Mount Everett	Western
3. Bartholomew's Cobble	Western
4. Beartown State Forest	Western
5. Monument Mountain	Western
6. Pleasant Valley Wildlife Sanctuary	Western
7. Warner Hill	Western
8. Saddle Ball Mountain	Western
9. Heart of Greylock	Western
10. Mount Greylock	Western
11. Berlin Mountain	Western
12. Spruce Hill	Western
13. Notchview Reservation	Western
14. Dorothy Francis Rice Sanctuary	Western
15. Granville State Forest	Western
16. Laughing Brook Wildlife Sanctuary	Central
17. Mount Tom	Central
18. Arcadia Wildlife Sanctuary	Central
19. Mount Holyoke	Central
20. Mount Norwottock	Central
21. Mount Toby	Central
22. Conway State Forest	Central
23. High Ledges Wildlife Sanctuary	Central
24. Mount Grace Grace State Forest	Central
25. Northfield Mountain	Central

DISTANCE (miles)	RISE (feet)	VIEWS	I	II	III	NOTES
5.0	840	★		★		Spectacular views over three states
7.7	2010	★			★	Spectacular views, Appalachian Trail
2.9	460	★	★			Unusual vegetation, neat rocks
7.8	1160	★			★	Wild woods, beaver ponds
2.7	900	★		★		Rocky summit and Indian legends
2.5	1000	★		★		Beaver-made wetlands
6.0	810	★		★		Appalachian Trail, woods
7.4	1770	★		★		Old roads and fir-topped mountains
4.5	1747	★			★	Explore state's highest mountain
8.2	2908	★			★	A long five-peak traverse
4.5	1720	★		★		Loop along the Taconic Crest Trail
2.6	680	★	★			Easy walk for all to great views
5.4	790			★		Woods and fields, nice trails
3.8	570			★		Several easy trails, woods and ponds
4.7	580			★		Beautiful river walk
3.0	320		★			Thornton Burgess stories locale
3.6	980	★		★		Views from rocky basalt ridge
1.5	80	★	★			Woods, wetlands, and river dynamics
2.7	1000	★		★		Loop along high ridge with views
3.1	820	★		★		"Horse Caves" of Shays's Rebellion
4.1	1040	★		★		Fire tower vista, conglomerate
7.7	1250			★		Woods roads, bear sighting here
2.5	610	★	★			View, many plant species
3.9	1138	★		★		Views, tall tower, and tree rings
5.9	1250	★		★		Many trails, visitor programs

DISTANCE (miles) RISE (feet) VIEWS DIFFICULTY (see page 16) I II III

50 Hikes at a Glance

HIKE	REGION
26. Northeast Quabbin	Central
27. Harvard Forest	Central
28. Mount Watatic	Central
29. Crow Hills	Central
30. Wachusett Mountain	Central
31. Wachusett Meadows Wildlife Sanctuary	Central
32. Great Meadows National Wildlife Refuge	Eastern
33. Charles W. Ward Reservation	Eastern
34. Hellcat Swamp Nature Trail	Eastern
35. South Plum Island	Eastern
36. Halibut Point	Eastern
37. Ravenswood Park	Eastern
38. Ipswich River Wildlife Sanctuary	Eastern
39. Middlesex Fells Reservation	Eastern
40. Rocky Woods	Eastern
41. Stony Brook Wildlife Sanctuary	Eastern
42. Moose Hill Wildlife Sanctuary	Eastern
43. Blue Hills Reservation	Eastern
44. World's End	Eastern
45. Whitney and Thayer Woods	Eastern
46. Great Island	Eastern
47. Wellfleet Bay Wildlife Sanctuary	Eastern
48. Marconi Beach	Eastern
49. Felix Neck Wildlife Sanctuary	Eastern
50. Caratunk Wildlife Refuge	Eastern

DISTANCE (miles)	RISE (feet)	VIEWS		I	II	III	NOTES
4.2	340	★	★				Man-made wilderness, old homes
4.4	470	★			★		Museum, fire tower, forest studies
2.8	800	★			★		Bird's-eye panoramas
4.4	1070	★			★		Mid-State Trail, rock-climbing cliffs
2.8	920	★				★	Views: Boston to Greylock
2.3	440	★				★	Beaver wetland to hilltop views
1.5	30	★	★				Wetland birds by the Concord River
4.0	600	★			★		Solstice stones and a northern bog
1.9	140	★	★				Sandy dunes and sea breezes
3.0	60	★	★				Sandy beaches and glacial geology
1.5	170	★	★				Granite shores and ocean views
3.5	390		★				Woods, wetland, quarry, erratics
3.3	240	★	★				Explore a grotto, eskers, and ponds
7.4	1540	★				★	Great views, long hike, volcanic rock
2.8	485	★			★		A stony whale and echoing pond
0.6	30	★	★				Wetlands: close-up and beautiful
3.5	585				★		In the woods: pines to swamps
4.1	1370	★			★		Rugged woods, many trails
4.0	370	★			★		Drumlin islands with landscaping
3.4	290	★			★		Dark woods and bright hilltop
7.5	230	★			★		Sandy trails and an old tavern site
3.0	150	★	★				Salt marshes and woodland trails
5.9	140	★			★		Beach hike to cedar swamp boardwalk
1.9	30		★				Coastal wetlands and wildlife
2.0	140		★				Fields, woods, streams, birds, muskrats

DIFFICULTY (see page 16)

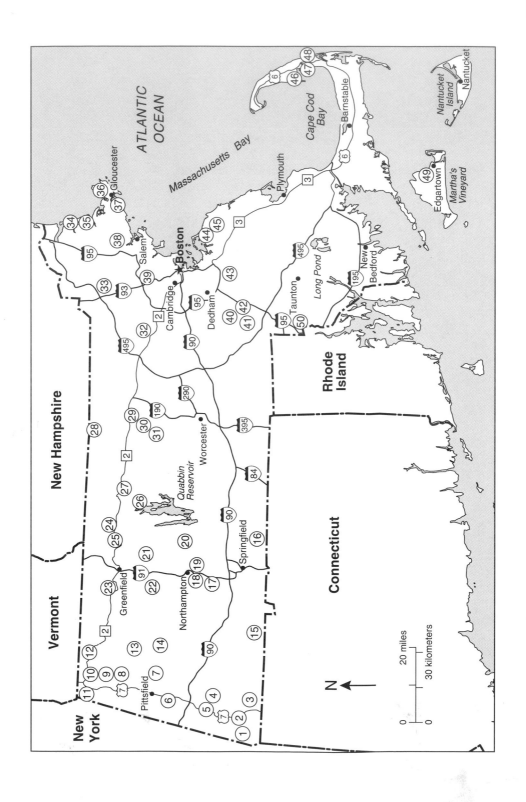

Contents

Eastern Massachusetts

Introduction

Massachusetts offers a surprisingly rich variety of beautiful places where you can hike in solitude or in company to refresh yourself both physically and spiritually. This guidebook tells you not only where to find and how to explore 50 of those beautiful places but also about the plants, animals, rocks, minerals, landscapes, and human artifacts that you may discover along the way. It will lead you along parts of the state's long and varied coastline; through swamps, marshes, and woodlands of many public and private parks, sanctuaries, and reservations; to spectacular views and summits in central and western Massachusetts; and along portions of the Appalachian, Metacomet–Monadnock, and Mid-State Trails.

Each hike is designed to fit into a day's outing, and many can be completed within a morning or an afternoon. We have included hikes at various skill levels, along with sufficient information for you to evaluate each hike's suitability for your own requirements. Equal space is devoted to the mechanics of locating and navigating each hike and to the natural history of the areas visited. Although the hike descriptions reveal only glimpses of the rich treasures that await your own explorations, we have tried to open a few doors to enhance your appreciation of the Massachusetts countryside.

The 50 hikes are grouped in this book geographically into western, central, and eastern regions. Within each region, hikes are numbered in a clockwise sequence, beginning in the southwest or west. A rough location for each hike is shown both on the state map that opens this book and on a generalized road map that opens each regional section. Specific driving instructions to the start of each hike are given in the text describing the hike.

For easy reference and comparison, we have listed certain standard information at the head of each hike. Total distance is the map distance of the hike route as measured on the pertinent United States Geological Survey (USGS) topographic map(s). Maximum elevation is the elevation above sea level of the highest point of the hike. Vertical rise is the sum of the elevation increases on the uphill portions of the hike as determined from the contours on the topographic map(s). Trailhead lists the latitude and longitude for the parking area. To help you select hikes for particular outings, we have included a summary table of the hikes beginning on page 6, along with an estimate of the overall degree of difficulty of each.

Hiking time was calculated from the total distance and vertical rise using a formula of ½ hour for each mile of distance with an additional hour for each 1,000 feet of vertical rise. This formula gives a minimum estimate of the time required for a hiker with some experience to cover the route, not counting time for stops. **Do not assume that the tabulated hiking time will accurately reflect the amount of time you will need to complete any particular hike until you have learned how your own pace compares with this formula.** Each hiker walks at a rate appropriate to her or his own interests and abilities.

The map listing is the quadrangle name of the current USGS topographic map that

Harvard Forest

covers the region of the hike. Most maps listed are metric 7½' x 15' quadrangles having a height of 7½ minutes latitude and a width of 15 minutes of longitude (in Massachusetts, roughly 9 by 13 miles). Relevant portions of these maps accompany the hike descriptions, with the hike routes indicated by heavy lines. Although it is possible to complete the hikes following only the directions given in the text, an ability to trace your progress on the topographic maps will not only enrich your appreciation of the countryside but will also provide an extra measure of safety for any outing.

If you wish greater map coverage, visit the U.S. Geological Survey web site at (http://mapping.usgs.gov/). There you will be able to obtain information about the latest maps and how to order them. For a paper index and ordering information, request a copy of "Massachusetts, Connecticut, and Rhode Island Map Index" (Publication MQTMAAPP30) from USGS Information Services, Box 25286, Denver Federal Cen-

ter, Denver, CO 80225 (telephone: 1-888-275-8747). Map information specific to Massachusetts may be obtained from the Earth Science Information Office, Blaisdell House, University of Massachusetts (http://riga.fnr.umass.edu/tei/esio/). Topographic maps may also be purchased from many local dealers. Check your telephone book (Maps-Dlrs. in the Yellow Pages) or examine the USGS list of dealers on the web (http://mapping.usgs.gov/esic/map_dealers/index.html). Easy-to-read maps for some state reservations are available from New England Cartographics, 425 State Street, Amherst, MA 01002 (413-549-4124).

The trailhead listing gives you the latitude and longitude of the parking area for each hike. We have added this information because of the popularity and availability of GPS (Global Positioning System) technology at increasingly modest cost. You do not need a GPS unit to navigate these hikes, and we did not use GPS to prepare them.

Nevertheless, GPS is very helpful in wilderness hiking and you may wish to practice the use of GPS on the well-charted paths of this book.

After you've done a few hikes, you'll learn what your own needs are when you're on an outing in Massachusetts. If you are not an experienced hiker, you may find it useful to read one of the many books available on hiking per se before setting out. All hikers require comfortable footgear appropriate to the terrain being traversed: Canvas walking shoes may do for dry, level ground, but a stiff-soled boot is recommended for rocky, uneven terrain. Clothing suitable to the season, elevation, and weather will make your hike more pleasant. Remember that temperature falls roughly 3.5 degrees Fahrenheit for each 1,000 feet of elevation increase. A raincoat or rainsuit is a useful precaution against windchill and sudden weather changes. In addition, most hikers will want to carry drinking water, insect repellent, and a compass.

New England hikers should be informed about Lyme disease and the deer ticks that can spread it. Deer ticks are tiny, not much bigger than the head of a pin, and difficult to spot. Like other ticks, they will try to attach themselves to your skin and suck your blood. If the tick is carrying the spiral-shaped bacteria, spirochetes, you can catch Lyme disease (named after Lyme, Connecticut, where it was first recognized in the United States). The best protection against Lyme disease is to wear long pants tucked into your socks, to spray your pants with a strong insect repellent, and to check your skin for ticks after each outing. Parents need to do this for their children. A vaccine against Lyme disease has been developed, but it is not yet completely effective. So keep your eyes open for deer ticks and see your doctor if an unusual circular rash appears.

One goal of this guide is to introduce you to some of the geology, biology, and history of the localities we visited. To realize this goal, you should travel at a pace that will permit you to observe the details of the plants, animals, and rocks along the trail. The text for each hike offers detailed information about a few items of interest and mentions many more. Most of the burden and joy of discovery remains in your hands, however, and requires your commitment to the challenge of the hunt. Field guides such as those in the *Peterson Field Guide* series (Houghton Mifflin) and the *Audubon Society Field Guide* series (Alfred A. Knopf) are invaluable aids in this endeavor. With a good field guide in your hands, you can turn forests into trees and meadows into wildflowers. For additional information particularly pertinent to Massachusetts, we recommend Neil Jorgensen's book, *A Sierra Club Naturalist's Guide to Southern New England.*

If you've already learned to hike, enjoy, study, and love Massachusetts trails, you will need no reminders of trail etiquette; it comes naturally to those who appreciate their environment. However, if you're new to the woods, please make a personal commitment to becoming an invisible traveler: quiet so as to be unnoticed by others on the trail and careful so as to be undetectable by others who follow the same route on another day. Many of the hikes are on public or private lands governed by certain regulations: Please obey them. Some of the hikes border or cross private land: Please respect the owner's rights. If each hiker removes their own trash, photographs rather than picks the wildflowers, and resists the urge to perpetuate their initials, pockets of wilderness may survive for generations to come. Enjoy the trail, but in ways that preserve the rights of others to enjoy it in the same fashion.

Introduction

For further information about hiking opportunities in Massachusetts, you may wish to write or call one or more of the following organizations:

Massachusetts Department of
Environmental Management
DEM Office of Public Information
100 Cambridge Street
Boston, MA 02202
617-727-3180
1-800-831-0569 (within Massachusetts)
http://www.state.ma.us/dem

Metropolitan District Commission
Public Information Office
20 Somerset Street
Boston, MA 02108
617-727-5215
http://www.state.ma.us/mdc

The Trustees of Reservations
Long Hill
572 Essex Street
Beverly, MA 01915-1530
978-921-1944
http://www.ttor.org

Massachusetts Audubon Society
South Great Road
Lincoln, MA 01773
617-259-9500
http://www.massaudubon.org

Appalachian Mountain Club
5 Joy Street
Boston, MA 02108
617-523-0636
http://www.outdoors.org

The 50 Hikes: A Quick Summary

How difficult you find any hike will depend on your abilities. However, to aid in your selection of outings, in the summary chart on page 6 we have divided the 50 hikes into three groups as follows:

I. Hikes accessible to most people and especially good for families with small children.

II. Moderately strenuous hikes for which some previous hiking experience is advisable.

III. Strenuous hikes for experienced, agile hikers.

Many of the hikes can be made less arduous by following shortcuts suggested in the text, which you should examine before you dismiss any hike or locality as being beyond your abilities.

Key to Map Symbols

--- main trail

••••• alternate or side trail

(P) parking

(T) trailhead

(R) rest rooms

(W) water

lookout

bridge

Western Massachusetts

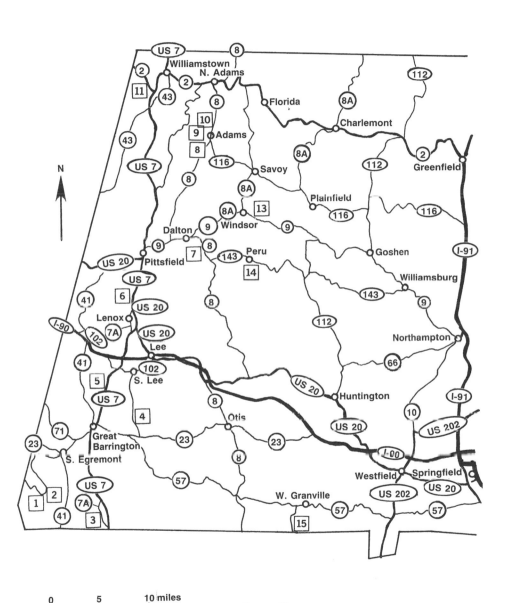

Western Mass.

0   5   10 miles

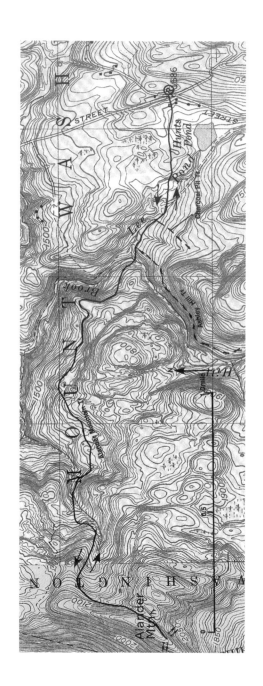

1

Alander Mountain

Total distance: 5.0 miles (8.0 km)

Hiking time: 3½ hours

Maximum elevation: 2,239 feet (682 meters)

Vertical rise: 840 feet (256 meters)

Map: USGS Ashley Falls (7½' x 15')

Trailhead: 42°05'09" N, 73°27'43" W

Nothing you encounter on the way up Alander Mountain can prepare you for the views from its summit. You will walk across beautiful flower-filled meadows, through a variety of woodlands where the sound of singing birds and splashing streams flavors the sylvan quiet, past sparkling rapids and clear, green rock pools and extensive stands of pink-flowering mountain laurel. But all these delights hardly hint that the top of Alander Mountain will give you the best views you can find anywhere in western Massachusetts.

Alander Mountain lies in Mount Washington State Forest, in the extreme southwestern corner of the state. To reach the trailhead, drive south on MA 41 past the intersection with MA 23 in South Egremont for 0.1 mile to a right turn onto Mount Washington Road, just beyond Mill Pond. Stay on the paved roads at all intersections with gravel roads—the name changes to East Street—and in 9.1 miles you will reach the forest headquarters. The parking area and public toilet are behind the building.

The blue-blazed Alander Mountain Trail, your route to the summit, heads west from the parking area across open meadows that soon merge with woodland. On early-summer days, you may be tempted to dawdle along this first stretch of your hike. Many flower species that bloom in succession through late spring and early summer at lower elevations seem to flower at the same time here in the high meadows, at around 1,700 feet. You can spend an enjoyable hour or so with a good flower guide, identifying heal-all,

Hikers on the summit of Alander Mountain

hope clover, speedwell, and many other species. Looking south, you will have splendid views over Hunts Pond to a narrow valley and encircling mountains.

The trail passes to the left of a large sugar maple, and soon the wide, gently undulating path takes you into a mixed second-growth woodland of small hemlock, white pine, both white and gray birch, black cherry, red maple, and quaking aspen. You will immediately recognize when you have reached the far edge of the overgrown former meadow, as the trail abruptly enters a cool, deep-shaded grove of mature hemlocks. Little sunlight penetrates the large conifers, and only a few sarsaparilla and ferns in better-illuminated patches manage to survive on the needle-carpeted floor. What a sharp contrast it is to the sunny meadows and mixed woodlands! But the hemlocks soon give way again to beech and maple, as the grassy trail passes through a stone wall and drops moderately into an-

other former meadow now in the early stages of reversion to woodland.

Looking west from this meadow, you will have your first view of Alander Mountain. The trail descends easily through many meadowland flowers, much meadowsweet, and an abundance of delicious blueberries and wild strawberries, toward a large pine that guards a former homesite. Pass to the left of the pine and cross the bridge over Lee Pond Brook. Watch for elderberry, purple-flowering raspberry, tall meadow rue, and blue European columbine near the stream. After walking through a short stretch of mixed woods, you will pass the narrow, poorly defined Charcoal Pit Trail on the left. You should stay on the Alander Mountain Trail as it descends gently, paralleling Lee Pond Brook on your right beyond the stone wall. After crossing over a small stream, the trail swings west and in 300 feet divides, with Ashley Hill Trail going left and your trail to Alander Mountain going right.

The trail drops to reach Ashley Hill Brook just upstream from its confluence with Lee Pond Brook. You may wish to linger here amid the rushing waters and sunbathe on the rock benches of this attractive and relaxing spot. Take a few moments to examine the remnants of a bridge over the stream immediately below the confluence of the two brooks. The old bridge abutments, made of large boulders, stand on the stream banks amid the hemlocks.

Beyond Ashley Hill Brook, your route follows an old road and climbs easily through woods dominated by hemlocks. After leveling off to cross a small stream, it again rises gently through mixed woodlands of hemlock and gray, yellow, and white birch. The trail soon flattens out again as it swings left over a rounded ridge, where an impressively steep slope to the right plunges down to Lee Pond Brook. Many birds spend the summer in these woods, and along here you may well spot the hairy woodpecker, pil-eated woodpecker, junco, veery, ovenbird, American redstart, blue jay, rose-breasted grosbeak, or scarlet tanager. Skirting the hillside, the trail slowly and hesitantly gains height, losing a little here and there as it crosses small stream valleys. The old road you are hiking and the many stone walls that crisscross the steep slopes provide ample testimony to the devotion and hard labor of the people who settled and farmed this land in the mid-1700s. After passing a side trail to a primitive camping area, your trail crosses a ridge and a small stream before climbing again through a gorgeous parklike stretch, where large hemlocks, birches, and beeches rise high above an understory of mountain laurel. If you hike Alander Mountain in early summer, you will walk from here almost to the summit with the delicate pinks of the laurel flowers at your side.

At the next stream crossing you will be at 1,650 feet, the same elevation as the parking area, so your 1.5 miles of up-and-down walking has brought you no net gain in height. The trail passes beyond the old road and soon follows a more prominent stream, crosses it near a confluence, then continues uphill between the two tributaries for 500 feet before turning sharply left. In another 400 feet the trail swings right, once again parallels a stream, and then forks. The way straight ahead climbs steeply, but briefly, up rocky ledges, while the way right takes you to the same spot by an easier route. The trail continues west up a moderately steep slope and then swings to the left near the base of a cliff. Narrow now, the trail climbs easily at first, but then steepens by the south end of the cliff. You will have a respite from this toughest part of your hike just below the top of the ridge, where the trail flattens out and passes by a pleasant cabin where you can spend the night free on a first-come, first-served basis. A sign for the Taconic Trail greets you just beyond the cabin, but you want the trail to the summit of Alander Mountain, which goes right a few yards farther along. Your path initially goes steeply to the right up rocky ledges and then climbs more moderately to the open summit.

What a place! Magnificent views extend in all directions. From the southeast to the south, Mount Ashley, Mount Frissell, and Brace Mountain stand all in a row; to the west lie the Hudson River Valley and the Catskills, to the northwest, Albany and the Adirondacks beyond; to the north, Mount Greylock (Hikes 8, 9, and 10); and to the east, Mount Everett (Hike 2). This is one time you will be glad you bothered to carry your binoculars to a mountaintop.

Scrub oak, blueberries, and bearberry grow in the summit area, and you may see and hear the common yellowthroat, rufous-sided towhee, and catbird among the shrubs. In summer, red-tailed hawks and turkey vultures soar close by, and viewing these birds is a spectacle in itself. You will want to linger in this elevated place to enjoy the views, the sunshine, and, no doubt, your lunch. When you are ready to leave, you should have no navigational problems following the well-defined trail down, and in an hour or so you will be back at your car.

2

Mount Race and Mount Everett

Total distance: 7.7 miles (12.4 km)

Hiking time: 5 hours

Maximum elevation: 2,602 feet (792 meters)

Vertical rise: 2,010 feet (612 meters)

Map: USGS Ashley Falls (7½' x 15')

Trailhead: 42°02'58" N, 73°28'01" W

Many trails in Massachusetts reward hikers with overviews of the surrounding countryside, but few offer the spectacular, continuous vistas found along the high portions of the Mount Race–Mount Everett ridge. Acres of bare rock and a precipitous slope to the east open a panorama that would otherwise be obscured by the normally luxuriant growth of trees and shrubs. The Appalachian Trail follows the Race-Everett ridge, and many hikers rate this stretch of the trail as spectacular as the much higher Mount Greylock portion to the north. In both areas, an unusually high ridge has been juxtaposed with an unusually low valley by similar geologic processes. As described, this hike works best as a one-way hike with two cars. However, if you have only one car, there is still a great hike to the Mount Race summit and back again along the Appalachian Trail (8.3 miles total).

To get to the Mount Everett area, follow the driving instructions for Hike 1, but turn left at the sign for the Mount Everett State Reservation (7.4 miles after turning onto Mount Washington Road). Drive 0.3 mile to a parking area at a gate that may be locked to prevent cars from ascending Mount Everett. The road beyond the gate will be your return route at the end of the hike. Leave your second car here. (If your time is limited or you have small children with you, consider hiking the road that leads to the top of Mount Everett. Rising nearly 800 feet in 1 mile, this road will get your heart and lungs pumping. Your effort will be rewarded not only by a great view at the top, but also by lovely woods and frog-filled Guilder Pond

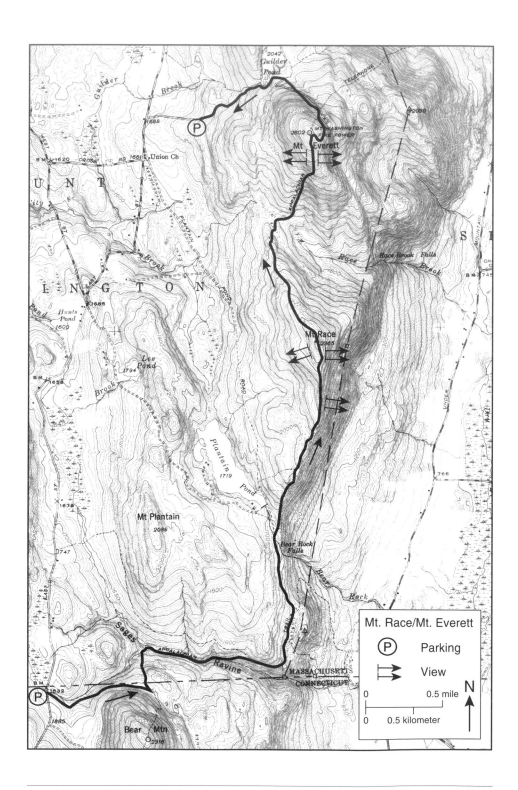

Mt. Race/Mt. Everett

Ⓟ Parking

▸ View

0 — 0.5 mile

0 — 0.5 kilometer

N

en route.) Return to Mount Washington Road, turn left, and continue south. In 0.3 mile, the main road turns right onto Cross Road at a church, but you should continue straight on East Street. The Mount Washington State Forest headquarters (and the start of Hike 1) will be on your right in 1.3 miles. Continue on East Street another 2.6 miles (gravel replaces asphalt in 0.4 mile) to a parking area on the left at the Massachusetts-Connecticut border.

A large sign announces that the Appalachian Mountain Club (AMC) maintains the parking area and trails here on land it owns. Follow a wide trail to the east around a gray metal gate as it winds through bright open woods thick with mountain laurel and through dark hemlock stands. You will soon come to a fork with a side path leading right to the Northwest Campsite and cabin of the AMC. Keep left with the main trail across a wooden bridge and along a slope as the stream drops away to your left into a deepening valley. The Appalachian Trail (AT) crosses your wide track as an equally wide track in a level area. Turn left onto the AT, following its white blazes north gently, then steeply, downhill into the hemlock darkness of increasingly deep Sages Ravine. Ignore another trail junction (Paradise Lane Trail) at the beginning of this downhill stretch.

Sages Ravine is filled with a lovely brook that offers pools to cool your feet in summer. Or are they lures for mosquito prey? Some are deep enough for a good soak or swim if you are small. Watch for folded outcrops of greenish schist, showing white quartz segregations typical of low-temperature metamorphic rocks. Holes in the rocks occur where calcite has dissolved in the acidic New England rain. There are lots of campsites here, but camping is restricted to one area due to overuse. Muddy sections and rocks slow your progress, but the trail is well used and clearly marked. Although you re-entered Massachusetts from Connecticut when you joined the AT, an AT sign welcomes you to Massachusetts as you cross the brook on large rocks and start your ascent of Mount Race.

The first uphill section is gentle, if rocky, with lush mountain laurel on this south-facing slope. Tall oaks tower over smaller maples and foot-high blueberry bushes. The AT makes a gradual 90-degree turn to the north to follow a wide, gently sloping bench. A cliff seems to rise on your left, which you soon climb along a gradual incline. Interestingly, you pass from younger (Ordovician) rocks to older (Cambrian or Precambrian) rocks as you go uphill, contrary to the expectation that younger rocks should be on top. This arrangement has been interpreted to mean that the rocks on top are part of a large slice that has been moved into place by faulting. Where the trail levels out somewhat, you cross a stream just above Bear Rock Falls. Follow the white-blazed AT uphill in the shade of tall hemlocks past a brown sign that announces Bear Rock Falls Campground. In summer you may hear the sounds of YMCA campers at Plantain Pond, far off to your left. Bedrock shows through the thin soil in many places as the path flirts with the edge of a cliff and views mostly hidden by trees. Ultimately (in about a mile) the soil gives out completely, and you emerge onto a ledge of bare rock that expands as you climb, eventually encompassing the entire top of Mount Race.

The view of the Housatonic Valley 1,500 feet below you to the east is truly awe-inspiring. So is the precipitous drop-off near the trail! Like most topographic features in Massachusetts, this large cliff is erosional in origin. Any rock above sea level will gradually be dissolved or broken and washed away by water, ice, wind, and gravity at a rate

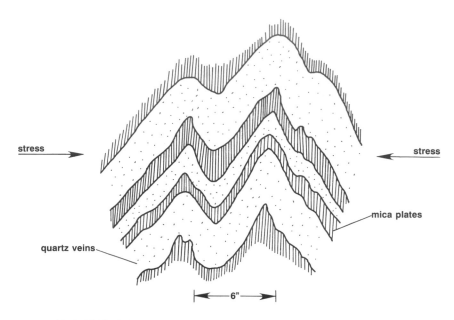

stress →

← **stress**

mica plates

quartz veins

|← 6" →|

Typical folds visible in the side of many outcrops when you are looking northward.

proportional to its elevation. Although erosion is slow in human terms—about ⅒ inch each century in this area—small differences in the rate of erosion of different rock types can lead to enormous differences in elevation over millions of years. The rocks you are standing on apparently erode more slowly than the rocks in the valley before you. The 1,500 feet of relief you see here could be produced in about 15 million years by a difference in erosion rates as little as 10 percent! Considering that these rocks are more than 400 million years old, it is perhaps surprising that these mountains exist at all.

If you can take your eyes off the wonderful view while climbing the open ridge, look carefully at the rocks at your feet. The sheen they display is imparted by tiny, glistening plates of the minerals muscovite and chlorite. These minerals grew while this rock, formerly a sediment, was buried to a depth of about four miles. Chemical reactions in the rock, driven by high temperatures and

pressures, produced the muscovite and chlorite and separated the quartz into prominently visible white veins. The entire mountain has been deformed by east–west stresses into folds that look much like the wrinkles that appear in a rug pushed from both ends. Folds large and small are delineated by the white quartz veins. Platy micas that grew while the region was being squeezed by some geologic vise were forced to line up in north–south ranks, paralleling the flanks of the folds (see illustration). Numerous examples of folding are visible on this bedrock ridge.

As you near the summit of Mount Race, notice how the trees in scattered pockets of soil are clearly stunted or dwarfed. In the harsh environment of this open ridge, the oak, birch, and pitch pine look more like exotic shrubs than trees. You should take a cue from the foliage and avoid Mount Race when the weather is foul; you will find little protection from a storm here. From the cairn-marked summit, the panorama extends for a full 360 degrees. Alander Mountain (Hike 1) lies immediately to the west; Bartholomew's Cobble (Hike 3) is a tiny bump in the valley to the southeast; Beartown State Forest (Hike 4) occupies some of the vast, forested expanse to the northeast; and Mount Greylock (Hikes 8, 9, and 10) caps a distinctive ridge to the north. Glaciers that 20,000 years ago not only filled the valleys but also covered Mount Race have smoothed and polished the rock on top into numerous dry, if slightly hard, picnic spots.

Unfortunately, it is not possible to ascend two mountains without a bit of descent in between. White Appalachian Trail blazes will guide you downward and across the col between Race and Everett. If you can take this hike in mid-June, you will find the mountain laurel bushes on the north slope of Mount Race crammed with blossoms. You may also recognize mountain ash here from

its distinctive compound leaves, red twigs, and gummy buds. As you lose elevation, the trees increase in stature only to become dwarfs again near the summit of Mount Everett. Trillium, bunchberry, and sarsaparilla grow where the trees are taller. In the col, you cross the upper reaches of Race Brook. If you come in spring or early summer, a detour onto the path following Race Brook down to its falls is strongly recommended. Although you must pay for the sight with a steep climb down and up several hundred feet, impressive cascades will reward your efforts.

Your climb up Mount Everett will be more difficult than that up Mount Race because of the steeper grade and the mountain already climbed. But many of the same treasures you found at the top of Mount Race await you atop Mount Everett, including views in all directions, blueberries, huckleberries, and scrub growth of gray birch and fire cherry. Following a New England practice of

Mount Race and Mount Everett from Hurlbut Hill

access for all, a road has enabled tourists to drive almost to the top of Everett, and the fragile summit environment has suffered. The hand of man is clearly at work around the somewhat dilapidated fire tower that crowns the peak but is closed to the public. However, any drawbacks are overshadowed by the stunning vista across portions of three states—Massachusetts, Connecticut, and New York.

Watch for the white blazes marking a right turn (east) and leading you past some final overlooks on your way down to the north. The Appalachian Trail briefly joins a wide trail between the summit and parking area but continues straight at the lowest switchback. Very clear grooves cut into polished bedrock in the woods here record the direction of ice movement (southeast) when glaciers last reigned. The Appalachian Trail crosses the paved summit road and descends to a picnic area (pit toilets available) next to Guilder Pond. Leave the trail there and follow the paved road 0.7 mile downhill to your car.

3

Bartholomew's Cobble

Total distance: 2.9 miles (4.6 km)

Hiking time: 2 hours

Maximum elevation: 1,034 feet (315 meters)

Vertical rise: 460 feet (140 meters)

Map: USGS Ashley Falls (7½' x 15')

Trailhead: 42°03'26" N, 73°21'02" W

Few localities in Massachusetts can claim the diversity of plant and animal species that has been observed in Bartholomew's Cobble. Even fewer concentrate so many species to such a high degree. Park wardens, visitors, and naturalists, notably C. A. Weatherby of Harvard University, have compiled a plant catalog of more than 700 species and a bird list of over 230 species sighted near this lovely Berkshire hill. Included are almost 50 species of ferns and nearly 500 of wildflowers. Clearly, Bartholomew's Cobble is a natural area worthy of some careful exploration. Although you can complete a circuit of this 277-acre property of the Trustees of Reservations in less than 2 hours, you should plan to spend at least half a day here. If you bring field guides to wildflowers, trees and shrubs, and birds, expect your day to be filled with challenge and discovery.

A circular, tree-covered hill of quartzite and marble forms the nucleus of this reservation on land farmed by George Bartholomew in the 1870s. Rising 100 feet above its embrace with the Housatonic River, the "cobble" probably evoked the image of a large cobblestone to early settlers. Walter Prichard Eaton, in his 1936 book, *Wild Gardens of New England,* described it as a "stone island ... rising from the alluvial bottom lands." The bottomlands are actually a flat-topped "sea" of sediment deposited at the bottom of glacial Lake Sheffield, which filled the Housatonic Valley 13,000 years ago. Finding itself in a flat-bottomed valley, the present-day Housatonic River seems unsure just which direction is downhill and

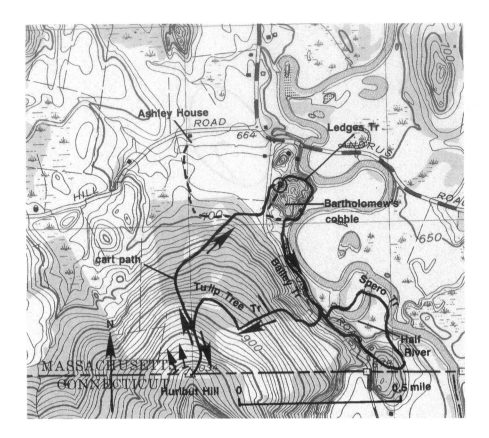

wanders about in drunken meanders that periodically short-circuit, leaving oxbow-shaped lakes to mature into swamps. Col. John Ashley was attracted by this oasis of flat farmland in the otherwise rugged Berkshires and in 1735 built adjacent to the cobble the first house in what is now Berkshire County.

To reach Bartholomew's Cobble, drive approximately 8 miles south from Great Barrington on US 7 through Sheffield to MA 7A, which forks to the right. Turn right onto MA 7A and travel 2.3 miles to the blinking light in the center of Ashley Falls. Turn right at the light onto Rannapo Road and follow it 0.9 mile to the first intersection, just beyond a large bridge. Turn left at the intersection onto Weatogue Road. A parking lot for the cobble is 0.1 mile on the left. A lovely new

visitors center has been built here since the last edition of this book was written. It is staffed by a warden or volunteers and open daily most of the year. A modest admission fee is charged to visitors who are not members of the Trustees of Reservations.

Well-marked trails begin at the north end of the grassy yard behind the visitors center. A sign on a wooden post identifies the beginning of Ledges Trail, your path. The clearly marked Ledges Trail circumnavigates the cobble in an eerie darkness created by hemlock trees, passing interpretive stops marked by numbered pillars. Acidic New England rain is neutralized by dissolving marble layers in the rocky cliffs, giving the soil on the cobble a higher-than-normal pH and favoring a distinct flora. Especially

Maidenhair spleenwort on moss-covered rocks

striking in May are clusters of red columbine set against the light gray rocks. Lush moss blankets the outcrops in many places, building soil to attract ferns.

The ledges themselves are part of the Stockbridge Formation, a sequence of shallow water ocean sediments, now mixed quartzite and marble, deposited on the edge of a continent in Cambrian time more than 500 million years ago. The marble portions are more easily dissolved in the rain, creating a weathered rock dotted with small holes, miniature caves for wood sprites. Radiating sprays of pearly white tremolite crystals up to 2 inches in length decorate the rocks in many places. You can see them low on the large rock to the left at the very start of the trail near the visitors center. Tremolite crystals, as well as contortions in the rock layering, attest to the high temperatures (perhaps 500 degrees centigrade) experienced by the rocks when they were buried beneath more than 4 miles of other rocks, now eroded away.

Not to be missed are the ant lions that may be in the sand at the base of a ledge by Station 12 on the eastern side of the main cobble. Each of these crafty larvae instinctively digs a cone-shaped depression in the sand. It then hides in the sand at the bottom, waiting to catch ants that tumble down the unstable slopes of an ingenious funnel to the lion's lair. Although these traps are much too small to trip you up, don't be caught by the poison ivy that thrives around the cobble. After looking for ant lions, you may wish to explore the flat, open field of Corbin's neck, in the center of a tight meander of the Housatonic River.

Returning to the trail, turn left onto white-blazed Bailey Trail, which leads south from Ledges Trail shortly after Station 13. Bailey Trail closely follows the west side of the river. Moist, fertile soil mantles the riverbank, supporting a plant community that contrasts sharply with that of the drier ledges. When the river is swollen with spring meltwater, it may wash over its bank, depositing a fresh layer of silt and sand. Here, where the river flows around a bend, water is driven by centrifugal forces against the western bank, which is undercut, causing conical wedges of soil to slump toward the water. Bailey Trail originally followed the bank closely, but has been moved uphill to drier, more stable ground and improved with small wooden bridges.

When you reach a trail junction in a stand of white pine, with Bailey Trail heading uphill to your right, continue straight to begin a 0.9-mile loop called the Sterling and Louise Spero Trail. (If you are short on time, turn right onto Bailey Trail to return to the parking area.) In a few yards, after descending to river level, turn left at a fork guarded by a magnificent eastern cottonwood tree with a prominent hole in the base of its trunk. The trail circles Half River, an oxbow lake that was undoubtedly the main channel of the river in John Ashley's time. You may find the tracks of raccoons (five toes) and other animals in the muddy approach to this pond. Paralleling the river, the trail meanders through woods, brush, and along mown paths across dandelion-dotted meadows.

As the trail leaves the river, it bends to the left up and into some rocky woods for a short tour of the side of another cobble, this time made of quartzo-feldspathic gneiss. After dropping briefly to cross a clearing, you will wind around boulders studded with red garnet crystals on the wooded slope above Half River. See if you can pick out the Stockbridge Formation rocks here, with their characteristic holes due to dissolved marble. The path descends to the large cottonwood tree, after which you retrace your steps 150 yards to the junction with Bailey Trail. Turn left at the junction and climb directly to graveled Weatogue Road, which you should cross to follow the white-blazed Tulip Tree Trail uphill into a forest kept free of underbrush by the darkness of more tall hemlock trees. Vines of wild grapes follow helical paths up some of these trees in search of the sun. At a large glacial erratic boulder (Stockbridge Formation), Boulder Trail departs right, but you should continue straight with Tulip Tree Trail. A sharp right turn and a downhill stretch precede your emergence into the sun along a clearing. Continue steadily uphill, passing another clearing and joining a cart path en route to the large field that covers the "summit" of Hurlbut Hill.

The summit is signaled by a square stone pillar marking the Massachusetts-Connecticut border and benches on which to sit and enjoy the unbelievable view across the wide Housatonic Valley and up to nearby Mount Everett (Hike 2). Plan extra time to savor this special place, which you may have to share with soaring hawks and grazing cows. When you must, retrace your steps along the cart path and continue downhill past Tulip Tree Trail all the way to Weatogue Road. Turn left and walk along the road for the last 150 yards to the parking area and your car. If you have time, visit the Colonel John Ashley House nearby. A guided tour of the house, preserved and restored by the Trustees of Reservations, is well worth the modest fee charged for entrance.

4

Beartown State Forest

Total distance: 7.8 miles (12.6 km)

Hiking time: 5 hours

Maximum elevation: 2,112 feet (643 meters)

Vertical rise: 1,160 feet (353 meters)

Map: USGS Great Barrington (7½' x 15')

Trailhead: 42°12'08" N, 73°17'19" W

Beartown Mountain, Wildcat Trail, Turkey Trail—these names evoke a feeling of wilderness that is quite appropriate even today for the high country east of Great Barrington. Bear sightings are not common, but neither are people sightings on the trails of Beartown State Forest. With more than 16 square miles of rugged woodland, Beartown is the third largest state forest in Massachusetts. Its only developed facilities are camping, picnicking, and swimming areas at Benedict Pond, and much of the forest remains quite inaccessible. In this hike, a part of the Appalachian Trail that traverses the forest has been combined with other trails and roads to create a circuit sample of this wild country with alternative routes for hikers of different interests and abilities.

The hike begins and ends at Benedict Pond. From the north or east, drive to the junction of US 20 and MA 102, just south of the Lee exit of the Massachusetts Turnpike, and then travel 2.5 miles west on MA 102 to South Lee. Turn left onto Meadow Street, cross the Housatonic River, then turn right immediately onto Beartown Mountain Road. Follow this road uphill past the forest boundary (1.5 miles) to a fork (2.5 miles). At the fork, turn right (downhill) onto Beartown Road and drive another 4.0 miles to Benedict Pond. Park on the left in a grassy lot just past the swimming area. If you're exploring the back roads of the Berkshires, take MA 23 east from Great Barrington or west from Otis to Blue Hill Road, 1.8 miles east of the junction of MA 23 and MA 57. Turn north onto Blue Hill Road and drive 2.1 miles to Beartown Road, where there are

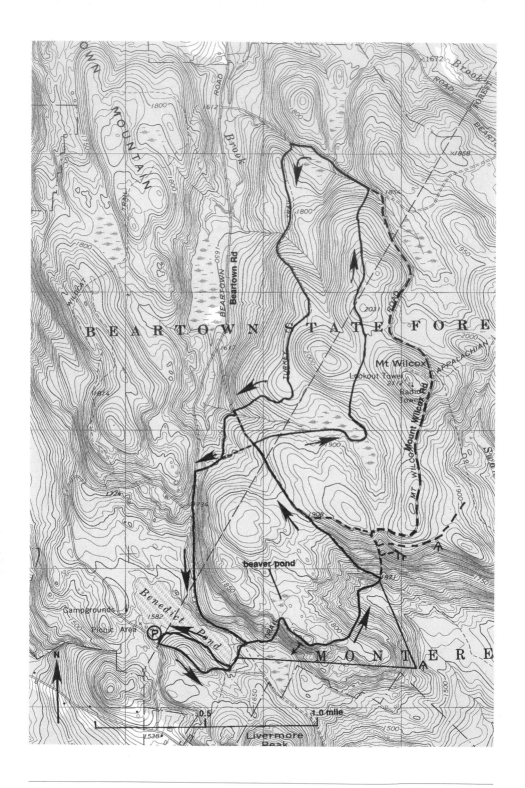

signs for Beartown State Forest. Turn right; in 0.4 mile watch for the grassy parking area on the right next to Benedict Pond. The state forest day-use fee will be collected by an attendant on summer days. Maps of the forest are available at a bulletin board near the entrance of the parking area.

A TO THE APPALACHIAN TRAIL sign indicates your route southeast from the bulletin board and uphill on the former route of Beartown Road. Moss and grasses grow in cracks where the asphalt has been raised and separated by the expansion of freezing water. Red oak, red maple, and white birch shade this road lined with bracken fern. Where the old road drops into a valley, turn left (northeast) onto the white-blazed Appalachian Trail, which quickly drops down to and along the southeast end of Benedict Pond. Spotted joe-pye weed mounts its fuzzy, pink flower clusters atop purple stems in the wet ground near the pond's edge. Boulders, logs, and a small bridge help you across the wet ground between east-tilted outcrops of gneiss. Past the pond, the trail jogs left across a bridge on an old road and then immediately right. Yellow flowers perched on a network of smooth, skinny, panicled hawkweed stems decorate the path in August.

For the next several minutes you will climb steeply up ledges of lichen-coated, Precambrian gneiss, situated so its clear layering is inclined to the northeast at an angle of 30 degrees. Red oaks tower above you, and shoulder-high mountain laurel thickets keep you from straying off the path. At the top of the ledges, the trail turns abruptly right (southeast) across a gully. Before you turn, however, walk forward another 50 yards to examine a former swamp, converted into a pond by beavers. The scale of their enterprise—pond, wood-earth dam, and enormous lodge—is impressive. A cho-

rus of twanging frogs celebrates the beavers' success. So do the blossom-covered (in June) mountain laurel plants that thrive in the increased sunlight along the shore.

Return to the Appalachian Trail and proceed across the gully beneath the white pines. The calories you spent in climbing the 300 vertical feet from Benedict Pond eventually yield some clear views at a rocky overlook. Mount Everett (Hike 2), in the southwest corner of Massachusetts, is the high point on the horizon. Another beaver pond is visible in the valley just below. If you are short of time or hiking with young children, this spot makes a good destination and turnaround point, but do be careful with children along the cliff. A major fault (no longer active) separates your Olympian perch from the valley to the west. Detailed geologic mapping in this region has demonstrated that the rocks holding up the high ground of Beartown State Forest are nearly twice as old (1,000 million years) as the rocks in the lowland before you (500 million years). Moreover, the young rocks apparently extend eastward beneath the older rocks. These observations imply that the Beartown gneisses moved as a gigantic rock slice a distance of tens of miles, from east to west, up and over younger rocks. The nearly horizontal surface of movement, called a thrust fault, intersects the earth's surface on the slope between you and the Housatonic Valley to the west.

After leaving the overlook, you'll soon ease downhill to the north into a broad valley filled with more tall oaks and large rocks. About 100 feet above the valley bottom, the trail crosses a grassy woods road beneath a low power line. Turn left onto the woods road, leaving the Appalachian Trail, and continue gradually uphill to Mount Wilcox Road. Now it is time to assess your stamina and choose among three routes. (1) For the shortest (2.2 miles), return to your car, turn

Beaver dam and pond

left, follow the gravel road downhill for almost 0.5 mile, then, where the road begins a bend to the left, turn left again onto a wide path. Skip to the last paragraph of this hike for the rest of the description. (2) For a longer (6.6 miles) hike that stays on clear but little-traveled roads, turn right and follow the gravel to the summit of Mount Wilcox—viewless except to those with access to the fenced fire tower. Continue past the road leading left to the fire tower and descend gradually to a road junction just past a bridge over a small stream. Bear left and skip the next paragraph to continue the description. (3) For the most challenging hike (5.9 miles), turn left, follow the gravel road downhill for nearly 0.5 mile, then where the road begins a bend to the left, turn right onto a wide path marked with a sign: SKI AND BRIDLE TRAIL. While it is not as well maintained as the Appalachian Trail, it can be followed and it leads to some lovely parts of the forest. This is the adventurer's route!

Red triangular blazes lead you uphill on an old road overgrown in places by ferns and other vegetation. Shorts are not advisable here, where the protection of pants is needed for blackberry thickets. A mixed hardwood forest punctuated by stands of spruce makes a good home for the birds and squirrels that now seem more numerous. Perhaps it was the bear droppings on the trail, the raccoon footprints in the mud, or the specially filtered sunlight—the feel of this route was definitely wild. The path detours to the right around a wetland. Deer tracks in the moist ground suggest that this might be a good place to spend some time watching for wildlife. After crossing a small wooden bridge, the trail runs to the left, keeping the cattails in sight at first, but eventually bending to the right and slightly uphill away from the water. A steady but gentle climb awaits you, interrupted by

soggy areas. Occasional red triangles confirm your route north, although it would be difficult to get truly lost here, with roads a short distance away on both the east and the west. In fact, Mount Wilcox Road is occasionally visible off to the right as the path descends to meet it. Waterproof boots may help for the stream crossing on mossy rocks that brings you to the gravel.

Turn left onto Mount Wilcox Road and walk mostly downhill for 0.5 mile to the first left turn onto a woods road (labeled Turkey Trail on the USGS map) that drops into a hemlock-darkened valley to cross the stream you have been following. A short, steep climb follows, in part on a pavement of gneiss smoothed by Pleistocene glaciers that also left boulders perched alongside the road. Tall sugar maples, other hardwoods, and white pines lend a parklike feeling to this part of the forest. Muddy ruts testify to the passage of off-road vehicles on this dirt track, although the traffic is light enough to permit grass to grow on some sections. As the path starts downhill to join Mount Wilcox Road again, the most used route turns to the right and you should also. When you reach the gravel, turn left, cross a small bridge, and then turn right to follow Turkey Trail along the stream.

Orange blazes here soon lead you away from the stream and up a muddy section to join a bridle trail on the remains of a road. You walk beneath a canopy of tall oaks towering over smaller maple and beech trees and descend to Beartown Road. Turn left onto the pavement, walk about 200 yards, then bear left onto an old road dividing a thick growth of sensitive fern and closed to vehicles by a brown metal gate. This level, grassy avenue was clearly built with considerable effort that involved cutting and filling along gneiss ledges, probably using Civilian Conservation Corps (CCC) labor during the

1930s. The remains of a CCC camp can be found along Beartown Road to the north. You may see purple heal-all flowers in the road as Benedict Pond comes into view. Various asters and common sunflowers highlight open areas as you near the intersection with the Appalachian Trail. Just across a small bridge, turn right onto the white-blazed trail that you walked earlier. For variety, at the next junction you may wish to turn right to follow the shore of the pond on a short blue-blazed trail back to your car.

5

Monument Mountain

Total distance: 2.7 miles (4.3 km)

Hiking time: 2¼ hours

Maximum elevation: 1,642 feet (500 meters)

Vertical rise: 900 feet (274 meters)

Maps: USGS Great Barrington (7½' x 15'), USGS Stockbridge (7½' x 15')

Trailhead: 42°14'33" N, 73°20'08" W

It must take a strange kind of courage to throw oneself over the edge of a high cliff, as legends tell us some Native Americans did from the top of Monument Mountain, a tale told most memorably in poet William Cullen Bryant's "Monument Mountain." Imagine the ritual that may have surrounded such a leap of faith as you climb past beautiful flowers, through deep, quiet woodlands, and over glistening white quartzite boulders to Squaw Peak, the high ridge of Monument Mountain. Here, bold cliffs and rock towers plunge down to the hard talus slopes at their feet. Here, you can sit in peace and safety, a mere step from oblivion, and enjoy warm sunshine, beautiful views, and the other good things of life.

The parking area for the trails of Monument Mountain, owned by the Trustees of Reservations, is on the west side of US 7, 3.6 miles north of its intersection with MA 23 in Great Barrington and 3.2 miles south of its intersection with MA 102 in Stockbridge. After examining the trail map and information board displayed adjacent to the parking area, walk south on a path that runs between the highway to your left and a steep hillside with a talus slope of large boulders to your right. The white-blazed trail passes through mixed woods of white pine, hemlock, white ash, red maple, and striped maple before joining the Indian Monument Trail as it enters the cool shade of large hemlocks and white pines. The trail swings sharply northwest up an easy slope through white pine, white birch, and mountain laurel, which blooms attractively in early summer. The trail reaches a fork, but you can go ei-

A family at the summit of Squaw Peak

ther way, because the branches soon rejoin as the route follows a braided pattern through a mixed wood of hemlock, white pine, oak, beech, and white birch. The steep slope on your right shields this peaceful trail from the noise of the highway and is also the source of the large boulders that have rolled toward the trail. The trail steepens slightly and crosses small outcrops of schist, a rock with prominent layering and micas quite unlike the quartzite that forms much of the rest of Monument Mountain. Soon the trail heads more to the northeast through deciduous woods of red maple, black and white birch, and white oak, and then curves easterly up a moderate slope to the top of a prominent ridge.

At this midpoint of your hike, the trail turns right and soon reaches an inscription in a large boulder of schist commemorating the donation of the area to the Trustees of Reservations by Rosalie Butler in 1899. Your route now heads southerly up a mod-

erate slope over rocky ledges of gneiss—a metamorphic rock with well-developed layers and easily visible and distinct quartz, feldspar, and mica. A little farther along, layers of quartzite—a hard, light-colored metamorphic rock composed largely of quartz—are interbedded in the gneiss. Following a pleasant stretch along the ridge, with views down wooded slopes on both sides, you reach a short, steep, rocky cliff composed entirely of quartzite. The slope soon eases, and you can enjoy the beautiful contrast of the greens of pitch pine, white pine, and mountain laurel against the dazzling white of quartzite boulders. The trail levels off as you reach an area of huge, jumbled quartzite outcrops that form the highest point of your hike. You may wish to scramble around on the rocks here, but be careful, as steep cliffs drop sharply on either side of the trail. From the summit, views extend west to the Catskill Mountains, north to Mount Greylock (Hikes 8, 9, and 10), and south to Mount Everett (Hike 2).

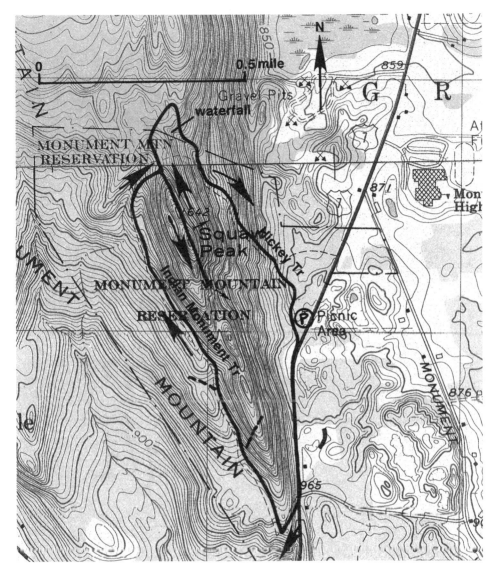

Continuing along the ridge, you descend into a col and then rise again to the top of Squaw Peak. If you continue past the top a short distance, you will reach an opening with views of Mount Wilcox in Beartown State Forest (Hike 4) to the east, Livermore Peak to the southeast, Butternut Ski Area to the south, and Mount Everett to the southwest. Your eye will be drawn, however, to the steep quartzite cliffs nearby and immediately beneath you. According to legend, Indians jumped, or were thrown, from these cliffs to appease offended gods. You may wish to explore the summit area and look for different views of the rock towers and the fissured and jointed cliffs, but, as earlier, be cautious or you may join some of those legendary Indians. If you feel less ad-

---

venturous, or if you feel hungry, this viewpoint also makes a fine lunch spot. You may see turkey vultures gliding by; these large black birds with bare heads have a distinctive rocking flight on upturned wings. Peregrine falcons once nested on the spectacular crags here before these fierce raptors were driven almost to extinction by indiscriminate hunting and environmental poisoning. Perhaps one day some offspring of the peregrines successfully reintroduced in Massachusetts in recent years may recolonize Monument Mountain and once more thrill human spectators with their flashing wings and high-speed hunting dives.

To continue your hike, walk back along the ridge, over the two prominent hilltops, and down to the trail junction where you first attained the ridgetop. At this junction, continue straight along the ridge. The clear, white-blazed trail follows the ridge down through woods of beech, oak, white birch, hemlock, and much mountain laurel. After crossing a quartzite knoll, the path descends a moderately steep, bouldery slope to cross a stream on a small wooden bridge, then rises a little before dropping to another stream. Here the path turns southerly (right) to follow this steep-sided, V-shaped valley, which was cut into the mountainside by the erosive power of flowing water. Soon you reach a small falls on your right, where water plunges out over a rock overhang sheltering a cool cave just to the right.

Beyond the falls, the trail angles across the slope before dropping to cross the brook on another wooden bridge. Following the right bank, the route continues moderately downslope alongside the deeply incised stream. Hemlocks dominate the woods in these darkened stream valleys, a common distribution in this part of the country. Soon the stream swings away to the east (left), and the trail drops easily through mixed woods. On your right you will see a great talus slope formed of boulders that fell from the quartzite cliffs above, including one enormous chunk whose thundering descent must have been an awe-inspiring sight. Leaving the talus, drop down through mixed woodlands on the well-worn path, letting the white blazes guide you, and go to the right around a flatter, muddy stretch. After surmounting one last rise, the broad trail brings you down to the parking area.

6

Pleasant Valley Wildlife Sanctuary

Total distance: 2.5 miles (4.0 km)

Hiking time: 2¼ hours

Maximum elevation: 2,123 feet (646 meters)

Vertical rise: 1,000 feet (305 meters)

Map: USGS Pittsfield West (7½' x 15')

Trailhead: 42°22'57" N, 73°17'59" W

In the fading light of a summer evening, a V-shaped ripple disturbs the smoothness of the still, dark water. Your heart beats a little faster and excitement mounts as you realize that your patience will be rewarded. A dark shape swims closer, and soon you can see the rounded head and prominent snout of a beaver breaking the surface of the pond.

Sixty years ago beavers were reintroduced to Yokun Brook, a mere 5 miles from downtown Pittsfield, the largest town in western Massachusetts, and since then their dams have reshaped the valley floor and created new and varied wildlife habitats. The Pleasant Valley Wildlife Sanctuary, which spans Yokun Brook, must be where many people catch their first sight of a beaver, but beavers are not the only attractions of the sanctuary. Numerous trails crisscross sunny, flower-filled meadows, rocky slopes, and rich woodlands, where with luck—and patience—you may catch sight of some uncommon birds as well.

To reach this Massachusetts Audubon Society sanctuary, drive south on US 7, 1.7 miles from its intersection with US 20 in Pittsfield, then turn west (right) onto West Dugway Road (sanctuary sign at the corner). If you are coming from the south, West Dugway Road is located 0.6 mile north of the intersection of MA 7A and combined US 7/US 20. The sanctuary parking area is 1.7 miles along West Dugway Road (signs will guide you at road junctions). The sanctuary is open daily in summer, closed Monday at other times, the trails from dawn to dusk and the office from 9 AM to 5 PM. Ad-

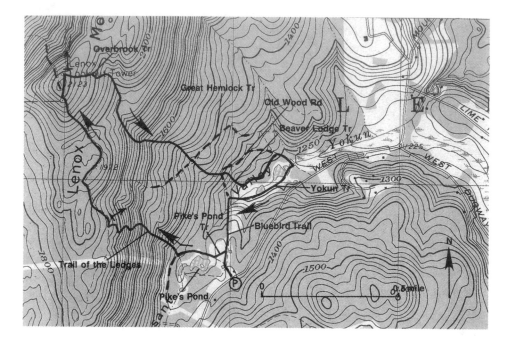

mission is free to Massachusetts Audubon Society members, otherwise $3 for adults and $2 for children (in 1998). Before starting out on the trails, visit the sanctuary office on the right, where you can obtain a free trail map and interesting leaflets about the sanctuary.

From the office, continue down a wide gravel path past a barn and rest rooms on the left. Your hike begins on Pike's Pond Trail, the mown path that branches off from Bluebird Trail in front of the Education Center and crosses a meadow in a southwesterly direction. You'll walk through a hedge of cherry, dogwood, and Tartarian honeysuckle into another former meadow where wildflowers, including black-eyed Susans, oxeye daisies, buttercups, goldenrod, and milkweed bloom amid the overgrowing blackberries. At the far side of the meadow, a narrow band of white pines, draped by grapevines, separates you from Pike's Pond. The trail skirts the pond, crosses boardwalks over wet spots, and brings you to a

bench that invites you to linger for a restful overview of the pond. Several large butternut trees line the pond, hanging their branches out over the water. Native Americans reputedly extracted oil from butternuts to use as butter and tapped the trees for sap as we tap maples to make syrup. Yellow-bellied sapsuckers appear to be the main exploiters of these particular trees, and a careful look should reveal neat rows of their drill holes in the tree trunks. Although these birds probably eat the sap released by their drilling, they may be just as interested in the insects that are drawn to the sweet liquid and become trapped in it.

Beyond the bench, a pair of bridges carry you over the outlet from Pike's Pond and adjacent wet areas to dry woods again. Follow Pike's Pond Trail past the intersection with Yokun Trail, which goes off to your right, cross two more small bridges, and soon you reach a junction where Pike's Pond Trail continues straight ahead. Your

Reflections on Pike's Pond

route, Trail of the Ledges, bears right and heads toward the Fire Tower.

Marked by blue blazes, Trail of the Ledges heads northerly away from Pike's Pond and begins ascending Lenox Mountain, easily at first, but the slope quickly becomes moderately steep. Maple, oak, gray and white birch, and beech dominate these woods, although you will find a few white pine and hemlock. After passing Waycross Trail on the right and ascending a steep stretch, the trail eases where Ravine Trail goes off to the right, and then follows a narrow valley for a short distance. Along the way you should look for the uncommon maidenhair fern, which is distinguished from other ferns by its dark stems. The trail runs along the base of small lichen- and moss-covered cliffs composed of schist: These rocks contain both muscovite, a silvery-colored mica, and biotite, a black mica. The trail climbs out of a small natural amphitheater, levels for a distance, ascends a short, steep slope, and then flattens by a damp stream valley that descends to the right. Ahead of you lies the steepest part of your climb as the trail winds upward among many rocky outcrops and small cliffs. Take care crossing the wet, mossy rocks, as they can be very slippery; also be alert for the blue blazes to guide you through the zigzags. If you lose the blazes, you have left the trail and will need to retreat to find it again. Through the steep part, the route is generally west, but at the top the trail swings sharply north, levels off, and in 30 yards reaches a look-off known as Farview Ledges. Your exertions have placed you 500 feet higher than your staring point, more than half of the height you need to take you to the top of Lenox Mountain.

You probably will want to sit for a while on the rocks in the warm sunshine and enjoy the view of distant hills to the east and southeast. This look-off will seem ideally located after your steep climb reaching it. Your rest here may be enlivened by visits from friendly black-capped chickadees, who would be very happy to share any snack you might be eating.

When you feel ready to begin the second part of your climb, look for the trail junction near the look-off. Here Laurel Trail heads off to the right (north), and you follow the blue-blazed Trail of the Ledges in a northwesterly direction up an easy slope. You will start in hemlocks, but as you climb to the drier upper slope, these give way to a canopy of oaks and birches

and a thick understory of mountain laurel, swamp azalea, striped maple, beech, chestnut, and hob-blebush. Among the many birds in these woods you may see or hear warblers, vireos, peewees, and woodpeckers; some trees display the large, rectangular holes made by the pileated woodpecker. In a few minutes you will reach a wooded ridge where the trail swings northeast, becomes generally level, and enters a hemlock grove. In summer, hermit thrushes live here, and you may hear their wonderful flutelike song or see them searching for food on the forest floor. Watch for the characteristic slow raising and lowering of this brown bird's reddish tail.

Shortly you will reach on the right a lookout over the hills and valleys to the northeast. After a restful pause to enjoy the views, descend gently among beeches to cross a small valley, rise over a rocky knoll, and drop again into another stream valley. After one more rocky top and another valley, you start your final ascent. The trail steepens, climbs a short rocky stairway where care is needed, especially when wet, and then levels off through a hemlock grove. From here, a few minutes of easy walking will bring you to the open summit of Lenox Mountain. The view westward stretches from the Catskills in New York around to the Taconic Range in northwestern Massachusetts, making an interesting backdrop if you choose this spot to eat your lunch. Nestling closer to the northwest lies Richmond Pond and the nearby Shaker Village.

After enjoying the summit area, follow the trail signs on the Fire Tower fence and the yellow arrows on the rocks to Overbrook Trail, which heads in an easterly direction into the woods. The slope down is moderate, following and crossing several small streams that flow over rocky ledges and waterfalls and along hemlock-lined ravines. Yellow blazes will guide you through the one or two obscure sections. At the first intersection, Laurel Trail goes right and Great Hemlock Trail goes left, but you should continue straight ahead. In a little while you'll reach an intersection with Ovenbird Trail. Stay left on Overbrook Trail and shortly you will pass Old Wood Road on the left, and in 40 feet you should bear left onto Beaver Lodge Trail.

Your route now follows a blue-blazed trail that takes you into the Yokun Brook valley, where the environment differs in many ways from the forested hillsides you have just traversed. Marbles, which are metamorphosed limestones, not schists as in the uplands, form the underlying bedrock here; because these softer rocks erode more easily, they help create the valley. They also counterbalance the usual acidity of the forest floor and create sweeter soils, where plants such as maidenhair fern and cranberry viburnum thrive. Lime-rich soils may also help to neutralize the impact of acid rain on the ponds and streams of the Yokun valley.

In 1932, beavers were introduced into Pleasant Valley Wildlife Sanctuary as part of a plan to create more varied wildlife habitats and to provide ponds for waterfowl. As you walk the Beaver Lodge Trail, bypassing the Old Wood Road that you will join later, you will see much evidence that the experiment was successful: several dammed ponds, lodges, and many trees felled by the sharp, busy teeth of beavers. Cattails, willows, and yellow water lilies grow in the swamps and open waters of the beaver ponds, and red-winged blackbirds, ducks, and bullfrogs live among the swamp vegetation. Trees growing alongside the ponds include sugar maple, American ash, various dogwoods, and black cherry.

After several stretches of boardwalk and a bridge over a small stream, the trail swings northeasterly to join Old Wood Road, which you now follow to the right. It will take you across a small bridge over a stream and then onto a longer bridge over a beaver pond. Just beyond the bridge, follow Yokun Trail right at the fork onto a narrow strip of land between two ponds. The trail heads southwest, flanked by a gentle slope on the left and beaver ponds and swamps on the right. A bit farther along you will reach another junction, where bearing right on a side trail will bring you to a bench to rest on and a closer view of a beaver pond, dam, and lodge. From here, too, you will have good views of the Fire Tower on Lenox Mountain and the ridge that you climbed earlier. If you come to this spot in the hour or so before dark, you will almost certainly see beavers swimming in the pond and perhaps coming ashore to retrieve branches for dam repair. Beavers will not be too perturbed by your presence, and if you watch quietly they may approach quite closely; if you do disturb them, they will slap the pond's surface with their tails and dive underwater in a warning flurry of sounds and splashes.

You may spend quite a while watching these fascinating animals, but eventually you should continue along the side trail back to the main path. Shortly, you will reach a junction where Alexander Trail bears left and your route, Yokun Trail, continues straight. The trail crosses a bridge over a small stream and soon reaches an intersection near a larger bubbling stream, where another wooden bridge may invite you to pause for a while before you turn left onto Bluebird Trail. Your path now heads uphill, in a southerly direction, through mixed woods and on into a former meadow, now being overgrown by smaller trees and shrubs. You will pass Alexander Trail on the left, and a little beyond, a line of red pines. Continue along the path and in a few minutes you will reach the sanctuary buildings and complete your hike.

7

Warner Hill

Total distance: 6.0 miles (9.7 km)

Hiking time: 3½ hours

Maximum elevation: 2,080 feet (633 meters)

Vertical rise: 810 feet (247 meters)

Map: USGS Pittsfield East (7½' x 15')

Trailhead: 42°27'25" N, 73°09'44" W

Although the forested hills east of Pittsfield are inviting any season of the year, the brilliant colors of hardwoods in fall make them irresistible. A gentle stretch of the Appalachian Trail opens these otherwise inaccessible woods to footworthy visitors and offers an outstanding view from the top of Warner Hill as a prize. Because there are no rugged sections, the trail here is especially pleasant. The hike may even be shortened if a second car is available. The route is a good sample of the easy-walking sections of the Appalachian Trail's 83-mile traverse of Massachusetts. Well maintained under the guidance of the Appalachian Trail Conference based in Harpers Ferry, West Virginia, the 2,050-mile-long Appalachian Trail offers dedicated hikers the chance to hike mostly in wilderness from Mount Katahdin in Maine to Springer Mountain in Georgia.

To reach the starting point for this hike, first locate the junction of MA 9 and South Street in Dalton. This junction is 1.1 miles west of the eastern junction of MA 9 and MA 8 and 1.2 miles east of the intersection of MA 9 and MA 7 in Pittsfield. Follow South Street south for 0.8 mile downhill, across the east branch of the Housatonic River, then up to Grange Hall Road. Turn left onto Grange Hall Road and travel uphill 1.1 miles to the Appalachian Trail, marked by a black pole on the left where the road begins to level out. You will find plenty of room for parking along the sides of this wide, quiet road. From the road, the white-blazed trail leads up a steep hill to the south.

If you wish to shorten the hike from 6.0 miles (3½ hours) to 3.7 miles (2¼ hours)

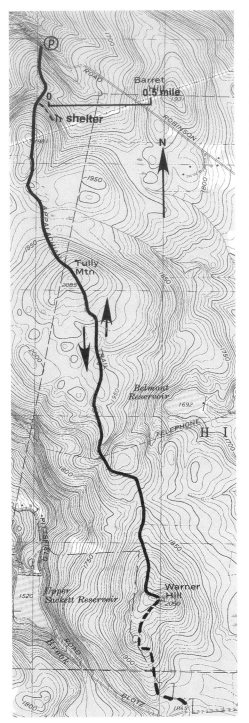

and can arrange for a second car, you can continue walking on the Appalachian Trail past the turnaround point on Warner Hill to its junction with Blotz Road. To get your second car to Blotz Road, continue on South Street past Grange Hall Road for an additional 0.8 mile to Division Road. Turn left and travel 1.6 miles on Division Road to Washington Mountain Road. At this T-junction, turn left and bear left again at a fork in 0.1 mile onto Kirchner Road (which becomes Blotz Road). The trail crosses Blotz Road along a nearly level stretch 3.0 miles from this fork.

The first 100 yards of trail south from Grange Hall Road provide the steepest climb of the entire hike. While catching your breath, look at the clusters of woodfern fronds or the outcrops of schist containing flattened quartz pebbles. Although most of the trail is on billion-year-old Washington gneiss, this first section passes over the 600-million-year-old Dalton schist and crosses the ancient erosion surface (an unconformity) that separates these units. This important geologic boundary is difficult to spot here, but the unconformity is well exposed in a cliff face along the Appalachian Trail a few hundred yards north of your car. The trail soon levels out, giving you a chance to appreciate the forest you have entered. Beech, birch, maples, and ash comprise most of the canopy, while the understory is predominantly green-trunked striped maple over a carpet of ferns.

As is typical for the Appalachian Trail, the path is well worn and clearly marked with white blazes. Scattered, smoothed outcroppings of rock and exposed tree roots serve as a pavement for the trail and indicate that the veneer of glacial till that blankets the bedrock throughout Massachusetts is particularly thin here. As the trail climbs out of a small gully, a blue-blazed

The Appalachian Trail

side trail leads 0.17 mile to Kay Wood Shelter and privy, built in 1987 along a small gneiss cliff by the Berkshire Chapter of the Appalachian Trail Conference. Continue on the white-blazed Appalachian Trail and you will soon cross a wide swath cleared for a power line, exposing views of Pittsfield and the Taconic Range to the west. Basking in the sun, blackberries thrive along this open slope. Look for them on the older, woody vines.

Shortly past the power line, the trail descends into a swampy area. Mud is a common peril for hikers of many areas in Massachusetts, where impermeable, clay-rich glacial drift has been deposited with no regard for the local drainage pattern. Climbing again, you reach the summit of Tully Mountain. Although Tully is higher than Warner Hill, the forest at the top precludes any vista. To reward your efforts, however, the gentle southern slopes of Tully nourish a lovely open forest of mixed hardwoods with a thick floor covering of hay-scented

fern for you to experience with your nose and eyes. Ruffed grouse may startle you here with their precipitous, crashing flight in response to your footfalls. At one point the trail jogs left briefly along a woods road that follows a crossing telephone line. The varying ages of hardwood stands along your route serve as reminders of man's influence on this woodland through past logging efforts. Even more striking are the old apple trees you will find in the saddle before the final ascent of Warner Hill. Stone walls, apple trees, and lilac bushes, left by previous residents, all look misplaced in this seeming wilderness you have, by now, purchased with your feet.

The summit of Warner Hill offers rocks, views, blueberries, blackberries, and controversy. The forest continually seeks to reclaim this hilltop and its panorama. In 1991 there was evidence of a fire, apparently set by hikers to maintain good views, and bushy new growth from the roots of scorched birches and cherries. Wander around to locate the best windows between the trees, and you will be rewarded with views of Mount Greylock 20 miles to the north and the hills of October Mountain State Forest in the south. Low outcrops of a rusty rock at the summit show the now familiar layering that is characteristic of gneiss, a type of metamorphic rock. The layering developed as the minerals that comprise this rock crystallized at high temperatures and pressures during a wholesale rearrangement of atoms (metamorphism) about 1 billion years ago. For this rock to be visible at the surface, several miles of overlying rock had to be removed by erosion or faulting. Although the evidence is not easily visible to untrained eyes, these old rocks actually rest on top of younger rocks—notably marble—which can also be found in nearby valleys (visit Bartholomew's Cobble, Hike 3, to see examples). The marble was deposited as limestone on the edge of a continent some 550 million years ago. Getting these old rocks on top of the younger ones required tens of miles of lateral movement of slices of the earth's crust over one another, a feat to be pondered.

If you brought a second car, continue on the Appalachian Trail down Warner Hill to Blotz Road, 15 minutes away. If not, retrace your steps to the north. The return trip is surprisingly different from the walk south. Looking in a different direction with the sun in another part of the sky will help you see much that you missed earlier.

8

Saddle Ball Mountain

Total distance: 7.4 miles (11.9 km)

Hiking time: 5½ hours

Maximum elevation: 3,240 feet (987 meters)

Vertical rise: 1,770 feet (539 meters)

Maps: USGS North Adams (7½' x 15'), USGS Cheshire (7½' x 15')

Trailhead: 42°36'05" N, 73°12'03" W

This long hike takes you past pretty streams, through a variety of woodlands that reflect the local microclimates, and to lookouts with near and far distant views. To reach the trailhead, follow the directions for Hike 9 (Heart of Greylock), but travel only 3.8 miles along Rockwell Road to the large parking area for Jones Nose, located on the right (east) side of the road. To begin your hike, exit from the east end of the parking area on Old Adams Road and continue gently downhill on the wide, grassy path. Soon you will pass around a metal gate sturdy enough to bar vehicular traffic. The small trees flanking the trail include white birch, cottonwood, and black birch above a dense understory of blackberry patches and tall milkweed. In fact, the upcoming stretch of your route makes a treat for tree lovers who embrace the challenges of tree identification.

The trail itself poses few challenges hereabouts as it meanders gradually downhill, with only scattered rocky outcrops of schist to roughen the smooth, grassy path. Deciduous trees of varying age and size comprise the forest on both sides of the trail. Scattered among the various birches, cherries, oaks, and maples you will find some old apple trees left over from a former orchard. You might want to specialize in maples along here, as three distinctive species can be found. Maples have leaves with rounded to pointed separated sections, known as lobes, which radiate from a point on each leaf. Twinned pairs of leaves extend out from the opposite side of a twig or branch. You should become familiar with the red maple, as you will see it on many different hikes in Massachusetts. Its leaves have three to five lobes, with a broad basal lobe and distinctive whitening on the underside of each leaf. Look also for the characteristic reddish twigs and buds that led to this species' name.

The trail drops downhill a little more steeply and passes many large white birch trees, including one triple-trunked specimen on the left that displays the pieces of peeling bark commonly found in this species. The downslope continues as the route swings southeasterly and soon you will reach another "maple opportunity," where striped and mountain maples stand side by side. Both are relatively small trees with leaves similar to the red maple in shape but considerably larger and green on both sides. The mountain maple has somewhat deeper teeth along leaf edges, but the easiest way to tell them apart is to study their trunk bark. One has dark brown to greenish bark and the other a paler green bark with narrow vertical white stripes along the trunk. You should have no problems figuring out which is which!

Shortly beyond the maple quiz, you will reach a major trail fork where a sign tells you that food and gasoline are available in Adams and, indirectly, that winter hikers may encounter snowmobiles. Here you take the left fork downhill and curve south through deciduous woodlands to shortly reach a T-junction. You turn left alongside, but above, a prominent stream valley that lies directly in front of you. In about 200 feet you will cross a south-flowing stream on a wooden bridge, then turn northerly and, for the first time on this hike, begin to go uphill, albeit only gently. You continue uphill for a while with the stream valley paralleling your route below you to the left and majestic birch and beech trees flanking the wide path. In only about 500 feet, though, the path curves easterly away from the stream and crosses a small ridge. For the next straightish stretch you will be heading generally east-southeast, with a few meanders to cross small streams. You will gradually gain height on this gentle rise punctuated by minor dips, but you will be only 150 feet higher than the ridge you recently crossed when you reach the Appalachian Trail (AT) some 3,500 feet beyond that crest.

Later you will hike part of the Appalachian Trail, but for now continue straight ahead for 100 feet of level going, which brings you to another trail junction. Here turn left to begin a generally level half mile or so that takes you to a wooden bridge over a tributary of Bassett Brook. Beyond the stream crossing, the trail drops gently for a while, steepens a little as you pass Silver Fox Trail coming in from the right, and then crosses a stream valley. In this part of your hike, in the headwaters of Bassett Brook, pretty streams feature prominently, and shortly you will reach a wooden bridge over another one. Bubbling water cascades over outcrops of schist and dawdles through cool pools amid the moss-covered rocks. You too should take your time to enjoy this lovely spot before following the trail for only a short distance to cross yet another stream valley. The path takes a jog to the south to follow the edge of a steep-sided, rocky gorge, but then changes its mind and turns northeasterly away from the glen. Beyond here the trail heads steadily downhill to one last bridge over a rocky tributary of Bassett Brook, and shortly thereafter to a fork where you go left and on for another 100 feet to a prominent trail junction. You will now leave the Old Adams Road and turn left onto Cheshire Harbor Trail (unmarked).

Here you are at an elevation of 2,035 feet and more than 300 feet lower than the trailhead. However, the easy downhill hiking

The view west from the northwest slopes of Saddle Ball Mountain

Saddle Ball Mountain

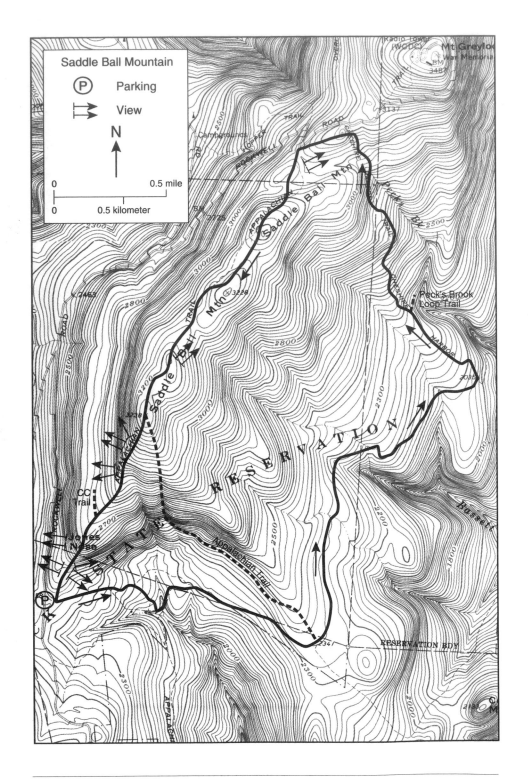

is over, at least for a while, and now you begin to gain some of the height that you need in order to attain the mountaintops later in your hike.

Your new trail heads moderately uphill in a north-northwesterly direction to begin a stretch of about 7,000 feet in which you will gain 1,100 feet in elevation. The unmarked and unblazed but well-defined path meanders somewhat on its upward way through deciduous trees made familiar earlier in your hike. You soon reach a moderately uphill stretch of about 600 feet where the trail crosses numerous outcrops of finely layered and somewhat contorted schists. After a stretch of almost level going, the trail approaches a prominent valley readily visible on your topographic map but variably so on the ground, depending on the season and foliage density. You will pass Pecks Brook Trail going downhill to the right and begin to drift away from Pecks Brook valley as the trail swings more to the left. In 150 feet or so, a sign directs you toward the "summit"—of Mount Greylock, however, and not today's ultimate destination. The path steepens beyond the sign and shortly you reach more schist outcrops in the trail. You have now reached the same elevation as the starting point of your hike—so it's all positive from here on! As if to reward you for your effort, the trail eases off a bit and enters a forest dominated by beech trees, with their pale gray trunks and egg-shaped leaves. The small triangular nuts of this tree ripen in early fall when numerous birds, squirrels, bears, and other animals feast on them. The trail wanders back and forth a little bit but generally heads north-northwest across the slope. The gradient alternates between quite gentle and moderately steep as the trail edges its way up the mountain. The southerly aspect of this side of the mountain favors a warmer and drier microclimate

than Greylock's north-facing slopes, and deciduous woods dominated by beech, admixed with some birch, extend almost to the top of the ridge to an elevation of 3,000 feet. On your way you will cross a few more schist outcrops and a wooden bridge over the upper reach of Pecks Brook. Some 1,000 feet farther along from the bridge and 200 feet higher, you will see a clearing ahead that turns out to be Rockwell Road. At this spot the Appalachian Trail heads south to provide your route for the next part of your hike.

Turning left onto the AT, the path immediately begins to rise to the top of a small, rocky knoll—at 3,140 feet, the first summit of today's hike. Notice the changed nature of the forest in this landscape, exposed to a much more rigorous microclimate than the slopes you recently ascended. Ground-hugging wood sorrel carpets the forest floor, and the mountaintop-loving balsam fir dominates the woodland. The trees are stunted by their severe living conditions in a process of natural bonsai formation. You will recognize the balsam fir by its soft needles, smoothish twigs, and upright greenish purple cones. The rather dark trunks are ornamented with resin blisters—the source of the Canada balsam familiar to geologists because of its use in the making of thin slices of rock for microscopic study. More immediately obvious here, these fir trees provide the distinctive and nostalgic aromas that permeate the forest and remind us that we traverse mountain highs. While in this mode, you should crush a small twig from one of the yellow birches that mingle with the firs on this knolltop, to release the sweet smell of wintergreen for another sensory experience. Assuming no intoxication from these olfactory experiments, you should head southwesterly down the bouldery trail, catching glimpses ahead of the domed shape of Saddle Ball Mountain. The crest of a broad ridge carries you down to a col where the route approaches Rockwell Road once again. After passing a side path to a parking area, the AT plunges south back into the woods. Beyond the col, the trail rises up a rocky stairway to an opening in the trees that affords unobstructed views toward the summit of Mount Greylock, with the War Memorial, communications towers, and Bascom Lodge clearly visible. Your path soon descends from this viewpoint summit and heads across a fir-dotted swamp on narrow footbridges. A barred owl lives hereabouts and you may hear its identifying calls, commonly rendered as *who cooks for you? who cooks for you all?* If you can generate a passable imitation, a real owl may engage you in an echoing conversation.

Leaving the damp area, the trail edges upward across the western slopes of Saddle Ball Mountain through a lovely balsam fir forest. The path flirts with the ridgetop but appears reluctant to follow the crest, perhaps because of its clothing of small, dense fir trees. This means that you will bypass "summit 3,228" on its western side and then angle back up to the crest of a better-defined ridge. The trail continues along the ridge and shortly reaches a rocky stairway that brings you to the top of a knoll at 3,240 feet in elevation, the highest point you will reach on this hike. Appropriately enough, views extend back from here along the mountain range to the summit of Mount Greylock. The trail heads down toward a small col, and on the way you can see ahead the last summit of this hike. You reach this by crossing a small stream and adjacent damp area in the col and then climbing past many boulders of bright white-vein quartz to the broad, ill-defined "summit 3,238." No views mark this mountaintop, but as you begin to drop down from it, the AT goes off

to the southeast. Your route continues straight ahead on the Jones Nose Trail toward the parking area, which a sign tells you is about a mile away.

The trail begins to drop moderately steeply down some smooth, rocky outcrops that can be treacherous when wet. Take care! Soon after safely negotiating this more tricky section, you will drop below the balsam forest that has been your companion for so long. Instead, you enter an area of low shrubs from which you begin to obtain views to the southwest around to the northwest. More rocky steps bring you into taller birch, beech, and maple trees and back into a shrubby, more open part. Eventually you will reach a short side trail to the right that goes to a rocky lookout. Views extend westward to the Taconic Mountains, which stretch along the Massachusetts–New York border, and farther to the southwest the peaks of the Catskill Mountains of New York State break the skyline. During your hike you have crossed numerous outcrops of schist, but at this spot you stand on a clean outcrop where you can more easily study the properties of this distinctive metamorphic rock. It's had quite a history! Beginning as soft sediment accumulating on the seafloor and then subjected to high temperatures and pressures as it became progressively more deeply buried, the rock hardened and new minerals grew in fine layers constrained by the pressure of overlying rocks. Micas were among the newly formed minerals, and they give schists their characteristic sheen. But now you see these transformed rocks on a Massachusetts mountainside, proof that massive mountain-building forces have uplifted them from within the earth's crust to form the heights over which we love to ramble. Food for thought as you return to the main trail and continue your downhill progress.

Another spur trail to the right takes you past a grove of red spruce trees to a second rocky lookout offering more restricted views. The trail continues down through deciduous woods containing some larger trees growing in the more protected spots. Soon after the path flattens noticeably, you will find a trail junction where CCC Dynamite Foot and Ski Trail goes off to the north, and your route back to the parking area continues straight ahead. After a spell of fairly gentle downhill, the trail steepens markedly and you find yourself progressing down the bridge of Jones Nose. As the gradient eases, once again you emerge into a former meadow now being colonized by a variety of shrubs, birches, and maples: a haven for many birds. But many open spaces remain, affording you views to the east, south, and west as you make your way to the starting point of your hike some 200 yards away.

9

Heart of Greylock

Total distance: 4.5 miles (7.2 km)

Hiking time: 4 hours

Maximum elevation: 3,487 feet
(1,062 meters)

Vertical rise: 1,747 feet (532 meters)

Maps: USGS North Adams (7½' x 15'),
USGS Cheshire (7½' x 15')

Trailhead: 42°37'56" N, 73°11'16" W

You could rightly call this hike a journey in contrasts. You will walk past a cascading stream into a deep ravine and on your way out wonder if the steep slope will ever end; later you'll stroll along gentle former carriage roads. You will walk in solitude through lush vegetation on mountain slopes and then wander over a summit clear of trees but heavy with human presence. You will enjoy the close-up beauty of miniature forest gardens, where woodland flowers bloom amid moss-covered rocks, and raise your head for far-flung vistas of distant mountains. These pleasures, and many others, await you in Mount Greylock State Reservation, as you explore the Heart of Greylock and ascend Mount Greylock, its most prominent feature and the highest mountain in Massachusetts.

Before you begin exploring Greylock country, you should stop at the visitors center, located in the southernmost part of the reservation. To reach it from the south, turn onto North Main Street on the east side of US 7 in Lanesborough, 3.2 miles north of the Pittsfield line. From the north, North Main Street is 11.6 miles south of the junction of US 7 and MA 2 south of Williamstown. Follow North Main Street 0.7 mile and turn right onto Quarry Road, and in 0.4 mile fork left onto Rockwell Road. The visitors center is 0.7 mile on the right. The reservation is open daily year-round, with the visitors center open daily from 9 AM to 5 PM. The center houses many very fine natural history exhibits and provides a wealth of information about the reservation, free trail maps, and rest rooms. To reach the hike's start, continue on

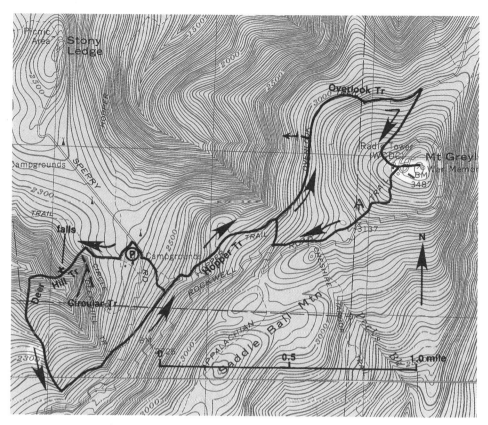

Rockwell Road another 5.7 miles to Sperry Road, which forks left, and then 0.6 mile down to Sperry Campground. You can park at the campground when Rockwell Road is open to cars, usually from May 15 to December 1. There is no daily parking fee, although there is a $4-per-night camping fee when the campsite is open (May 15 to October 15).

Leaving your car, turn left onto the gravel road past Campsite 2 at the end of the parking area. Signs here direct you toward several trails, including your eventual route, the Deer Hill Trail. Uncommon for Massachusetts, on this hike you will start at the high elevation of 2,400 feet and head downhill toward your first destination—Roaring Brook. Proceed to the end of the gravel road as it curves left, then go right and cross a wooden bridge over a small unnamed stream. In 50 feet turn onto the combined Deer Hill and Roaring Brook Trails. The path heads easily downhill, passes the turnoff to Circular Trail on the left, and crosses the brook on a second bridge. Once across the stream, turn left onto Deer Hill Trail as it splits from the Roaring Brook Trail, which continues straight ahead. The trail drops gently at first through a mixed woodland of hemlock, spruce, yellow birch, beech, and striped maple, but the slope soon steepens. The stream flowing alongside begins to hurry in response to the increased gradient and plunges over rocky steps in sparkling cascades. You will need to pay attention to the trail as it drops over rocky ledges and down steep, slippery, needle-covered

A storm approaching the second overlook from the west

slopes. Soon after you reach a hemlock grove, the Deer Hill Trail zigzags across the hillside and brings you to the base of the 40-foot-high Deer Hill Falls. As you carefully work your way down the steep slope, you will pass small cliffs of micaceous schists and glimpse the falling water through the hemlocks. A short side path leads to a close-up view of the falls, where you may wish to try your photographic skills. Here the hemlocks have grown large and mature because these inaccessible slopes were too steep even for the 19th-century lumbermen who cleared much of formidable Greylock itself.

The slope below the falls eases somewhat at first, and the narrow trail swings right across the hillside away from the stream before zigzagging steeply down the precipitous slope toward a wooden bridge over Roaring Brook. The large, rectangular holes excavated in some of the maples and beeches bear witness to the hunger pangs

of pileated woodpeckers. You may see these crow-sized black-and-white birds flapping through the trees or digging vigorously into a tree trunk. On close view you will almost certainly spot the bright red crest on their heads. The tributary that you followed down from the campground joins Roaring Brook a little way upstream from where you eventually meet it. Rocky pools, small cascades, and rapids make this place an especially attractive spot to gather your strength for the steep climb out of the valley.

Beyond the bridge, the narrow trail winds steeply uphill, at first through shrubs and deciduous forest but eventually in a more open hemlock forest. You may well need a reason to pause on this testing part of the hike: In June and July, blooming wood sorrel could be just the excuse. This low-growing plant with white and pink flowers on stalks above cloverlike leaves thrives in the damp forests of New England mountains. You will find it a familiar friend by the end of your hike. The trail heads in a southerly direction and at first flirts with a nearby stream tumbling down the hillside. When you reach a new shelter, rejoice—the steepest slope is behind you.

From here the trail climbs steadily up a more moderate slope punctuated by both steeper and compensating easier stretches. Now in better-illuminated mixed woodland, the forest floor resembles a garden in late spring and early summer, as trillium, starflower, clintonia, wood sorrel, and Indian cucumber root come into flower. Eventually the trail reaches a junction where the Deer Hill ski trail goes right, but you turn left to follow a wide old woods road as it contours around the hillside close to the 2,500-foot level. A mildly undulating 0.7 mile of enjoyable hiking past rocky cascades and across wooden bridges over small streams will gain you 40 feet in elevation and bring you to the gravel road from Sperry Campground. Your car waits 0.5 mile to the left down this road if, for any reason, you wish to shorten your hike after this first 1.3 miles.

Deer Hill Trail continues on the other side of Sperry Road, and the friendly old road brings you easily uphill for 0.3 mile to the intersection with Hopper Trail, which comes up from Sperry Campground. Later in the day, you will follow this trail down to the parking area. For now, however, follow it to the right as it climbs a moderate slope in a northeasterly direction for a while, levels briefly, and then swings east to resume its climb. Where Hopper Trail bends sharply right (south), your route, Overlook Trail, leaves to the left (north) as a rather hidden path marked by blue blazes and trail signs nailed to trees.

Overlook Trail starts by dropping to a brook with a bouldery bed and small waterfalls, but beyond the stream the gently undulating path follows a shelf around the hillside without gaining much height. Some openings in the trees allow good views northwest to Stony Ledge. Notably luxuriant vegetation grows along here: a canopy of spruce, yellow and gray birch, and beech over an understory of red, striped, and mountain maple, hobblebush, and mountain ash. The forest floor is sprinkled with a variety of woodland flowers; wood sorrel on a mossy rock provides a delicate example of beauty on a small scale. You should take the time to explore the short, prominent side trails to the left to obtain some fine views. Stony Ledge is noticeable to the west; farther away to the northwest the Taconic Range reposes in splendor along the Massachusetts–New York border; and to the north, across the deep valley called The Hopper, Mount Prospect rises with its well-defined south ridge. The view can be very dramatic when broken clouds trail across the mountains or a thunderstorm approaches from the west. Return to Overlook Trail, which gradually swings eastward, slowly gaining height. The way becomes narrow, bouldery, and shrubby in places but always remains clear, well defined, and free of navigational difficulties. After what may seem a long time, you eventually reach the paved Notch Road, which leads to the top of Mount Greylock.

Your route to the summit, however, follows a former carriage road. To reach it, cross directly over Notch Road and follow the blue blazes and signs for Overlook Trail. Go straight ahead on a narrow trail, and in 50 feet turn right. You'll head southwesterly up a long, easy slope through woods of yellow birch, mountain ash, mountain maple, and conifers. After a straight stretch of 0.3 mile, the old carriage road turns eastward and continues as a pleasant wide path through ferns and woods of mountain ash and delightfully aromatic balsam fir. When the trail ends, pass left around a TV tower and follow the Appalachian Trail to the summit of Mount Greylock and the War Memorial, which you will see ahead of you.

By walking about the mostly treeless mountaintop, you can find different vantage points that together will give you views in all directions. You will have particularly impressive ones from the rocky ledges on the east side of the summit. From here you look eastward over the town of Adams nestled in the Hoosic River valley and to the Hoosac Range beyond, and northward to the Green Mountains of southern Vermont. In summer, you may hear white-throated sparrows and common yellowthroats singing from perches on nearby shrubs, while overhead red-tailed hawks and turkey vultures may be gliding by on outspread wings. You may wish to visit Bascom Lodge, located a little below the summit on the south side, where you can obtain refreshments, gifts, and weather and trail information. The lodge, open from mid-May to late October, has overnight accommodation for 38 visitors.

To begin your descent, return to the TV tower and continue straight ahead on the white-blazed Appalachian Trail, not the Overlook Trail that you came up. The trail descends on an easy grade in a southerly direction and in 0.4 mile reaches the paved Notch Road. Notice that at the beginning of this stretch on the higher, more exposed part of the mountain, red spruce, balsam fir, and a few mountain ash predominate, but farther down, in more protected areas, these species abruptly give way to birch, beech, and cherry. Walk diagonally across the road and pick up the Appalachian Trail again. It leads you past a pretty pond amid spruce and fir on the right and downhill to a fork where you leave the Appalachian Trail and take the right fork onto the Hopper Trail. The trail descends on an easy grade and soon skirts Rockwell Road near a hairpin bend where the Hopper Trail turns sharply right and heads toward Sperry Campground.

Leaving the roadside, the trail again drops gently in a northerly direction for 400 feet and then turns sharply left. Overlook Trail, your route up the mountain, leaves to the right here. Retrace your earlier route down the easy grade for 0.5 mile, then bear right onto Hopper Trail where it leaves the wide old road. A sign for Hopper Trail on a maple tree will confirm your route. About 0.2 mile along this well-used path, you will reach a gravel road where a right turn and 100-yard walk will bring you to Sperry Campground and your car.

10

Mount Greylock

Total distance: 8.2 miles (13.2 km)

Hiking time: 7 hours

Maximum elevation: 3,487 feet (1,062 meters)

Vertical rise: 2,908 feet (885 meters)

Map: USGS North Adams (7½' x 15')

Trailhead: 42°37'56" N, 73°11'16" W

This hike to the top of Mount Greylock, the highest mountain in Massachusetts, will take you over 8 miles of trail, including parts of the famous Appalachian Trail, deep into a stream valley, and across a total of five mountaintops. It will test your endurance, and you should try it only if you are an experienced hiker and in good physical condition. Give yourself plenty of time to enjoy this long hike, and keep an eye on the weather. But when you are ready for it, this hike up Mount Greylock will give you a real feel for the mountainous land encompassed in the more than 10,000-acre Mount Greylock State Reservation—as well as great personal satisfaction.

This hike begins and ends at Sperry Campground in the midst of the reservation (see Heart of Greylock, Hike 9, for driving directions). After parking, turn left onto the gravel road and walk downhill past Deer Hill Trail on the left. In the first 1.2 miles you will descend 1,100 vertical feet from your parking place (elevation: 2,400 feet) to Money Brook, at the bottom of The Hopper. Soon your route, the blue-blazed Hopper Trail, goes right from the gravel road near Campsite 10 and in 40 feet continues straight ahead in a northerly direction where a self-guiding nature and historical trail branches right. Follow the well-defined trail, which poses no navigational problems, as it drops steadily northward. On the way down you will glimpse massive, wooded mountains through the trees to the east, including your eventual goal, Mount Greylock, which is easily identified by its TV transmitting tower. The hillsides display a wide variety of trees,

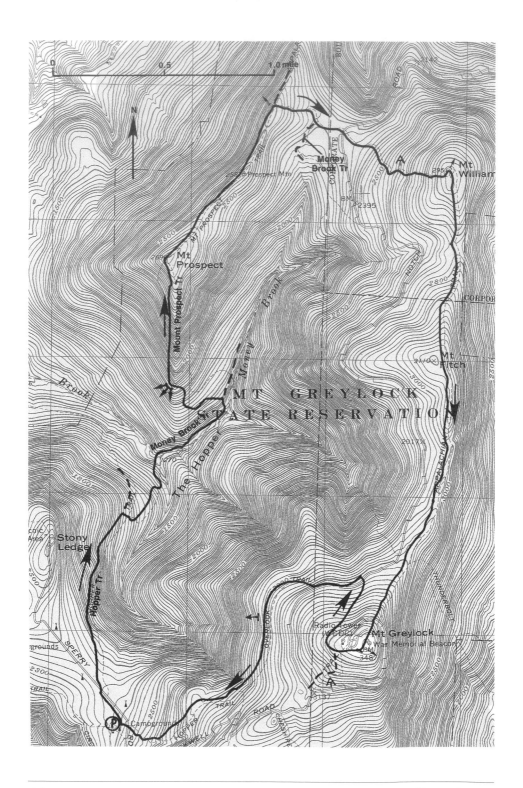

Mount Prospect from near Halley Farm

including white and yellow birch, striped and sugar maple, beech, and white ash, but notice how the mix of species changes as you descend. At lower elevations hemlock replace the spruce that grow abundantly higher up. In places the trail has been built up and widened by flat rocks—remnants of a former road that once connected Williamstown and the farms on Sperry Road. Enough sunlight reaches the woodland floor to encourage a rich display of flowers; look for partridgeberry, Indian cucumber root, wood sorrel, trillium, Canada mayflower, clintonia, wood nettle, field garlic, and white baneberry. Where the trail swings northeast you will find lots of pale touch-me-not, or jewelweed, growing in a damp area. This tall plant, with many yellow, spurred flowers, blooms through much of summer; its ripe fruit capsule pops when touched, dispersing its seeds over a wide area and giving rise to its common name. You will also see more jack-in-the-pulpit here than on most trails in Massachusetts.

Beyond the jewelweed patch you should leave the Hopper Trail, which goes straight ahead, and turn right onto the cutoff trail to Money Brook Trail, signposted and marked by blue triangular blazes. The path winds easily downhill through attractive woodlands of large maples, beeches, gray birch, and, lower down, some oaks. The most common fern at your feet is the maidenhair, and overhead in the summer ovenbirds, robins, and wood thrushes sing from the trees. As you approach a stream, the deciduous trees give way to large hemlocks, and soon you will reach an overview through the trees of a steep-sided valley. The trail turns left and parallels this valley for a while before edging down to cross a small splinter of the stream you have been following and then over a bridge across the broader stream, a tributary of Money Brook. Straight ahead beyond this tributary you quickly reach a trail junction.

To your left a bridge crosses Money Brook, but you should follow the Money

Brook Trail to the right (upstream). This area provides a reminder that bridges come and go as a result of the interaction of building humans and eroding stream floods and they may not prove reliable long-term navigational aids. In about 500 feet you will cross a small tributary of Money Brook and then rise through deciduous trees into a hemlock forest. In another 700 feet the trail levels off, and a little farther along it descends back into deciduous trees and soon reaches a major tributary of Money Brook. Approximately 150 feet farther upstream, you cross Money Brook and soon the blue-blazed trail climbs steeply up a stairway of rocks and then a bouldery slope. Keep a sharp lookout here for a T-junction, where you should turn left onto the Mount Prospect Trail. The trail heads generally southwestward for several hundred feet across a moderate slope through deciduous woodlands before turning more northwesterly. A short, steeper, rocky stretch will bring you to the crest of a well-defined ridge.

You have reached the south ridge of Mount Prospect. Before you begin the long ridge climb to its summit, take a few moments to enjoy the view through the trees. To the southwest lies Stony Ledge; to the southeast, Mount Greylock; and to the east, Mount Fitch. These mountains surround the steep-sided, glacially carved valley known as The Hopper, through which you have just traveled. Although you will see few oaks on most of this hike, both black and white oaks grow abundantly on this drier and warmer, steep, south-facing slope. Other plants to look for include lowbush blueberry, cow wheat, bush honeysuckle, Indian pipe, and swamp azalea. You may be glad to have something to stop and examine on this steep section, which can seem longer than its true distance of only 0.5 mile. The slope eases a little by a look-off where you can catch your breath and enjoy views to the west over a valley to the Taconic Range beyond. As you approach the summit of Mount Prospect, the slope eases and the ridge broadens, while the trail, somewhat overgrown by raspberries and hobblebush, narrows.

Although well marked by a rock cairn, there are no views from this first summit of your hike, and you will soon want to continue easily down the broad ridge on the other side through maple, beech, and yellow birch. After dropping only 100 feet or so in elevation, the trail climbs to the top of Prospect Mountain, the next summit on the ridge. Here you will have restricted views to the southeast of Mount Fitch and more southerly of Mount Greylock and the War Memorial on its summit. From the summit, the well-defined trail follows a fairly narrow ridge through woods that become more varied as red spruce and mountain ash mix among the maple, oak, beech, and birch. About 0.4 mile beyond the summit of Prospect Mountain, the woods open up to offer fine views west to the Green River and the Taconic Range beyond, and northwest and north to Williamstown, the Hoosic River valley, and the Green Mountains of Vermont.

Here, too, Mount Prospect Trail joins the Appalachian Trail, which you will now follow to Mount Greylock. Turn right (east) and, guided by white blazes, follow the trail easily down into a mixture of small spruces and large oaks. Straight ahead you will have your first glimpses of Mount Williams, the next peak on your circuit, before you descend through the trees past scattered outcrops of schist. The trail soon enters a mature spruce forest. Shortly, you will reach a trail intersection where Money Brook Trail goes right and your route, the Appalachian Trail, left in a northeasterly direction into a dense spruce forest. Beyond these dark woods the trail swings easterly onto a wide, former woods road that takes you through mixed woodlands to paved Notch Road.

Across Notch Road you will find the continuation of the white-blazed Appalachian Trail. Mount Greylock is still 3.0 miles distant and you have two more peaks to climb before you get there. At first the trail wanders easily up through a woods of red spruce and a few yellow birch, but the slope soon steepens and the spruce thins out as you pass into mixed woodlands with beech, maple, and gray birch. After hiking 0.5 mile from Notch Road and gaining 650 feet in elevation, you will reach the summit of 2,951-foot-high Mount Williams. From the partly cleared top you have good views northeast toward North Adams and the Green Mountains.

Your route continues southward down a broad ridge through maple, beech, and much hobblebush. In some of the schist exposed along the trail, you will find contorted and folded layers—testimony to the powerful forces that metamorphosed these rocks. About 0.4 mile from the summit of Mount Williams, you will reach a col where a trail goes right for 800 feet to Notch Road and Bernard Farm Trail comes up from the left. Continue your hike by making a 0.5-mile-long, gradual ascent up a quite narrow ridge to Mount Fitch. You'll pass the 3,000-foot contour on the way for the first time on this hike. Although the beech, maple, cherry, and birch do not grow very tall along this rather exposed ridge, unfortunately they still block the view.

The trail skirts the featureless top of 3,110-foot-high Mount Fitch, drops easily into a sheltered col where the trees grow taller, and then rises abruptly up a short,

steep, bouldery step. Between here and Mount Greylock, your fifth and final peak, you climb easily through very attractive woodland. You may wish to dawdle through the forest of spruce, hemlock, mountain ash, and yellow birch and admire the natural gardens of wood sorrel, club moss, and clintonia amid moss-covered boulders and rocky ledges of schist. In summer, background music may be provided by a hermit thrush as it sings its haunting, clear, flutelike song from some spruce tree. Soon the trail widens and begins to climb quite steeply toward Mount Greylock. Already you can see the top of the War Memorial on its summit. When you reach paved Notch Road, turn around and look back northward to Mount Fitch and Mount Williams and the route you have just hiked. The Appalachian Trail continues steeply up on the other side of the road to an unfortunately located parking lot, which you bypass, to reach the top of the 3,487-foot-high mountain. By walking about the cleared summit you can have, on a clear day, views eastward to central Massachusetts and around into neighboring New Hampshire, Vermont, New York, and Connecticut (see Heart of Greylock, Hike 9, for more information about the summit area).

Your return route follows the Overlook and Hopper Trails, which are more fully described in Hike 9. When you are ready to leave the summit, walk down to the TV building and turn right onto blue-blazed Overlook Trail, which will soon bring you to Notch Road again. A trail sign and blue triangular blazes show you where the Overlook Trail picks up beyond the road. Continue down through the woods another 0.9 mile to Hopper Trail—do not miss the fine views described in Hike 9—turn right, and in 0.7 mile you will be back at your car.

11

Berlin Mountain

Total distance: 4.5 miles (7.2 km)

Hiking time: 4 hours

Maximum elevation: 2,798 feet (852 meters)

Vertical rise: 1,720 feet (524 meters)

Map: USGS Berlin (7½' x 15')

Trailhead: 42°42'08" N, 73°16'09" W

The open summit of Berlin Mountain offers a 360-degree panorama of the Taconic Range in portions of three states. Even this unobstructed view, however, does not penetrate the curtain of time to reveal the complex and exciting geologic history of the Taconics. Studies of Taconic rocks in a continuous 150-mile belt extending from Sudbury, Vermont, to Poughkeepsie, New York, show that these mountains are built with rocks that are older than the rocks on which the mountains rest. This unlikely state of affairs—older rocks on top of younger rocks—developed during a major event in the geologic history of North America known today as the Taconic orogeny.

Five hundred million years ago, the site of Berlin Mountain looked much like the Caribbean does today: Limestone and coral reefs had developed in warm, shallow water near the eastern edge of the continent. Farther east, silt and mud were being deposited in deeper water. This situation continued until about 460 million years ago, when the tranquillity of the region was crudely interrupted as the deeper-water sediments were moved westward in a series of enormous slivers up and over the shallow-water limestones. Whatever caused this movement, possibly the collision of a chain of volcanic islands with the east coast of North America, also moved the 1-billion-year-old crystalline "basement" rocks that were under the sediment west and over the limestone in slices, which today constitute the high country of Beartown State Forest (Hike 4), Warner Hill (Hike 7), and Mount Greylock (Hikes 8, 9, and 10). The lime-

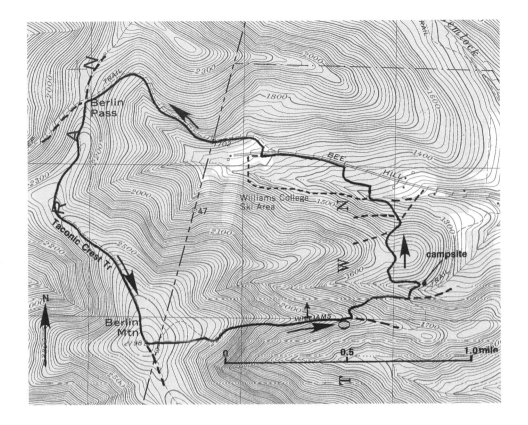

stones, now marble, can be seen in the quarry near Adams at the base of Greylock. At Berlin Mountain, the only obvious evidence of this amazing history is the character of the rocks along the trail: minerals that formed from deep-water silts during a moderate heating, small folds, and sedimentary layers that are no longer horizontal. Nevertheless, it is exciting to sit on top of Berlin Mountain with some knowledge of the natural drama behind the scenery before you.

To reach the trail up Berlin Mountain, drive to the junction of MA 2 and US 7 south of Williamstown, then travel west on MA 2 for 0.3 mile. Bear left onto Torry Woods Road. At a junction in 0.4 mile, continue straight; drive another 0.8 mile and keep left, going uphill on Bee Hill Road for a final

0.9 mile to a small parking area on the left. This is the parking area for the Williamstown Rural Lands Foundation (WRLF) Trail, a 1.4-mile interpretive loop trail that is a good alternative if you don't care to tackle the full hike. A small sign at the parking area proclaims the Class of 1933 (Williams College) Berlin Mountain Trail, which is your return route. Lock your car and continue on the gravel road uphill, in August among yellow buttons of common tansy, Queen Anne's lace, white snakeroot, and other flowers. In 0.4 mile you will arrive at a large open area being invaded by gray birch and aspen. This was the parking lot for a ski area operated by Williams College. The ski lift is gone, but a prominent ski trail remains to guide your eyes upward toward Berlin Mountain. Turn

Berlin Mountain   71

The Taconic Range from Berlin Mountain

right as you enter the open area and look for a gravel road leading uphill to the north. (Turn left onto the WRLF Trail here to return to your car if you wish.)

Walk north on the old road leading to Berlin Pass through a hardwood forest of maple, birch, oak, ash, and beech. This road is still passable by four-wheel-drive vehicles, although it is hard to believe that it was ever passable by anything else. Try to imagine urging a team of horses or oxen to pull a wagon up this steep incline en route from Williamstown to Berlin, New York—no doubt a common ordeal 200 years ago. Outcrops of greenish rock are abundant, both alongside and as a natural pavement for the road. A short distance up the trail, you will enter New York State (no change of pavement flags the border here). The jade green color of the rocks is due to a platy, iron-bearing mineral called chlorite. Chlorite joins the mineral muscovite, a mica, in giving the rocks a silvery sheen that catches the

sunlight and signals metamorphic rock called phyllite. Both minerals have grown with their plates parallel to a general layering in the rocks, tilted to the southeast and highlighted by white quartz layers and lenses.

Your arrival at Berlin Pass is heralded by the appearance of stunted trees and an abundance of shrublike fire cherry, mountain ash, and gray birch. No doubt the wind truly whistles through this pass many days of the year. At the pass, you will turn left onto a dirt road running along the wide ridge to the top of Berlin Mountain. First, however, take a moment to go right to a small clearing for a preview of sights to come. Here the horizon is dominated by Mount Greylock to the east. Pink-spiked meadowsweet crowds this clearing in competition with farkleberry and some delicious blueberries. Now cross the pass and walk south along the dirt road, which is marked with the white blazes of the Taconic Crest Trail.

As you walk uphill, trees rise to more normal heights, accommodating a veritable chorus of birds. Some perennial large puddles and messy detours record the passage of off-road vehicles, but the road dries out as you begin a more steady climb. Blackberry treats ripen in sunny openings along the road in August. Layering in rock outcroppings cuts obliquely across the road here, rather than roughly paralleling the road as it did earlier. It is the road that has changed orientation, however, for the rock layers have the same southeasterly inclination. The top of Berlin Mountain is largely treeless, although a crowd of spruce trees is encroaching. Expansive views are offered in all directions. Particularly prominent are Mount Greylock to the east, Pownal Dome to the north, and the Taconic Range stretching to the south. If you come in late July or August, a feast of blueberries and more blackberries may await you in the summit clearing.

When you've had your fill of scenery and berries, look for a wide grassy path parting the hay-scented ferns and leading east-northeast downhill. Fifty yards below the summit clearing, turn right onto a good trail with faint red blazes and follow it downhill through a wood of gray-trunked American beech. The path descends a narrow ridge, steeply in places. Recent logging had disrupted the path somewhat in 1998, but the logging road follows the east-trending ridge and so should you. Where the trail levels somewhat and passes a grove of hemlock trees, begin watching for older blue blazes along with the newer, reddish orange ones. Approximately 100 yards past the hemlocks, turn left with the blue blazes onto a path alongside the logging road. In another 50 yards this path, and its blue blazes, turns left and drops you quickly, first to the northwest and then, via a switchback, to the northeast into a valley. Do not take any trail that descends from the logged ridge right and to the south.

On this north-facing slope, beech trees give way to hemlocks, then white and yellow birch and green-striped maples. Patches of shining club moss, woodfern, and Christmas fern line your route. Maples dominate in the valley where the trail widens into a woods road. In about 200 yards the next turn, to the left, down and across a small stream in the valley bottom, is poorly marked and easy to miss. The turn is in a wet spot on the road near the point where the brook drops noticeably away from the road. If the valley begins to widen and the road swings northward, you have gone too far. Prominent rock outcrops of now familiar greenish rocks are cut by the brook where the trail crosses.

Across the brook is a campsite that has been used by the Williams College Outing Club, the organization responsible for the blue blazes. From here to your car, the path is a comparatively new trail designed to avoid private land downstream. Because the route is somewhat tortuous, you must pay attention to the blue blazes. Turn left at the camp and follow the blue blazes upstream a short distance, then walk up and across a flat hill to the north. Next go downhill in a troughlike path, past a trail joining from the left, then make a sharp left turn with the blue blazes. A sequence of turns (right, left, right) guides you steadily downhill to a stream crossing, with clear water to tempt bare, tired feet. Just before the stream you join the WRLF Interpretive Loop Trail mentioned at the beginning of this hike. On the far side of the stream, walk up into a crowded stand of young birch, beech, and maple stilts. If you watch carefully for the blue blazes, you will soon navigate the several remaining turns to arrive at a gravel road. Turn left to find your car, now just 100 yards away.

12

Spruce Hill

Total distance: 2.6 miles (4.2 km)

Hiking time: 2 hours

*Maximum elevation: 2,566 feet
(781 meters)*

Vertical rise: 680 feet (207 meters)

Map: USGS North Adams (7½' x 15')

Trailhead: 42°39'29" N, 73°03'19" W

Eighteen hundred feet above the Hoosic River in North Adams, the rocky summit of Spruce Hill commands an impressive view of Massachusetts's marble valley. It seems almost unjust that this Olympian roost is accessible by only modest effort over such a short trail. But when placed in a regional context, the Spruce Hill panorama is revealed to be a view into a "grand canyon" cut into an uplifted erosion surface. Pleistocene glaciers have deepened the canyon and steepened its sides. Thus, for an awesome view, all you have to do is walk up to the edge of the canyon and look down. For the price, well within reach of most people, the view is a steal.

Spruce Hill is located in Savoy Mountain State Forest in the town of Florida. On the USGS topographic map, part of the trail is shown to be in Florida State Forest, which has now been assimilated into Savoy Mountain State Forest. To reach the trailhead from the north, locate the intersection of MA 2 and Shaft Road on MA 2, just 2.0 miles west of the Whitcomb Summit lookout tower (alternatively, 0.6 mile east of the West Summit lookout tower). Drive southeast on Shaft Road past a road entering from the left at 0.5 mile and past a road entering from the right at 1.5 miles. At 2.1 miles, turn right along with Shaft Road and travel 0.9 mile to a bend in the road by a swamp, just past the brown Savoy Mountain State Forest headquarters buildings. Park your car in the wide pull-off area. If you are coming from the south, begin at the western junction of MA 8A and MA 116 in Savoy and drive 0.4 mile east on MA 116 to Center Road, where there is the first of several signs for Savoy Mountain State Forest. Turn left onto Center Road and drive 2.9 miles to a T-junction. Turn left onto Adams Road and in 0.2 mile right onto New State Road. (A right turn onto Adams Road at the T-junction leads, in 0.6 mile, to a very rough paved road to a fire tower atop Borden Mountain.) From the junction of New State Road and Adams Road, drive 1.5 miles north (past the badly rutted road to lovely Tannery Falls at 1.3 miles) to a T-junction. Turn left onto Burnett Road. In 0.5 mile, turn right with the main road onto Florida Road. You will reach the trailhead in another 2.3 miles, after passing the South Pond campground and the North Pond swimming area.

From your car, walk west on a wide dirt path that is the old Florida–Adams road. Perennial large puddles may host a community of tadpoles or a few newts. The trail to Spruce Hill (named Busby Trail on some maps and signs after an early landowner, George Busby) begins in a few yards (the first right) as a less traveled road heading north into a woods filled with eastern hemlock and yellow birch. A sign here in 1998 announces SPRUCE HILL HAWK LOOKOUT. Blue blazes confirm your route, but the path is well trodden and clear. You will pass under two sets of high-voltage power lines leading southwest from the former Yankee Atomic nuclear power plant in Rowe and the Bear Swamp pumped storage facility. Between the two sets, you may have to walk to the left of the main track, which can be quite boggy. If the sun is shining, the trail will sparkle with reflections from mica crystals in the soil. Periodic clearing of brush along the transmission lines stimulates a vigorous growth of raspberries and blackberries—you will find more than you can eat in early August, but be sure to wear long pants to protect against thorns if you plan any serious browsing in this brier patch.

Beyond the second power line, the trail begins the business of climbing. Several 1990s clearcuts open the trail to light and remind you of the multiple uses included in the mission of state forests. You will walk along an unusual trough in the hillside filled with maples, which contrast with the spruce on either side. Larger than required by the stream within it, this trough may be the channel of a former glacial meltwater stream. In spring, white Canada mayflower, starflower, and yellow trout lilies festoon the forest floor. Low ledges on the left exhibit samples of the quartz- and feldspar-rich metamorphic rocks of the Cambrian Hoosac Formation, named for the Hoosac Range in which you are walking. Just past the ledges, a well-preserved cellar hole marking the homesite of some earlier settler can be found on the right. A switchback soon signals a steepening of the grade that continues the rest of the way to the summit. Do not turn on a level, and therefore inviting, cross trail that you meet at a prominent stone wall.

While catching your breath along this final 400-foot ascent, look at the delicate ferns that grace the trail. You should be able to distinguish two common varieties: the low, lacy hay-scented fern, which grows in thick mats, and the taller, coarser cinnamon fern that grows in clumps. The last few yards to the summit are quite steep, but have been improved by a new path with steps and switchbacks. Follow the blue blazes beside and up a long outcrop of Hoosac schist to emerge from the woods into a wonderful clearing on the north end of Spruce Hill. If you've chosen a day in early fall for your hike, you will probably find others here watching for the southerly migration of hawks. And for good reason! There is a 180-degree view, from the Taconic Range, Williamstown, and North Adams in the west to the Green Mountains in southern Ver-

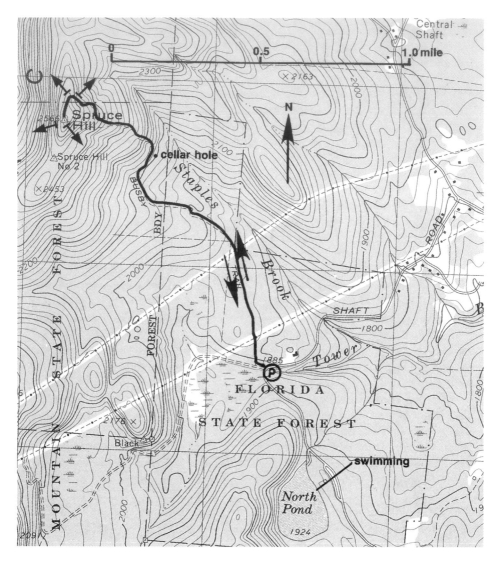

mont to Mount Monadnock in southern New Hampshire. For southerly views, follow the trail a few more yards across the summit to the very steep cliff on the south end of Spruce Hill. There you will see better the most impressive valley occupied by the Hoosic River and by the towns of Adams and North Adams. Just across the valley, Mount Greylock (Hikes 8, 9, and 10), adorned with the scar of a May 13, 1990, landslide, towers above everything. South of Adams, several square miles of open fields provide a glimpse of what much of the Berkshires must have looked like 160 years ago, before the human exodus to more fertile land in the West. These fields stand in stark contrast to the continuous forest to the south and east.

A variety of geologic factors have combined to produce this deep valley. First, a layer of erosion-resistant rocks caps a layer of erosion-prone rocks. The erosion-resistant rocks are the ones you are standing on: metamorphic rocks containing quartz, feldspar, white mica, chlorite (greenish mica), and red garnet. The erosion-prone rocks are marbles, the white rocks visible in the quarries to the southeast across the valley. Second, the rock layers have been bent upward into a large arch centered on the valley, bringing the softer marble closer to the surface. Third, a prehistoric Hoosic River was captured by the less resistant rocks in the center of the arch and cut the path of the present valley. Finally, glaciers deepened the valley, perhaps by a large amount, and steepened the valley walls. The marble in the valley is actually younger than the rocks on Spruce Hill and those on Mount Greylock. Implications of these age relations are discussed in the Beartown Mountain and Berlin Mountain hikes (Hikes 4 and 11). This marble is quarried in Adams to be crushed and spread on fields or lawns to dissolve in rainwater and raise the pH of normally acidic New England soils.

Seventeen hundred feet almost directly below you is the Hoosac tunnel of the Boston and Maine Railroad. Nearly 5 miles long, it connects the Hoosic and Deerfield River valleys. Built between 1851 and 1875 at a cost to the commonwealth of Massachusetts of more than $17 million and a tragic 199 lives, this engineering marvel was the source of much political controversy, pitting communities that would benefit from the rail traffic against those that would not. Enjoy the summit on a calm, sunny day, and you will find it hard to leave. However, the dwarfed maple and cherry trees suggest that your stay will be short if the wind is blowing. Return to your car by the same clear path that brought you here.

13

Notchview Reservation

Total distance: 5.4 miles (8.7 km)

Hiking time: 3½ hours

*Maximum elevation: 2,297 feet
(699 meters)*

Vertical rise: 790 feet (241 meters)

*Maps: USGS Cheshire (7½' x 15'),
USGS Pittsfield East (7½' x 15')*

Trailhead: 42°30'13" N, 73°02'11"W

Notchview Reservation in the heart of the Berkshires must be one of the best-kept secrets in Massachusetts. With more than 3,000 acres, Notchview is larger than most tracts of land accessible to the public in this state. Yet in spite of its size, Notchview is not heavily used, and many days of the year you may well find that you are the only human visitor. The low use may be because Notchview does not have facilities for camping, swimming, boating, fishing, or snowmobiling, which tempt many people into the out-of-doors. If you want solitude, however, and a chance to walk or cross-country ski in the Berkshire woods, the 25 miles of well-maintained trails in Notchview are unsurpassed.

A small, unobtrusive sign marks the entrance to Notchview on the north side of MA 9, 1.0 mile east of the intersection of MA 9 and MA 8A in Windsor. A parking lot and the Budd Visitor Center are located 300 yards east of the entrance. Named for Arthur D. Budd, who bequeathed Notchview to the Trustees of Reservations in 1965, the visitors center offers rest rooms, and in winter a place to warm up or wax skis. A trail fee is collected by a warden (or a hollow metal post) from visitors over 12 who are not members of the Trustees of Reservations. All the trails are shown on a map of the reservation that is posted at the northeast end of the parking lot; copies of the map are available in a wooden box. The route described here provides a good overview of the reservation. However, do not hesitate to choose different trails if you want a shorter hike. Most trails are clearly marked with signs and yellow blazes.

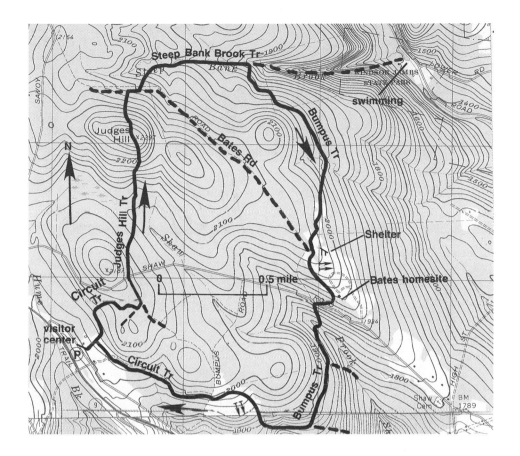

From the parking lot, walk north along a white fence into the woods. Just as you enter the trees, turn left onto Circuit Trail. At the first junction, which you reach shortly, go straight with the Circuit Trail. Here and throughout much of Notchview, the trail passes through a forest of mixed hardwoods dominated by maple and birch and scattered stands of spruce. Your route follows an unusually wide swath cut in the woods to facilitate cross-country skiing. At the next fork, bear right (to skip a skier's switchback), climb gradually past a small clearing that harbors blueberry bushes for a late-July treat, and wind through a spruce woods past a variety of club mosses. Bear left

at the next junction, left at a fork, and then in 25 yards left once more onto Judges Hill Trail.

The wide, mown path that leads to Judges Hill evokes the same tranquil feelings lent by an old garden lane, feelings that are reinforced by long-forgotten apple trees. Soon the trail crosses little-used Shaw Road (dirt) and continues gently downhill toward the north. A patch of spotted touch-me-not (also called jewelweed), with pendantlike, orange, spotted flowers in July and seedpods that explode at a touch in late summer, signals a moist stretch of trail ahead. Even during the drier times of summer this slope may be soggy, as myriad tiny springs leak rainwater stored in the po-

Old chimney on Judges Hill

rous blanket of sand and gravel left by melting glaciers on the hill above. Heal-all, a wild mint, carpets the path with dense, oblong heads of tiny, hooded violet flowers in midsummer.

The trail crosses a small bridge over the beginnings of Shaw Brook and ascends the drier slope of Judges Hill to the highest point of your hike. At the top are the remains of a fieldstone foundation and fireplace. The chimney is particularly impressive because there is no evidence that mortar of any kind was used in its construction. Mortarless construction was possible because of the flat rocks available to the builders. The building stones are metamorphic rocks, found locally, that have broken along planes defined by platy, white mica crystals (muscovite). The micas grew in this fashion while the rock was being squeezed at high temperatures (see Mount Race and Mount Everett, Hike 2, for an explanation of this process). Like ancient pressure weather vanes, micas record the once prevailing di-

rection of maximum stress. Although the summit of Judges Hill is now wooded, try to imagine how spectacular the view here was some 150 years ago, when most of this and the surrounding hills were cleared of trees. A dense growth of young American beech trees shades the path as you leave the ruins and begin the descent to the north. Extensive patches of hay-scented fern border the trail down.

At the end of Judges Hill Trail, turn right onto Bates Road, an old stagecoach route. Most hikers should follow Bates Road approximately 1 mile to a large open field on the left (and skip to the next paragraph). If you are comfortable with topographic maps and want more adventure, turn left onto Steep Bank Brook Trail in about 150 yards just before Bates Road crosses a small stream. This trail has been neglected in recent years and was not well marked in 1998. Steep Bank Brook Trail follows a small stream that becomes larger as several

Western Massachusetts

other streams merge with it along your route. If in doubt about your route, stay close to the stream. Ferns thrive in this valley, including cinnamon fern, New York fern, Christmas fern, and spinulose woodfern. Like most ferns, these species are fairly distinctive and easy to identify with a field guide. Shortly beyond the point where the trail begins to get more difficult, with numerous stream crossings on abundant and occasionally slippery rocks, you will reach a junction with Bumpus Trail where a stream enters from the right in a prominent valley. Take Bumpus Trail right (south), up the steep bank. (If you're really adventuresome, consider continuing about 1 mile farther downstream on Steep Bank Brook Trail for a swim in the pond dammed from the Westfield River in Windsor State Forest. Be forewarned, however, that any cooling you experience may be lost on the climb back to this junction.)

Bumpus Trail winds along a maze of stone walls, through thick hardwood forest, under tall spruce, through dark hemlocks, and past bracken fern and interrupted fern. Red-circle blazes mark the route, but are not as frequent as you might wish. Some sections follow overgrown logging roads. Yellow clintonia flowers in May and navy clintonia berries in July offer spots of color in the pervasive green. Bear right when you meet the blue blazes of a Windsor State Forest trail. Eventually Bumpus Trail enters a large clearing (bordered in part by glossy buckthorn), around which it winds counterclockwise on a mown path. (If you took the Bates Road shortcut, you'll rejoin Bumpus Trail by turning left into this open field, which

is visible just after Minor Trail leaves on the right.) This field, which offers a fine view of the notch cut by the Westfield River to the southeast, is a good spot to rest or eat your lunch. If you wish, you can use the table at the three-sided Thomas Carl Pierce Shelter at the northwest end of the main field. In several places, glacially smoothed outcrops of schists form the surface of the field, reminding you why most Berkshire farms were abandoned long ago. A tree-lined drive in the southeast corner of the field leads to the former front door of the home of General Bates (after whom the road was named). Goldenrod and purple cow vetch decorate the meadow in August.

Look for Bumpus Trail leading into the woods south from the Bates home, downhill to the west, and across Shaw Road near its junction with Bates Road. A large patch of sensitive fern adjoins the trail where it meets Shaw Road. After descending to cross Shaw Brook, you will climb gradually for about 0.3 mile to a right turn onto an old, grass-covered road guarded on both sides by stone walls. Emerging from the woods, you will wind counterclockwise around a hay field for another look at the notch from another shelter and bench. At the end of the field (and Bumpus Trail), go straight onto Circuit Trail, which heads into an array of planted spruce. As you walk along the dirt road here, watch for low rock outcrops on the right as a service building comes into view. An inspection of the rocks will reveal lovely red garnet crystals. Continue past the service building through more spruce, and along the edge of a grassy field to the Budd Visitor Center and your car.

14

Dorothy Frances Rice Sanctuary

Total distance: 3.8 miles (6.1 km)

Hiking time: 2½ hours

Maximum elevation: 2,120 feet (646 meters)

Vertical rise: 570 feet (174 meters)

Map: USGS Pittsfield East (7½' x 15')

Trailhead: 42°25'25" N, 73°02'11" W

If you want a family outing that includes a gentle walk in the woods, head for the delightful Dorothy Frances Rice Sanctuary for Wildlife in the small town of Peru. Six color-coded loop trails, each approximately 1 mile long, lead from a central parking area to various corners of the 273-acre sanctuary. Comparatively low-relief combined with well-maintained, wide trails make the hiking here particularly pleasant if you're accompanied by small children. Come in spring for colorful wildflowers, in summer for air-conditioned woods and delicious blueberries, in fall for glorious colors. With habitats ranging from swamps and ponds to thick brush and dense forest, ample opportunity exists to view a wide variety of flora and fauna, from ferns to flycatchers.

To reach the Dorothy Frances Rice Sanctuary, drive to the crossroads town of Peru on MA 143, west of Worthington and east of Hinsdale. From the triangular common and white church in Peru, drive south on South Road 1 mile; the entrance of the sanctuary is straight ahead where South Road makes a 90-degree right turn to the west. In 0.4 mile, the gravel entrance road ends at a small parking area adjacent to a tiny visitors center/warden's cabin. The gate to the entrance road may be closed during the winter, but courteous hikers are welcome year-round. Administered by the New England Forestry Foundation, the sanctuary was created by Oran and Mary Rice in memory of their daughter Dorothy, who died of tuberculosis in 1925, just two years after her graduation from Smith College in Northampton.

Wild animals like the Dorothy Frances Rice Sanctuary and, if you are lucky, you may see some of them. During one visit, we noticed a small wire fence around the vehicle owned by the resident warden. The fence was an attempt to ward off local porcupines, which apparently consider the rubber parts of a car to be something of a delicacy. Tires are convenient and tasty, but various hoses are also in demand for nighttime dining. Road salt contained in the rubber may be the critical seasoning. If you can arrange to come in early August, plan to bring your own appetite for a less exotic feast of highbush blueberries, which thrive near the parking area and along some of the trails.

A large, painted sketch map of the sanctuary trails is mounted next to the parking area, and copies of the map may be available in the visitors center. The route described below combines portions of all six trails to make a counterclockwise circuit of the entire sanctuary, but because each trail is fairly short, well blazed, and easy to follow, do not hesitate to try any that suit your fancy. Please note, however, that only the full circuit has been sketched on the accompanying map.

To begin your sanctuary explorations, walk north from the parking area along a mown path marked with blue blazes. Proceed into mixed spruce woods where the path is lush with hay-scented fern. Tiny jungles of 1- to 2-inch-high *Polytrichum commune,* or common haircap moss, will cushion your steps in many places here and throughout the sanctuary. Towering over the moss jungles, but only a short step up in scale, are forests of ground cedar and running pine, similar 6-inch-high club mosses that look like miniature branching evergreens. The runners for ground cedar are deeply buried, while those for running pine creep along the surface. Both provide cover for many small toads that may be found along the trail in late summer.

Because this circuit is composed of sections of many trails, you will encounter numerous trail junctions. Bear right at all trail forks. Your first major turn will be from the Blue Trail to the Orange Trail. The blazes for the Orange Trail are situated so that they are clearly visible when you are walking this particular loop in a clockwise direction, so you may find them hard to spot. The path is quite clear, however, and will lead you to a magnificent stone wall at the northern edge of the sanctuary, along an eerie wetland, and back to the Blue Trail, where you again turn right.

Stay with the Blue Trail as it winds partway up and down a small ridge. Along the way a vista opens to the south where the foresters have clear-cut a section. You may see thick mats of two different downy-needled club mosses with erect (shining club moss) or branching (staghorn club moss) stems. As you approach South Road at the entrance gate, the trail passes a prominent white birch standing over the stone-enclosed outlet of an old spring on your right. Make a left turn and follow the entrance road you drove earlier. In about 200 yards, stop to visit a small pond hidden by arrowwood, chokecherry, and willow shrubs on the left. Beavers are often living in this pond, which they deepened by careful dam work. An impressive beaver lodge was visible in 1998. Along the road, 4-foot-high fronds of interrupted fern, so called because of the brown clusters "interrupting" the ladder of leaflets on fertile leaves, grow in circular groups.

At the first path on the right, where two stone walls meet to form a corner, turn right, off the road, across one stone wall, and onto the obvious mown path of the Yellow Trail. Thick growths of young maples, cherries, and birches line the trail here, making a tunnel in what was probably an open field as recently as 30 years ago. Apple trees and

Beaver lodge in beaver pond

highbush blueberries remain as signs that this area was once someone's home. Look for ripe blackberries when you slow to avoid the sharp thorns of the stalks that crowd the trail. Sizable bear droppings here reminded us that there are other visitors who like to browse. Follow the Yellow Trail as it wends its way around an open area resulting from storm damage and cutting. After climbing a short uphill stretch, make a sharp right turn onto the Red Trail. Stone walls border the route on both sides here, indicating a former road. As the Red Trail departs to your left, keep to the right to follow the White Trail. You now enter an older, taller forest, cross a brook on the roots of a yellow birch growing on the remains of an old stone bridge, and begin a climb that angles steadily along and up the side of a ravine. After an abrupt turn to the left (north) with the White Trail, begin watching for the Red Trail again. You reach the junction shortly after you cross a tiny, trickling brook. Turn right.

The Red Trail will lead you southeast up and across a ridge, northeast down the other side, then northwest up and down again. White-tailed deer may be hiding in the woods nearby; three were spotted together here on one visit. Occasional ribs of bedrock protrude through the veneer of unsorted gravel and silt left by melting glaciers. Watch for the Pink Trail as you descend gradually to the northwest. Turn right near a large contorted beech tree to cross a boggy section filled with moisture-loving sensitive fern, which you can recognize by its coarse, winged leaflets that are not divided into subleaflets. Ferns that have no subleaflets, such as sensitive fern, are called once-cut; ferns that have leaflets divided into smooth-edged subleaflets, such as interrupted fern, are called twice-cut; ferns with lacy subleaflets, such as those on the hay-scented fern, are called thrice-cut. This categorization greatly simplifies fern identification. Follow the Pink Trail up and down to a steeper climb partway up French Hill.

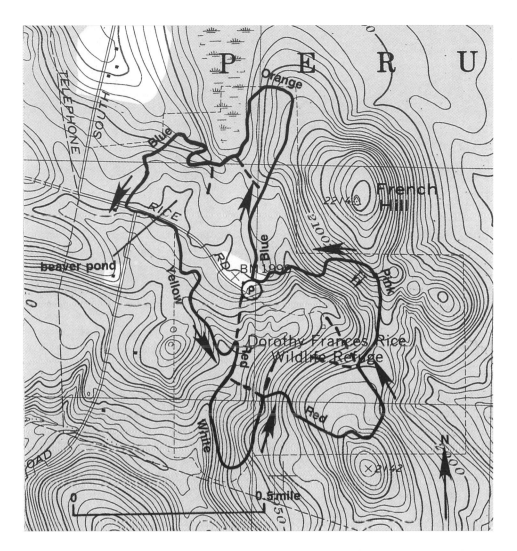

An opening in the trees near the top of French Hill affords a fine vista west across the sanctuary and beyond to Warner Hill (Hike 7). Outcrops of mica schist of the 500-million-year-old Cambrian Hoosac Formation can be seen at the clearing and elsewhere along the Pink Trail. This same rock unit is found in a north–south band that crosses Massachusetts and passes through this spot as well as through Notchview Reservation (Hike 13) and Spruce Hill (Hike 12). Red garnets pepper the schist with a shape and color reminiscent of the pomegranates after which they were named. Continue along the Pink Trail, which runs mostly downhill from the overlook, back to your car. If time remains, take a short walk along the start of the Pink Trail (not on the described circuit) to two ponds in a large meadow for some salamander sleuthing.

15

Granville State Forest

Total distance: 4.7 miles (7.6 km)

Hiking time: 3 hours

Maximum elevation: 1,285 feet (391 meters)

Vertical rise: 580 feet (177 meters)

Map: USGS Southwick (7½' x 15')

Trailhead: 42°03'47" N, 72°57'59" W

If you've ever wanted to slide on a smooth rock surface over a waterfall and plunge into a deep pool of water, visit Hubbard River in Granville State Forest on a hot summer day. The rock slide may not be as long as those in the movie versions of the *Swiss Family Robinson* or *South Pacific,* but the thrill of the ride is very real. Located adjacent to small picnic and camping areas, this unique swimming hole has surprisingly few visitors much of the time. Many other small cascades and enticing pools highlight Hubbard River as it descends an impressive valley. A hike down the Hubbard River valley and back on old woods roads following a broad ridge makes an interesting and varied circuit to get you ready for a swim. Bring old canvas shoes for wading, along with your hiking boots.

Granville State Forest nestles up to the Connecticut border southwest of Westfield. From the white church in the tiny community of West Granville (5 miles west of Granville), go west on MA 57, 0.9 mile to West Hartland Road, where you'll see a sign for the forest. Turn left and travel 1.1 miles downhill into the state forest. Leave your car in the small parking area on the left 50 yards past the new bridge (1997) over Hubbard River. A state forest day-use fee may be collected in the summer. Walk back across the bridge and turn right (south) onto the paved road leading to the Hubbard River Campground. The pavement ends at a circle in 0.4 mile, but the road bears left, continues along the river, and eventually shrinks to a trail.

Rare blue blazes mark the route, but the path here is easy to follow. Initially, the trail

Hubbard Brook

Granville State Forest

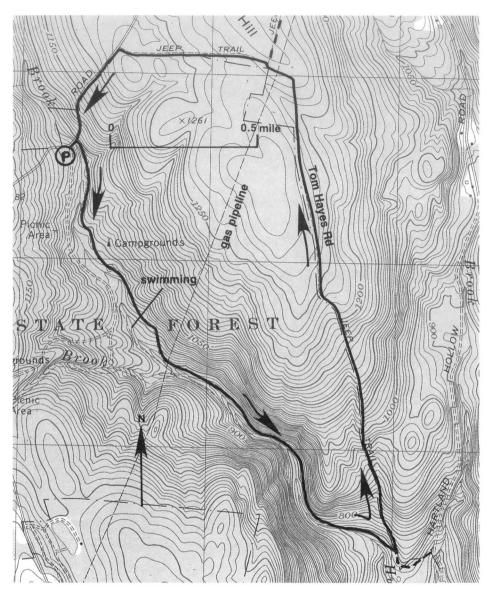

hugs the stream. When it begins to climb a small rise and bend left away from Hubbard River, follow one of the small side trails on the right to overlook the special swimming hole. A deep pool receives water and swimmers that plunge over a 6-foot-high precipice. Water in the river is orange-brown in color, probably because of vegetable tannins leached from humus derived from tannin-rich eastern hemlock, the predominant tree in the valley. Hemlock, which keeps the valley cool and dark, is easy to recognize by its flat needles with blue-striped undersides that grow in rows like the barbs of a feather. Maple, birch, and beech trees are scattered among the hemlocks.

Hobblebush, a common viburnum shrub with large, opposite, oval leaves, grows in the shade here, its white flower clusters in spring leading to green, then red, berry clusters in summer.

Return to the main path, but be sure to make regular detours out onto the rocks that line the stream, watching for poison ivy lurking in the shadows. Polished by flowing water and ice and scrubbed during spring floods, slippery streamside outcroppings of bedrock display a number of interesting geologic features. At the swimming hole and for some distance downstream, the rocks are gneisses that resulted from the metamorphism of other rocks, probably granite, more than 1 billion years ago (see Warner Hill, Hike 7). Dikes of granite pegmatite are clearly visible, particularly at the bottom of shallow pools, as white bands a few inches wide cutting haphazardly across the north–south lines on the surface of the gneiss. The dikes were formed when molten rock invaded the solid gneiss along cracks. The name "pegmatite" is used to mean that the crystals of the rock are large and easily visible. You may see sunlight reflected off flat cleavage surfaces of inch-long, milky white feldspar crystals in the pegmatite dikes, analogous to the sparkling surfaces of mica plates.

Among the moss-covered rocks you'll find dark green Christmas fern, so named because its leaves are green at Christmastime and its "eared" leaflets look like hanging Christmas stockings. Ignore possible turns on an orange-blazed trail left and on a straight track following a gas pipeline. As you continue downstream, the valley narrows between steepening slopes. In places the path is well above the cascading stream that carved this route. You cross an important geologic boundary, spanning at least 500 million years, between Precambrian gneisses and Cambrian schists. This boundary would have been easy to locate 550 million years ago, when fossiliferous marine sands and silts were being deposited on top of the gneiss. Today, however, the boundary is hard to locate because both the sediment and the gneiss have been subsequently metamorphosed and look rather similar. Eventually the valley broadens in anticipation of merging with the Pond Brook valley to the east, and the old road you are following bends east and away from the river. Here, beneath towering red oaks, the trail meets Tom Hayes Road. Make a hard left turn (north) onto this gravel road. (If you go right, you will encounter some wide, frog-filled puddles as the road makes an extended bend to the left on its way to meet closed Hartland Hollow Road in about 400 yards.)

Tom Hayes Road is a fairly straight track heading about 15 degrees west of true north and will be your path for about 1.5 miles. It is a route used by all-terrain vehicles and snowmobiles, but we have never seen any in our many visits to the forest. The clear path soon detours to the right from the original straight road because of severe erosion. If you don't take the detour, you will see small gullies in the road grow into a 10-foot-deep ditch as you climb uphill, rendering the road impassable to four-wheel-drive vehicles and difficult even for hikers. Although you may want to do much of your walking on the newer bypass track, do take time to examine the spectacular erosion. Cavernous gullies are the inevitable fate of unattended, unditched gravel roads in hilly terrain, for the road will capture any stream of rainwater runoff that comes its way. Destruction of the road has provided a great opportunity for anyone interested in surficial geology. In the sides of the gullies, profiles of the forest soil and usually hidden glacial deposits ("till") are exposed. At the top of each profile is a layer of black, decayed forest debris. Next is a layer, typically sandy clay, where the glacial till has been leached by infiltrating rainwater. Below this layer is a zone, typically a rusty color, where some of the elements leached from the layer above are precipitated. Finally, the unaltered, unsorted clay, sand, and gravel of the drift are exposed. If you look carefully, you can find many variations in the glacial deposits, from hard clay to soft sand to a mix of coarse pebbles, boulders, sand, and clay. Because the glacier moved generally south, glacial till is commonly thickest on south-facing slopes like this one.

Hemlock is the dominant tree along the uphill stretch of Tom Hayes Road. An enormous (5-foot-diameter) branchless chestnut trunk stands next to the eroded old road as a monument to the former monarch of the New England forest. As the road crests the hill, the hemlocks are replaced by mixed hardwoods: beech, birch, maples, ash, and oak. Increased light fosters abundant plant growth on the forest floor that was so barren beneath the hemlocks. Here the new track on the right rejoins the original road and you may again see blue blazes marking the forest boundary. In the nearly level topography of the hilltop, the road becomes an avenue with stone walls on both sides, broken occasionally to mark routes to old cellar holes. As in much of western Massachusetts, this once well-settled land was largely abandoned in the mid- to late 1800s. Imagine the view the residents must have had when most of the surrounding countryside was clear of trees. Muddy spots in the woods road capture the footprints of current residents of this lovely forest, including deer and raccoons.

After a gradual downhill run followed by a short uphill stretch, the road makes an abrupt turn left (northwest) and crosses an open gas pipeline cut. Sixty paces past this cut, bear left (west) as the more obvious route bends right. The forest boundary and blue blazes also go left. You continue due west on the less traveled road, initially through a dark hemlock woods, for 0.5 mile to paved West Hartland Road. This final section is a bit wet and muddy. Use the paths on the left to avoid some of the large puddles. The glaciers evidently dropped a lot of moisture-retaining clay here! At least the moisture fosters a good mushroom crop to decorate the trail. You will reach the pavement at the highway sign marking the forest boundary. Turn left for a 10-minute walk downhill to your car. To enjoy that well-earned swim, walk (or drive) 0.7 mile downstream (south) on the paved road on the west side of Hubbard River. The swimming hole is on the left where the road widens to accommodate parking.

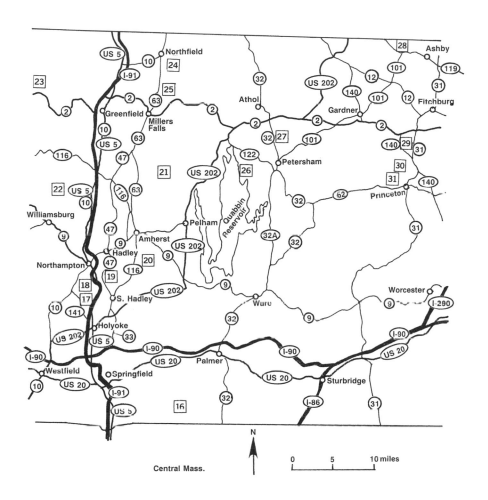

Central Mass.

N

0   5   10 miles

16

Laughing Brook Wildlife Sanctuary

Total distance: 3.0 miles (4.8 km)

Hiking time: 2 hours

Maximum elevation: 510 feet (155 meters)

Vertical rise: 320 feet (97 meters)

Map: USGS Hampden (7½' x 7½')

Trailhead: 42°03'53" N, 72°24'15" W

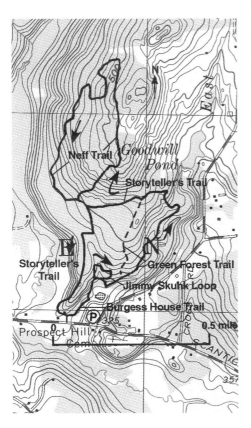

The past, present, and future are firmly intertwined in the relationship between the Massachusetts Audubon Society's Laughing Brook Wildlife Sanctuary and Thornton Burgess, famed writer of children's books. Burgess purchased the Storyteller's House on Main Street in Hampden in 1928. He used it as a summer home for many years and lived there permanently toward the end of his long life. Many of the fictional habitats and locales for the adventures of Peter Rabbit, Reddy Fox, and friends were based on the land that now makes up the sanctuary. Following Burgess's death in 1965, the Massachusetts Audubon Society created this sanctuary so that present and future generations can explore the real-life places that inspired Burgess: the tranquil wooded hillsides, sparkling streams, and surprising geologic wonders, all complemented by the cheerful songs of birds. The hike described here offers a good sampling of the main part of the sanctuary, which lies north of Main Street. Although not described here in detail, the short trails south of the road also make for interesting explorations. Highlights include the Scantic River, designated a scenic river in 1982 and featured as the Big River in Burgess's stories; a "high-water" and a "low-water" trail along the river to emphasize the importance of flooding; a boardwalk through a red maple swamp; and a flower-filled meadow.

The Laughing Brook Sanctuary is located in Hampden a few miles southeast of Springfield. To reach the sanctuary from I-91, take exit 4 (south) or exit 2 (north) onto MA 83 and go south on MA 83 for 0.6 mile to a left turn onto Sumner Avenue. Stay on Sumner for 2.5 miles, then bear right onto Allen Street and proceed toward Hampden for 5.8 miles to a left turn onto Main Street. A Massachusetts Audubon Society sign on the corner will direct you to the sanctuary on Main Street, 2 miles beyond the turnoff. The sanctuary is open Tuesday through Sunday and holiday Mondays from dawn to dusk. Admission is free to members of the Massachusetts Audubon Society and residents of Hampden, $3 for adults, $2 for children under 14 and senior citizens. You should make a point of visiting the splendid Education Center (Tuesday through Saturday 10 AM to 4 PM; Sunday 12:30 to 4 PM), where you will find a well-stocked Audubon Shop, some fine displays, and rest rooms.

After you have enjoyed the displays, walk out of the back door of the Education Center to begin your exploration of the sanctuary. (Or circle around the left side of the building to the same spot if the Education Center is closed.) Ahead you will see an information board, where you can borrow a trail guide complete with a map of the trails. Go right onto Smiling Pond Path and walk past the cedar- and willow-fringed pond. Soon you will reach a pond overlook that allows you open views over the small pond and the chance to look for some of its inhabitants, such as belted kingfishers, bullfrogs, and bluegills. Leave the pond area by following the wide trail over a wooden bridge that crosses East Brook. About 50 feet beyond the bridge, go right onto the narrower Green Forest Trail, which branches off the main gravel path. On this part of your hike you will be guided by blue blazes—remember that blue blazes direct you away from the parking area, whereas yellow ones guide you back to your starting point. The trail passes through stands of red maple and white pine. Stay right at the first trail inter-section, where the appearance of hemlock marks your approach to streamside. The trail follows East Brook in an easterly direction and you will have lots of opportunities to view deep pools and shallow riffles where the water gurgles over large, rounded boulders in the streambed. After passing an old stone wall on the left, you will enter a cool stretch where small hemlocks shade the forest floor and large oaks tower over everything. Ovenbirds and veeries live along here in the summer months, but they are more likely to be heard than seen. Soon you will see a large boulder looming on the far side of the stream. Notice that it has a covering of liverwort on its streamside faces. This huge glacial erratic was transported and dumped here by an enormous ice sheet that scraped over the region during the last ice age, less than 20,000 years ago. Also here you can examine a nice example of a stream meander, complete with a point bar and an undercut bank (this kind of river geomorphology is described more fully in Hike 18, Arcadia Wildlife Sanctuary).

Following your brief excursion into geology, continue along the trail as it bends left away from the stream and climbs gently past numerous glacial erratics scattered on both sides of the trail. Your path curves right at an intersection back toward the gurgling brook for an instant review of undercut banks with their tumbling trees, a large meander, and a bouldery point bar at the base of a sloping house lot. The trail parallels the stream and takes you to a damp area where skunk cabbage grows in the black mud and stepping-stones keep your feet dry. Continue along the stream bank, being careful not to stumble over the many moss-covered tree roots that cross the trail hereabouts. Your route climbs gently into a drier area and then does a sharp switchback to the left to avoid running straight into the stream. At this turn a red maple tree is riddled with holes drilled by a pileated woodpecker, and you will be saying goodbye to East Brook until almost the end of your hike.

The trail winds easily uphill past a vernal pond through hemlock, oak, and white pine to a confrontation with a stone wall at the top of a hill. Here you must turn sharply left near a large old oak tree and head westerly along a level path, soon leaving the stone wall behind. Another stone wall appears where the path bends left and in 100 feet reaches an intersection. Going left here on the continuation of Green Forest Trail will take you back more directly to the parking area. But the hike route goes right and follows the blue-blazed Storyteller's Trail, which undulates toward the next trail junction, some 600 feet ahead. On the way you will pass large outcrops of granitic gneiss, marked by the prominent alternation of dark- and light-colored minerals. Careful observations of the abundant glacial erratics scattered around the sanctuary will show that many of them are the same lithology as these outcrops, and it is not hard to figure out where some of them came from. Having reached the intersection, turn right onto Neff Trail to begin a 1.5-mile loop that eventually will bring you back to this spot. To shorten your hike, you can go left here and pick up the route details by skipping the next two paragraphs.

Assuming that you wish to hike the longer loop, take the blue-blazed trail to the right and in 100 feet or so branch right again at a trail fork. The path passes a fine white birch at trailside and meanders easily uphill past scattered erratics and gneiss outcrops. You walk through mixed woodlands of maple, oak, hickory, white pine, and hemlock, and a careful search should reveal Indian pipe growing on the forest floor. After leveling off, the trail crosses a stone wall in

a hemlock grove and then a second wall where the route begins to descend so gently as to be almost imperceptible. A long northerly stretch takes you through a more remote, less traveled part of the sanctuary where you may expect to see more wildlife amid the mixed forest and by the old stone walls that mark the boundaries of former farm fields. Dark green Christmas ferns dot the forest floor and flocks of chickadees, tufted titmice, and red-breasted nuthatches scour the treetops for food, while screeching blue jays protest your intrusion. Eventually the trail crosses yet another stone wall, but here turns sharply left into a grove of hemlock trees. In the cool shade, little sunlight reaches the forest floor, severely limiting the number of plants that can grow. Creeping pine figures prominently among those that flourish here. As you travel the indistinct path through this dark forest, keep a sharp lookout for yellow blazes (you are now returning) on tree trunks to guide you on your way.

The route turns more southerly, but wanders around past stone walls and through alternations of shaded hemlock groves and more brightly illuminated patches of maple and oak. Since you turned toward the south and the parking area, you now are guided by yellow trail signs. After 0.2 mile of generally southward travel, the trail turns sharply right near a patch of mountain laurel and heads westerly and then northerly downhill through a hemlock forest. This marks only a temporary diversion, however, and the path soon returns to a general southerly course. Following a gentle downhill stretch through oak, hickory, and maple, the trail levels off to pass a swamp on the right and then contours around the hillside through an area where many stone walls crisscross the woodland. Just beyond a damp patch, the trail turns sharply left past abundant Christ-

Liverwort on a glacial boulder

mas fern and climbs uphill to the east. Ahead lies about 800 feet of gently undulating trail as your route winds generally toward the southeast and the intersection where you began the 1.5-mile loop.

Go right here and in 200 feet you will reach Storyteller's Trail; those who chose the shorter hike can pick up the trail description here. The trail heads right (south) through mixed woodlands and soon crosses a small swamp on a wooden boardwalk before turning right for a 400-foot stretch of level going to the west. Beyond here the trail makes no more westerly swings and heads generally south and then southwest for the next 0.25 mile. At first, the wide, grassy trail passes through pleasant oak woodland that affords glimpses through the trees of the nearby Wilbraham Mountains to the west. Along here the route follows a southwest-trending ridge with a steep slope to the west and a more gentle incline on the east side. Farther along, the ridge narrows

and the trail swings over to the east side to look down a now steepened slope to the sanctuary buildings visible through the trees. The trail continues down the nose of the narrowing ridge of glacial gravels dumped here by a melting ice sheet, passes a nature study workshop athwart the ridge, and nudges to the right down a steep stone stairway. At the base of the stairs, turn left onto Burgess House Trail and, after passing some buildings including the Storyteller's House, cross a wooden bridge over the East Brook. Follow the creek upstream to an intersection with Smiling Pond Path, where you can turn right through a tunnel of shrubbery to the rear of the sanctuary buildings and the parking area.

To continue your hike, take the left turn over a wooden bridge that gives you views out over the pond to the right and on across a boardwalk to yet another bridge that goes left to span East Brook. The Jimmy Skunk Trail begins here, taking you first up a wooden stairway to a platform that overlooks East Brook. Just beyond the overlook, the trail loops right and takes you past a multilevel observation platform and on down to the beginning of the Green Forest Trail. A right turn here continuing on Smiling Pond Path quickly brings you back to the Education Center.

17

Mount Tom

Total distance: 3.6 miles (5.8 km)

Hiking time: 3 hours

Maximum elevation: 1,200 feet (365 meters)

Vertical rise: 980 feet (298 meters)

Maps: USGS Easthampton (7½' x 7½'), USGS Mount Tom (7½' x 7½')

Trailhead: 42°16'03" N; 72°38'12" W

The Mount Tom Range stands high and abrupt above the Connecticut Valley, and from the tops of its precipitous cliffs expansive vistas extend over the Berkshires and the Pioneer Valley of western Massachusetts. The range owes its stature to volcanoes that erupted almost 200 million years ago, spewing out lavas that cooled to hard basalts. These volcanic rocks resist erosion better than do the adjacent, softer sedimentary rocks and remain as high ground when the softer rocks are worn away. You can hike along the Metacomet–Monadnock Trail in Mount Tom State Reservation and examine the rocks and views for yourself.

To reach the reservation, turn onto Smiths Ferry Road from US 5, 1.8 miles south of the Holyoke-Easthampton line. Follow this road for 0.3 mile to the entrance booth, where you will be charged $3 per car during the summer months and on fall weekends. Just beyond the entrance, you will pass Lake Bray on the left and from there drive the reservation road as it winds uphill for another 1.6 miles to a small rotary. Park in the area to the right and then walk left at the rotary, and in 0.1 mile turn left again onto a side road that leads you past a maintenance building.

Bypass the gate just beyond the end of the maintenance area and continue for 300 feet to the Metacomet–Monadnock Trail. Turn right here where Quarry Trail continues straight ahead. You will be guided by the white blazes of this trail for the rest of your hike to the top of Mount Tom. The trail heads south easily uphill through mixed woods of hemlock, white pine, maple, oak,

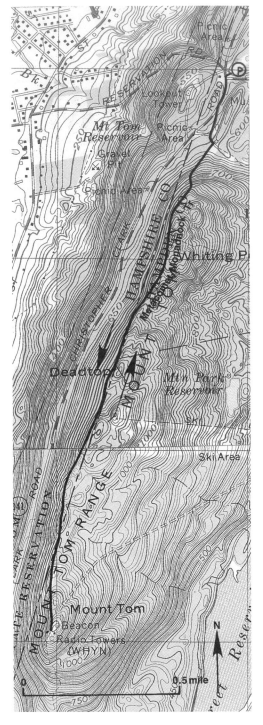

and black and white birch. Growing on the forest floor among bushes of mountain laurel and mapleleaf viburnum, you will find Indian cucumber root, starflower, teaberry, and lowbush blueberry.

The trail soon steepens and, after making a sharp left turn, begins to gain height quickly. Fortunately, interesting rocks crop out along the trail, and you can catch your breath while examining them. The first occur to the right of the trail near the sharp left turn. These rocks have the characteristic layers, known as beds, of sedimentary rocks. If you look carefully, you will find finer layers that slope at different angles to the bedding surfaces. These structures are called cross-beds, and were formed when sand was carried and deposited by an ancient river almost 200 million years ago. That was the time when dinosaurs roamed a valley that existed here long before the present Connecticut Valley was created.

As you climb the steep slope, keep a sharp lookout for more of the cross-bedded sandstones. If you're alert, you will find on the upper part of the slope, instead of sandstone, a dark, hard, nonlayered rock. These rocks formed when liquid rock broke through the earth's surface and flowed as lava over the river-deposited sediments. Thus, on this slope you have clear evidence of a dramatic shift in environments, from rivers to volcanoes. Somehow, ancient rivers seem appropriate here, but to picture volcanoes erupting in this Massachusetts valley requires a more vivid imagination. Near the top of the steep slope the trail curves to the right over rocky steps, but before you make the turn, look carefully at the rocks themselves. In them you will find small holes, known as vesicles, that were formed when bubbles of gas were trapped in the upper part of a lava flow. Volcanic basalts form the bedrock for the rest of your hike, and you will clamber over numerous outcrops of them.

A basalt tower overlooking Easthampton

Mount Tom

The slope now eases, and in a few minutes you will reach the first of many excellent look-offs. The west side of the ridge you will follow has many vertical cliffs and very steep slopes; you can stand, however, in complete safety on some very spectacular and precarious-looking clifftops. Westward you look down on the valley towns of Easthampton and Northampton and beyond to the forested Berkshires. The exposed ridgetop sports a growth of quite small red oak, red pine, and hornbeam, which you can identify from its shreddy bark and pointed, fringed leaves. The trail continues in and out of trees as it climbs steadily along the cliff edge. Each look-off gives ever more extensive views, and on clear days you can pick out Mount Greylock to the west, numerous northern peaks, and even Mount Monadnock in southern New Hampshire to the northeast. Soon the trail climbs steeply up two successive gullies in basalt cliffs and brings you to the summit of Whiting Peak, a wonderful spot to sit in the sun and admire the most extensive vistas you've seen so far.

The trail briefly descends from Whiting Peak, rises again to the top of towering cliffs, and descends once more. The red-blazed D.O.C. Trail goes off left but you continue straight ahead to begin the long ridge climb to the summit of Dead Top. In addition to the wide views, you can see the upper part of the Mount Tom ski area nearby and even closer at hand some shrubby scrub oak, sweet fern, and lots of blueberries. From Dead Top, the trail drops easily down an open ridge. Along here you should look carefully for a white arrow directing you down a small cliff. It marks your route to the summit of Mount Tom, but before you take it, look along to the left to find a granite boulder perched atop the basalt cliff. How did a granite boulder arrive in such a place?

You are looking at a spectacular example of a glacial erratic, a boulder brought to this spot by an ice sheet and dumped here when the ice melted. It is compelling evidence that ice once flowed over this mountain range, which is something to think about as you walk through verdant woods and cross the sun-warmed rocks. If you look carefully at the rocks, you may find scratches and grooves on polished surfaces where the heavy, stone-laden ice scraped its way over.

When you have thought enough about ice sheets, follow the arrows down the cliff and continue along the cliff edge, where you will be impressed by the sharp, nearby drop-off. Follow the trail's white blazes carefully as they guide you in and out of the woods, up and over rocky steps, and eventually to the top of a knoll, where a blue-blazed trail joins from the left. You will cross the knoll at the edge of a cliff that has a precipitous drop to the right and extensive views, including your first sight of Mount Tom itself, straight ahead. From here the trail continues its up-and-down pattern, without much overall change in elevation, bringing you ever closer to your now visible goal. False foxglove, meadowsweet, and purple-flowering sheep laurel all grow plentifully along the ridge. Beyond open ledges, the trail cuts left into the woods and climbs to the top of Mount Tom, with its sprouting of comunications towers. From the rocky summit area you can look south along the continuation of the basalt ridge, west out over the Berkshires to Mount Greylock (Hikes 8, 9, and 10), and north along the Pioneer Valley, the Connecticut River, and the Holyoke Range to Mount Holyoke (Hike 19).

To return to the parking area, retrace your route. You may be surprised how different the cliffs and ridge look when viewed from the opposite direction. Your trip down should take a little less time than your journey up.

18

Arcadia Wildlife Sanctuary

Total distance: 1.5 miles (2.4 km)

Hiking time: 1 hour

Maximum elevation: 140 feet (43 meters)

Vertical rise: 80 feet (24 meters)

Map: USGS Easthampton (7½' x 7½')

Trailhead: 42°17'21" N, 72°38'44" W

Standing on the observation tower at Arcadia Wildlife Sanctuary, located on the Easthampton-Northampton town line in the lowlands of the Connecticut Valley, you look out over an ancient oxbow lake of the Connecticut River, now partly filled in to form Arcadia Marsh. Before you begin your hike, you should make a side trip to see a much younger oxbow, and later on your hike you can study river processes in a brook that serves as a small-scale model of its big sibling, the Connecticut River. Along the way you will follow the route of a 19th-century trolley line and a colonial stagecoach road and pass the site of a former amusement park. Imagine the bustle of these earlier times, compared to nowadays, when you can enjoy the peace and stillness of a wooded wildlife sanctuary.

To reach this Massachusetts Audubon Society sanctuary in Easthampton, turn from US 5 onto East Street, 0.3 mile south of the Northampton-Easthampton line and 0.1 mile north of the Holyoke-Easthampton line on US 5. In 1.2 miles, turn right onto Fort Hill Road (sanctuary sign on corner) and follow the signs for 0.9 mile to the sanctuary. Before driving to the parking area, continue straight ahead on Old Springfield Road and park just before a bridge over the Mill River. You can stand on the bridge over the mouth of the river and look west, upstream, into Arcadia Marsh (Hulbert's Pond on the USGS map). Mill River drains the marsh and flows into the oxbow—the wide, curving stretch of water behind you enjoyed by canoeists, fishermen, water-skiers, and boaters. Many of these recreationists may be unaware that

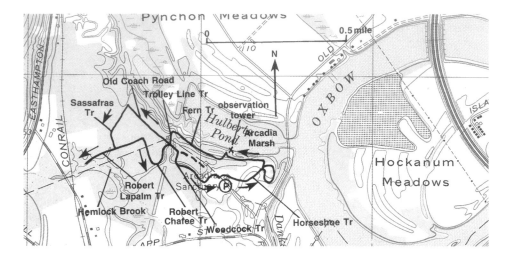

until 1841 the Connecticut River flowed through the oxbow in a great meandering loop. Then the flooding river took a shortcut across a narrow neck of land that separated two close reaches of the river and permanently abandoned its former course, leaving it as a loop-shaped lake. Oxbows form commonly as part of meandering river systems. They remain as lakes for a while, but slowly flood-carried silt and decaying vegetation shoal them, and then marsh plants colonize the mudflats. Further shallowing allows shrubs and trees to change the marsh to a swamp, and eventually the wetlands become dry bottomlands. Ned's Ditch and Arcadia Marsh once formed part of a single meander of the Connecticut River that has undergone much of the natural sequence of oxbow formation and infilling. The Mill River flows along Arcadia Marsh, though, complicating the riverine landscape.

Following this introduction to river mechanics, retrace your route and park in the sanctuary parking area. Admission is free for Massachusetts Audubon Society members; otherwise, adults are charged $3 and children under 14, $2 (in 1998). The trails are open daily dawn to dusk except Monday.

In the Nature Center building, open daily from 9 AM to 3 PM except Monday, you will find natural history displays, books for sale, leaflets, trail maps, and rest rooms.

This hike begins by the Nature Center. Walk past the hummingbird garden, turn left at the end of the building, then bear immediately right onto Tulip Tree Trail at the first trail junction. For much of the first part of your hike, you will be walking through shrubs and trees planted especially to provide food and shelter for wildlife, particularly birds. Many of these plants—among them dogwood, crab apple, honeysuckle, and apple—bloom gaily in late spring and early summer, releasing cascades of color and perfuming the air with heady fragrances. In fall and winter, the ripened fruits and berries attract and sustain dozens of birds—a birdwatcher's delight. On your left, just after the turn, banks of jewelweed, or spotted touch-me-not, draw the ruby-throated hummingbirds, which sip nectar from these orange flowers. The trail tunnels through overarching shrubs and trees, passes a small cabin on the right, and soon reaches an intersection. Continue straight ahead on Horseshoe Trail. After passing a plantation

Central Massachusetts

of white pines on your right, the trail makes a sharp left turn. Before you take this turn, however, follow the short spur ahead to the edge of a meadow, where bobolinks nest in early summer. From here the basaltic cliffs of the Mount Tom scarp (Hike 17) stretch tall against the southeastern skyline.

Return now to Horseshoe Trail and follow it through plantings of fruit and berry trees, past a small meadow on the left brightened in spring and early summer by a multitude of wildflowers. Stay straight ahead at a trail junction and then, just beyond a trailside bench, turn right onto Old Orchard Trail, which loops counterclockwise through a former orchard, taking you past verdant growth of sumac, apples, grapes, and ferns. For a short distance the trail follows a small valley deeply incised into clays

that were deposited in an ancient glacial lake. A stand of Norway spruce marks the end of the loop. This makes a good spot to watch the many colorful warblers that forage in the spruces on some early mornings in late April and May.

At the junction a little beyond the spruce trees, turn left onto Horseshoe Trail. Continue ahead, passing an orchard on your left, to a junction by a large white pine; turn right and then left past a bench and onto Fern Trail, an aptly named path where, among other species, you can find ostrich fern. The trail angles down across a steep river terrace, but soon levels off where it skirts Arcadia Marsh—visible through hardwood trees to the right. To your left look for small bladdernut trees, identified by opposite compound leaves with three leaflets, white

Canoeists in Acadia Marsh

stripes on gray-green trunks, and pale green, lanternlike fruits that develop from clusters of drooping white spring flowers.

Soon you will reach a short spur over a wooden bridge to an observation tower that provides excellent views over Arcadia Marsh. As you climb the tower, note the markers showing the height of floods for 1936 and 1984, graphic reminders that the river considers this land part of its domain. The tower was built to provide wide-ranging views of the marsh and the plants that grow there, as well as of visiting birds and other animals. You may see ducks, Canada geese, herons, egrets, and many other birds out on the marsh, as well as muskrat and occasionally deer. You can also peer into the upper foliage of the floodplain forest of black birch, silver maple, and shagbark hickory and look for warblers, woodpeckers, nuthatches, and other small woodland birds that live there.

Return to Fern Trail and continue to Trolley Line Trail, the wide, straight, former route of the Northampton-to-Springfield trolley. To the right you can see the remnants of the trolley-line bridge over the Mill River. Skunk cabbage and jack-in-the-pulpit grow alongside your route as Trolley Line rises gently to intersect Old Coach Road, once the route of the Northampton–Springfield stagecoaches of colonial days. Turn right onto this former road and go easily uphill through a wood of black birch and black locust. In the late 19th century an amusement park and bandstand were located near here to attract more customers to the trolley. The trail soon levels off and follows the edge of a river terrace that slopes steeply to your right. The flat area to your left, now covered by white pine and oak, was once open meadows and used for farming. Pass Robert Chafee Trail and in about 500 feet turn left onto Sassafras Trail (a sign is nailed to

a tree) and head southerly through mixed woodlands, which include, of course, the sassafras tree; look for its mitten-shaped leaves. You will soon intersect Robert Lapalm Trail; turn right and follow this path until it passes close to Hemlock Brook, bordered, appropriately, by hemlocks.

The large scale of major meandering rivers often makes it difficult to grasp their overall characteristics unless you fly above them or study them indirectly by using maps. Hemlock Brook, on the other hand, serves as a small-scale model that you can see and understand from ground level. Notice how the stream channel follows a sinuous path formed by successive meanders. When the water flowing downstream reaches a meander, most of it swings to the outer part of the curve, where it flows faster and deeper. This action causes undercutting and erosion, which in turn produces a steep bank and undermines the roots of streamside trees, which eventually tilt over or even fall into the channel. As the outer part of successive curves in a meandering path switches sides, so the undercut alternates from one bank to the other. On the inside curve of a meander, the water flows more slowly, dropping any sand it carries there to form a point bar. This feature, too, alternates sides on successive curves. Ripple marks often cover the sand surface, and these are sometimes preserved in ancient fluvial rocks. Two successive meanders can form such large loops that the undercut banks come close to each other, and you can easily see how further erosion leads to the river itself taking a shortcut and abandoning the meander, which then forms a small oxbow lake.

If you dig around in one of the undercut banks of Hemlock Brook, you will find it composed of clay. Squeeze some of this fine sediment in the water, and you will see a turbid cloud of suspended clay flowing downstream. In contrast, if you drop a handful of sand from the point bar into the water, it will sink to the bottom and leave the water clear. About 14,000 years ago, much of the Connecticut Valley was occupied by a lake left behind as the ice sheets melted. In spring, rushing meltwaters brought a mixture of pebbles, sand, and clay to the lakeshore; the sand and pebbles were immediately deposited at the lake's edge, but the clays spread out as a turbid suspension in the lake waters. When the lake froze each winter, the suspended clays sank slowly to the lake floor, eventually to become this stream bank, after the lake had drained away, of course.

When you have finished this bit of geologic research, retrace your steps along Robert Lapalm Trail, pass Sassafras Trail, and continue to a T-junction with Robert Chafee Trail. Turn right, following the trail through white pines, and bear left onto the Robert Chafee Trail where Fire Road goes right. Where the trail swings sharply left, you are skirting the edge of a steep river terrace. In about 400 feet you should make a sharp right turn and follow a log stairway down the slope; turn left onto Trolley Line, and in 100 feet you'll reach Old Coach Road once more. Turn right to climb an easy slope through a tunnel of hemlock. After 100 feet on level ground, you should turn right onto Woodcock Trail. The trail soon reaches a bench at the edge of a steep slope, where you can sit and look out over a swamp and wait for birds to resume the activities that you disturbed. Notice the sharp changes in forest here: white and pitch pines on the flat higher area, oaks on the dry south-facing slope, red maples and gray birch in the swamp. The trail continues along the edge of a terrace and soon drops through hemlocks to a junction. Turn left onto the trail that winds through the Cornelia Mendenhall Native Garden, and soon you will reach Old Coach Road yet again; turn right and walk 200 feet to the parking area.

19

Mount Holyoke

Total distance: 2.7 miles (4.3 km)

Hiking time: 2½ hours

Maximum elevation: 960 feet (292 meters)

Vertical rise: 1,000 feet (305 meters)

Map: USGS Mount Holyoke (7½' x 7½')

Trailhead: 42°17'19" N, 72°36'05" W

Even from the height of a satellite, the broad, flat-bottomed Connecticut Valley lowland appears as a prominent north–south rift in the rolling topography of central Massachusetts. Equally striking is the Holyoke Range, also visible from space, which stands as an anomalous east–west ridge jutting across this valley. Spectacular views from the serrate crest of this range easily merited the arduous journey by train, ferry, buggy, and tram taken by many of the thousands of visitors to the hotel that crowned Mount Holyoke from 1851 to 1938. Today, similar outstanding views merit the climb proposed in this hike. Although no one will serve you dinner at the top, as someone would have 100 years ago, along the way you'll encounter a potpourri of natural delights, from lava flows to newts, with enough to satisfy your intellectual appetite, if not your gustatory one.

To reach the start of this outing from the north, drive to the junction of MA 9 and MA 47 in the center of Hadley and wind south 4.9 miles on MA 47, watching the skyline ahead for the Summit House, to which you will climb. Turn sharply left opposite a cemetery at a sign marking the South Hadley town line. (Alternatively, from the junction of MA 116 and MA 47 at the common in South Hadley, drive 2.7 miles north on MA 47. Turn slightly right at the Hadley town line, opposite a cemetery on the left.) Park along the road on the right in 0.1 mile, just before a high-tension line. Please respect the private property that borders the road.

Your route begins on the right and is marked by the white blazes of the Metacomet–Monadnock Trail, which here starts

The Connecticut River from Mount Holyoke

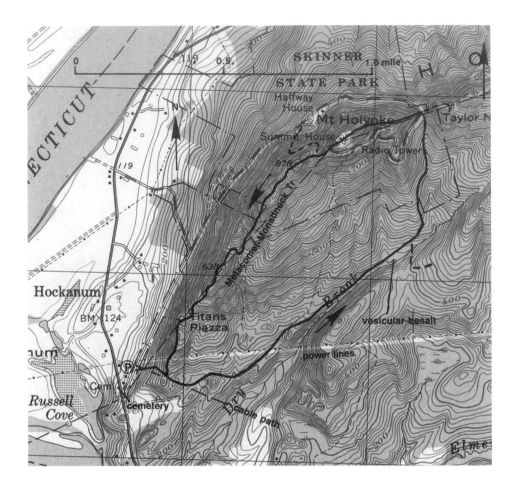

its run along the entire crest of the Holyoke Range en route from Mount Metacomet in Connecticut to Mount Monadnock in New Hampshire. You will be confronted immediately with a scramble up an angular ledge of black rock. Vertical fracture planes in the rock impart a columnlike appearance to its face. This feature, called columnar jointing, is produced by the contraction of solidified lava during cooling and is prominently displayed at many famous localities nationwide, such as the Devil's Postpile National Monument in California and the Palisades along the Hudson River in New York. The rock itself is a 190-million-year-old basalt

lava flow that will be underfoot throughout most of your hike.

The path follows a line of hemlock trees uphill to an open area next to a cabin. Turn right at the cabin to follow the wide swath in the woods cut for a buried telephone cable marked by concrete posts. Here, armed with similar, alternately positioned leaves, Solomon's seal and false Solomon's seal challenge you to distinguish between them. Yellow flowers or blue-black berries dangling beneath each leaf identify Solomon's seal, whereas terminal clusters of white flowers or brown-speckled white berries characterize false Solomon's seal. At the second concrete post, atop a basalt-supported rise, the white-blazed trail turns left (this is your return route) but you should continue straight, following the buried cable and occasional red blazes.

A few yards east on the cable path, large boulders of a pink, pebble-bearing sandstone rest on the smoothed top of basalt outcrops. These red rocks are samples of a sandstone layer that normally is found only below the basalt layer. The nearest sources for the boulders are sandstone outcrops on the steep northern face of the Holyoke Range. Therefore, transport of some kind is required to explain the presence of the red rocks here on top of the basalt. The river of ice that covered this range for much of the last 100,000 years is the most likely explanation for moving the boulders south up and over or around the range to this spot. When the path drops to a level area, at another post marking the path of the telephone cable, turn left (northeast) onto a trail that soon swings left to skirt a small, hidden pond. Wet ground here favors a garden of ostrich, sensitive, and other ferns. Your path becomes a woods road as you walk past hemlock trees, more basalt outcrops, and into some hardwoods. Mountain laurel and witch hazel highlight the red-blazed road.

An open power-line cut gives you the chance to see, in effect, both sides of the Holyoke Range at once. Originally a horizontal sequence of sediments interrupted by several lava flows filled the Connecticut Valley. Several blocks of sediment layers were tilted, probably while the ancient valley was still being formed (see Mount Toby, Hike 21). Uplift and erosion over the last few millions of years have removed a considerable thickness of sediment, leaving only comparatively resistant rocks to form the hills we see today. The Holyoke Range is the erosional expression of one south-tilted sediment block, capped by an erosion-resistant basalt layer. The top of the basalt layer forms the 10- to 15-degree slope on the south side of the range. This is the slope you can see up the power line to the west. Where the basalt layer ends to the north, the sandstone below is rapidly eroded, creating a very steep or clifflike slope. Visible to the east along the power line is a smaller version of this north-facing scarp, reflecting a second, thinner basalt layer that rests on top of the main one. A short sequence of sand layers separates the two lava flows. In a north–south cross section, the range looks like two books, a thin one on top of a thicker one, both inclined to the south.

Continue past the power line, past more basalt outcrops, beneath hemlocks and tall, old white pines toward Dry Brook. Around the brook, this valley instills a pleasant feeling of solitude, perhaps due to the prominent ridges that contain it. During a 1991 visit, five deer wandered through this woods at midday while we watched from a log seat. The woods road eventually reaches the valley bottom, where Dry Brook has been tempted into a more sinuous track. You may wish to poke around the trickling stream for newts or rocks. Here Dry Brook runs along the very top of the main lava flow. Look for examples of "vesicular" basalt, basalt that is full of holes left by gas bubbles frozen in the frothy surface of the flow. On the hill across the brook to the south, moss-covered outcrops of thin-layered sandstone confirm that you have reached the top of the basalt.

After your stop to enjoy this secluded valley, continue upstream and watch for a prominent intersection with another woods road. Turn left and begin a steady climb to the north. In several sections the ground is the smooth, bare, south-tilted surface of the basalt. Soon you will enter a north-trending valley filled with mature oaks and maples. At one point, the trail turns right and descends briefly, trading elevation for a good stream crossing on a small bridge. The trail follows this lush valley to Taylor Notch in the crest of the range and emerges onto the paved Mount Holyoke summit road. Watch for cars hurrying around the bend through Taylor Notch. If you want to confirm that there is sandstone beneath the main basalt layer, follow the pavement a few yards to the north to see some good outcrops. Otherwise, cross the road and follow white-blazed Metacomet–Monadnock Trail steeply uphill to the west and then on to the Summit House.

The building before you on the top of Mount Holyoke is all that remains of a series of Summit Houses, beginning with a cabin in 1821 and culminating in a 35-room hotel. Following severe damage to the hotel during the 1938 hurricane, J. A. Skinner donated the property to the state, making possible the formation of Skinner State Park. The state has restored the remaining Summit House to suggest some of its former glory. The structure is open daily in summer months, depending on the budget of the Massachusetts Department of Environmental Management. Inside, a few small exhibits will help you envision some of the past. Even if the building is closed, you can ascend to the wide veranda, look over the precipice to the north, marvel about the view up and down the Connecticut Valley, and appreciate the experience of more than 3 million people who rode the tram up the cliff to this spot. Because a road now leads to the summit, you may have to share this view with others. Nevertheless, there is plenty of impressive scenery to go around, and solitude lingers just down the trail.

From the Summit House, continue to follow white-blazed Metacomet–Monadnock Trail down from the top and southwest along the ridge. You immediately cross the rust-colored surface of more basalt, smoothed here by glacial ice so thick (10,000 feet?) that it was able to flow over the top of Mount Holyoke as water flows over a boulder in a stream. When the trail drops into a col, be sure to follow the white blazes up again to the southwest. Do not take the well-traveled route that leads west from the col and down to the foot of the old tram. Oaks share the ridge with hickory and ash and, in some summers, gypsy moths. Many places along the ridge offer lookouts. At one point, where the main trail swings left, a smaller trail leads right to a clearing formerly used by hang-glider pilots for take-off. Winds that must rise to climb over the range provide the sort of updrafts needed for successful hang-gliding starts and long flights. Poison ivy, white snakeroot, and staghorn sumac have all found niches along the ridge. A good view south is available as you cross Titan's Piazza, another smoothed basalt surface. Columnar joints in the rock make this surface look like polygonal patio stones. Although the trail makes a few unexpected turns along the way, the white blazes are always clear. After you cross under some power lines, you will descend to meet the buried telephone cable path you followed earlier. Turn right and follow the white blazes to your car.

20

Mount Norwottock

Total distance: 3.1 miles (4.9 km)

Hiking time: 2½ hours

Maximum elevation: 1,106 feet (337 meters)

Vertical rise: 820 feet (250 meters)

Map: USGS Mt. Holyoke (7½' x 7½')

Trailhead: 42°18'17" N, 72°31'39" W

Views from the top of the Holyoke Range in central Massachusetts have dazzled hikers and tourists for more than three centuries and, for millennia before that, Indians. With the range cutting directly across the flat-bottomed Connecticut Valley, these small mountains offer scenery that outclasses their modest height. Mount Norwottock is named for the Algonquin Indians who lived in the valley north of the Holyoke Range when European settlers arrived; *Norwottock,* more commonly written Nonotuck, means "The Midst of the River." Just below the summit are some overhanging cliffs and large clefts collectively known as the Horse Caves. This name refers to the reputed use of this location by rebels (and their horses!) hiding from the state militia during Shays's Rebellion in 1787. When all these features are combined with others into a modest hike, Mount Norwottock becomes irresistible.

From the eastern intersection of MA 9 and MA 116 in Amherst, drive 5.0 miles south on MA 116. Turn left into a paved parking area marked by a brown sign for the Holyoke Range State Park. (Alternatively, from the intersection of MA 47 and MA 116 in South Hadley, drive north 4.3 miles to a parking area on the right as you begin your descent from the Notch.) Inside the attractively landscaped Notch Visitors' Center, which is sited above the parking area, you will find a ranger, interesting displays, and rest rooms. You may wish to explore the blue-blazed, 0.75-mile-long Laurel Loop Nature Trail at the beginning of your hike. The nature trail, orange-blazed Robert Frost

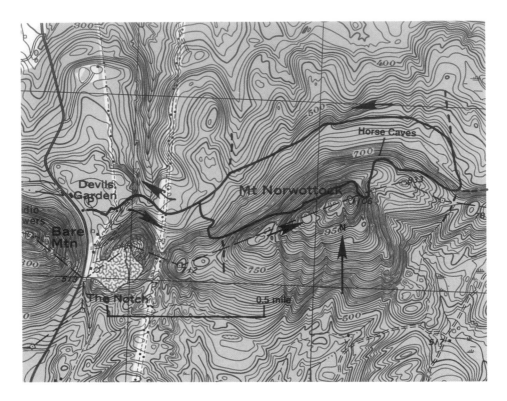

Trail (your return route), and white-blazed Metacomet–Monadnock Trail (your route now) all begin together on a wood-chip-covered path adjacent to the Visitors' Center on the far side of an asphalt circle drive.

As you start down the trail you will be shaded predominantly by oak trees, which seem to be a favorite food of gypsy moth caterpillars during their periodic defoliating outbreaks (see Middlesex Fells Reservation, Hike 39). Chestnut oaks and young chestnut trees, the latter heedless of the blight in their future, cohabit here with similar but easily distinguished leaves. Mountain laurel blooms well in the open cut under some telephone lines and grows abundantly all over Mount Norwottock. After plunging through the darkness of a stand of hemlock trees, you emerge to meet a gravel road. Turn left at the gravel road and then right immediately onto another road, both surfaced with crushed black rocks from a nearby quarry.

When you reach a power-line cut, you will see a large and unnaturally steep pile of crushed black rocks off to your right. The rocks are waste (tailings) from an active quarrying operation uphill to the south, where portions of the 190-million-year-old Holyoke Basalt lava flow are being removed. One of the major characteristics of igneous rocks, rocks that have crystallized from a cooling magma, is a uniform texture and absence of layering. There is no layering in the Holyoke Basalt, but there is plenty of fracturing. Because of contraction upon cooling, this several-hundred-foot-thick lava flow developed countless tension fractures, most oriented vertically—perpendicular to the surface of the flow. These fractures permit this otherwise very strong rock to be broken into the small pieces required for road building and other construction applications. Where the lava flow can be viewed in cross section, the fractures may make the rock look like ordered columns or posts of various sizes, as you will see along this hike. Beneath your feet you can see sparkles of sunlight reflected from the cleavage planes of plagioclase feldspar and clinopyroxene crystals on the freshly broken, unweathered surfaces of the gray-black basalt. Outcrops and other older surfaces of the basalt are commonly brown with rust.

Follow the road under the power line and across a swampy area into the woods. The white- and orange-blazed trail climbs gently here to bring you to an important trail junction. When you reach the junction, turn right, uphill, following the white blazes. A sign promises that this is the Metacomet–Monadnock Trail to Mount Norwottock and the Horse Caves. Your return will be along the level orange-blazed trail, which continues straight. You now begin the steepest part of the hike. Sassafras, recognized by its three distinctively shaped leaves, grows as small shrubs beneath the mixed hardwood trees and hemlocks. Many tree roots, near the surface because of the rocks beneath, provide welcome footholds. When you reach the ridge, the trail turns to the left (northeast) to follow the high ground. Keep to the left with the white blazes at a junction with blue-blazed Southside Trail.

As you walk along the ridge, you will alternately cross or pass outcrops of uniform, rusty-weathering, dark basalt and of pinkish, layered, pebble-filled sandstone. These outcrops are clues to a geologic puzzle. In broad design, the Holyoke Range is a south-tilted layer cake: The bottom layer is the pebble-bearing sandstone (New Haven Formation) and the top layer is the basalt lava flow (Holyoke Basalt). The range is high because the basalt is very resistant to erosion (see Mount Holyoke, Hike 19). Based on this simple model, your hike should have begun on sandstone and crossed one contact onto basalt as you climbed. The alternate outcrops of sandstone and basalt mean that the sandstone-basalt contact has been shifted up and down here along small faults running across the ridge. Faults are surfaces along which there has been movement, probably with accompanying earthquakes. Having a model (a working hypothesis) makes it easier to recognize the outcrops here as anomalies and, therefore, to find the faults.

You will be guided up and down over several knobs along the ridge. Keep an eye out for the poison ivy that grows in places along the trail. Small, white wood aster flowers will greet you in late summer. The summit, formerly crowned by a 30-foot-high open metal observation tower, is only slightly higher than the two knobs that precede it. Good views to the north toward Amherst can be found near the base of the old tower and to the east a few steps down the trail. Keep back from the edge of the high cliffs at these overlooks. Watch for hawks spiraling upward on thermal plumes along the ridge.

The white blazes lead you right from the summit and then rather steeply down to the east. After crossing a draw, the trail swings around to the left and along the base of a basalt cliff among huge blocks of basalt that have evidently fallen from the cliff face. As you move toward the north face of the mountain, the talus is much smaller and harbors some poison ivy. Where the trail levels out, you will see thinly layered outcrops

Overhanging ledges at the "Horse Caves"

Central Massachusetts

of the sandstone, which means you have walked over the basalt-sandstone contact and down into the lower layer of the geologic layer cake. The path descends through a cleft in a large outcrop to an impressive exposure of the sandstone, overhanging in places. Look closely at this cliff face and you can read a record of 200-million-year-old streams: lens-shaped cross sections of stream channels, cross-bedding that indicates the direction of water flow, ripple marks, flood deposits full of pebbles, and much more.

Downhill movement of building-sized chunks of rock has opened crevasses that invite exploration. You may want to bring a flashlight to get a good look. This is the location labeled HORSE CAVES on the state park trail map, although there is no cave that could hold a horse. According to local lore, participants in Shays's Rebellion (1786–87) stayed near this spot to hide from the state militia raised to suppress the insurgency after their attack on the Springfield Armory. The rebels were local farmers who could not raise enough cash during the post–Revolutionary War depression to meet heavy state tax bills or to repay their debts to merchants and banks. Rather than come to the aid of its less affluent citizens, the merchant-controlled government of the newly liberated state passed laws that encouraged foreclosures and led to the imprisonment of many soldiers who had previously fought for the colony's freedom. Daniel Shays of Pelham and thousands of others felt driven to protest, eventually with violent actions, what they felt to be government injustice.

After exploring the area of the Horse Caves, follow the trail downhill to the right and across the hollow that might have been the location of the Shays camp. The trail widens to logging-road size, descends to meet a ravine opening to the southwest, and bends left to follow the ravine to a pass. At the pass you encounter first a junction with a blue-blazed trail leading right: Keep left with the white blazes. In a few yards, after crossing a boundary onto Amherst Conservation Land, the white blazes of the Metacomet–Monadnock Trail turn right toward Rattlesnake Knob. You should continue straight, leaving the white blazes and following the orange blazes of the Robert Frost Trail. In wet ground at the bottom of a downhill stretch, turn left to begin a fairly level, easy walk west with the orange blazes. Large sections of trees here were defoliated by gypsy moth caterpillars in 1991, but seemed quite healthy in 1998. Eventually, you will descend to cross a stream and turn left onto a woods road that follows the water gently uphill. (A right turn would take you onto the blue-blazed Northside Trail.) Soon you will reach a junction you passed earlier in the hike and rejoin the white blazes. Remember to jog slightly right under the power line and to jog left at the T-junction with the gravel road, retracing your steps from the beginning of this outing. The Visitors' Center is now only a few steps away.

21

Mount Toby

Total distance: 4.1 miles (6.6 km)

Hiking time: 3 hours

Maximum elevation: 1,269 feet (386 meters)

Vertical rise: 1,040 feet (317 meters)

Maps: USGS Williamsburg (7½' x 15'), USGS Greenfield (7½' x 15')

Trailhead: 42°30'12" N, 72°31'50" W

Even the most casual observer of a map of the world cannot help but notice the complementary outline of the east coasts of the Americas and the west coasts of Europe and Africa, like pieces of a giant jigsaw puzzle. Until the late 1960s, however, the suggestion that these continents were once part of a single landmass was regarded by most scientists as preposterous. Now, supported by extensive evidence gathered by deep-sea drilling and geophysical surveys, most geologists consider the slow movement of continents a virtual certainty. Although the Atlantic Ocean is the most obvious result of the forces that separated northwest Africa from Massachusetts, other consequences abound. Of particular interest in Massachusetts are the Connecticut Valley lowland and Mount Toby, a broadbased mountain that presides over the Connecticut Valley a few miles north of Amherst.

Two hundred million years ago, the supercontinent Pangea, consisting of Eurasia, Africa, and the Americas, all stuck together, was split down the middle by a series of fractures and began to pull apart. Many of these fractures (faults) joined to form the major rift that became the Atlantic Ocean (which is still growing wider at a rate of 1 to 2 inches per year). Other faults leading from the main rift into one continent or another became dead ends. The Connecticut Valley lowland is bounded on the east by one such fault and owes its existence to the breakup of Pangea.

As the Atlantic opened, movement on the Connecticut Valley's eastern border fault lowered and tilted western Massachusetts relative to eastern Massachusetts. The val-

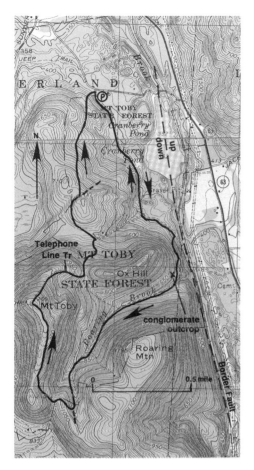

Although it was once filled with sediment, the Connecticut Valley is a lowland today because the sedimentary rocks that formed from the sand and mud that filled the rift valley are less resistant to erosion than the igneous and metamorphic rocks of the surrounding hills. Mount Toby is something of an exception. It is underlain by a coarse, erosion-resistant variety of sediment, known as the Mount Toby conglomerate, and stands as a prominent ridge within the lowland. Sedimentary fragments ranging in size from sand grains to large, angular boulders are visible in the Mount Toby conglomerate along the trail to the top. Boulders such as these would be broken up if carried very far by a stream. Thus, the sediment source and fault must be nearby. In fact, the fault is located in the valley followed by MA 63 just east of Mount Toby, where you can find conglomerate rocks adjacent to much older metamorphic rocks.

The Mount Toby trailhead is located on Reservation Road just off MA 47, 3.9 miles north of its junction with MA 116 in Sunderland immediately past the Montague town line and sign and 0.9 mile south of its junction with MA 63 in Montague. From MA 47, travel 0.5 mile east on Reservation Road to a small parking area on the right just past a large brown sign proclaiming your arrival at the Mount Toby Forest. From the parking area, walk back to the entrance road, south around a metal gate (watch for poison ivy), and into the woods along a level dirt road bordered in midsummer by white snakeroot flowers. Just past the gate on the right is an orange-blazed trail that will be your return route. On the left, you will pass a plantation of red pine dating from 1924 and then a plantation of white pine adjacent to a plot of a naturally seeded white pine. On the right, you will pass a large, shaded, moss-covered outcrop of Mount Toby conglomerate; large

ley that formed at the fault filled with erosional debris from the highland rising to the east (see illustration). This sediment, consisting mainly of stream deposits of sand and silt, accumulated to a depth of five miles or more near Hartford, Connecticut, less to the north and west. Thus, at the fault, the western block must have sunk five miles or more, relative to the eastern block, in thousands of earth-shaking increments of inches to feet every hundred years or so over millions of years. Particle size in the sand deposits decreases westward across the valley, confirming that the sediment source was in the east.

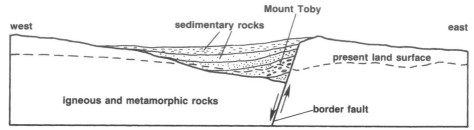

west   sedimentary rocks   Mount Toby   east

present land surface

igneous and metamorphic rocks

border fault

A schematic cross-section of the Connecticut Valley showing the distribution of sediments with respect to the border fault and the present land surface.

pebbles of glittering schist and black-and-white-layered gneiss are visible. See if you can identify some of the many species of ferns, such as bracken, interrupted, silvery spleenwort, Christmas, New York, and hay-scented. Canada mayflower and partridge-berry hug the earth beneath the pines.

Past an open area guarded by shagbark and pignut hickories, you'll spot Cranberry Pond if you look down side trails to the east. Another outcrop is nearly invisible in the trees on the right. Note the telephone lines that leave the road to follow a cut uphill to the southwest, as they mark a possible return route. Here the road bends left downhill, then begins to climb through a forest of white, black, and yellow birch; red and sugar maples; red oak; and hemlock. Although several paths enter from various directions, stay with the obvious main road. Just as you finish the first steep uphill stretch, you will find a well-exposed outcrop of conglomerate on the right. The unweathered rock was exposed by blasting during road construction; you can see the remnants of vertical drill holes in the rock. Angular, poorly sorted boulders of igneous and metamorphic rocks up to 2 feet across proclaim a nearby source and, as you now know, the rupture of a continent.

As the road levels out, you will come alongside Roaring Brook, which can roar in spring but only gurgles in fall. If you have plenty of time and energy, you may wish to follow the brook downstream to a cascade where boulders 3 to 4 feet across are visible in the conglomerate as you approach the ancient fault. The road to the top continues following Roaring Brook until the water is no more than a trickle and then turns abruptly right (uphill). Do not take the lesser road that goes straight (south) and becomes a path. From this uphill turn, you have about 0.8 mile and 300 feet remaining to climb on a generally more gentle grade than you experienced along the brook. A fire tower waits to lift you above an otherwise viewless clearing at the summit.

Views from the tower on a clear day reach from Mount Monadnock and Wachusett Mountain (Hike 30) in the east to Mount Greylock (Hikes 8, 9, and 10) in the west and are particularly good up and down the Connecticut Valley. To the south is the Holyoke Range, capped by a resistant layer of basalt, anomalously jutting across the valley. The basalt erupted as lava shortly after the deposition of the Mount Toby conglomerate and probably used the border fault as a conduit to the surface from its source in the upper mantle. The notch separating the once continuous rocks of the Holyoke and Mount Tom Ranges (Hikes 19 and 17), and used by the Connecticut River, has been cut through the resistant basalt. This water gap is evidence that the Connecticut River, or some more ancient river, was lowered onto the basalt as erosion gradually excavated the present valley.

From the fire tower, follow a trail northeast beneath the telephone lines very steeply downhill in a thicket of young hardwoods competing for the sun. In June, patches of blackberries covered with white blossoms and clusters of mountain laurel burdened with flowers highlight your descent. Goldenrod, rough-leaf and purple-stemmed asters, and spotted touch-me-nots are among the wildflowers that crowd the trail in late summer. At one point the trail makes a sharp turn left at a T-junction, but the telephone lines identify the correct path for you. Past this junction, watch for a sharp turn left into the woods with the orange blazes, which you will follow to your car. (Alternatively, you can continue to follow the telephone lines on a broader track downhill to a left turn onto the entrance road you walked earlier.) The orange blazes mark the northernmost section of the Robert Frost Trail, which runs from Mount Toby through Amherst to Mount Norwottock (Hike 20). Not far past the turn is a fine conglomerate outcrop where you can see the filled channels of streams that were here 200 million years ago. Take your time and enjoy the downhill ramble that takes you to the entrance gate where you began the hike.

Sunbeams on the Mount Toby Road

22

Conway State Forest

Total distance: 7.7 miles (12.4 km)

Hiking time: 5 hours

Maximum elevation: 1,355 feet (413 meters)

Vertical rise: 1,250 feet (381 meters)

Map: USGS Williamsburg (7½' x 15')

Trailhead: 42°25'46" N, 72°42'28" W

Conway State Forest is one of the least developed of the 128 Massachusetts state forests and parks: It has no campgrounds, no picnic areas, no swimming areas, and often no visitors. It is the shortage of visitors that makes Conway particularly well suited for a quiet outing in the woods. Although no hiking trails are shown on the Massachusetts Department of Natural Resources state forest recreation map, a great hike is possible on what the Conway map terms "woods roads." These former cart paths, logging roads, and other wood trails are now neglected and passable only by off-road vehicles. Walking is easy on these wide paths, giving you plenty of opportunity to examine the forest as you pass.

To reach the trail that will lead you into Conway State Forest, follow MA 9 to Williamsburg. In the center of town, MA 9 makes a 45-degree turn. If you are coming from the east, take the right fork at this turn (which is almost straight); if you are coming from the west, turn sharply left. Drive across a small bridge and turn right onto East Main Street. At the first opportunity, turn left onto Nash Hill Road, heading uphill. After traveling 0.9 mile, turn left with the pavement, staying on Nash Hill Road. The pavement turns to gravel in patches and then completely, 2.2 miles from the start of Nash Hill Road. Drive 0.8 mile on the gravel, now called Depot Road on the map, to a less used gravel road that forks to the left. Park here in a pullout to the left of the fork.

From your car, walk north between two stone walls on the smaller gravel road, which is labeled HENHAWK TRAIL on the USGS topographic map. In the first hundred yards or so you will pass a wide variety of flora typical of the forest ahead, including white pine, red oak, white ash, shagbark hickory, American beech, witch hazel, spotted touch-me-not (also called jewelweed), Christmas fern, hay-scented fern, silvery spleenwort, and marginal woodfern. Please respect the rights of landowners whose private land borders portions of this established trail.

Soon a large outcrop will be visible just off the path to the left. If you take time to examine these rocks, you will find that the bulk of the outcrop consists of Williamsburg granodiorite, an even-textured igneous rock that crystallized from a liquid several miles below the earth's surface some 360 million years ago. The granodiorite contains the micas muscovite and biotite in addition to the usual quartz and feldspar, signifying that it is comparatively rich in aluminum and was probably formed from the melting of schists formed from clay-rich sedimentary rocks. You may find inclusions of unmelted schist in the granodiorite as well as veins of pegmatite containing large crystals of quartz, feldspar, and muscovite. Watch out for poison ivy in the woods near the outcrop!

White, black, and yellow birch are all here, with trunks the color their names imply. The black and yellow birch have wintergreen-scented twigs. Keep to the left at the first fork just past an open area, and watch for white snakeroot flowers in late summer. Lavender flower clusters of the mint selfheal hug the ground in and beside the road. Grapevines with stringy, campfire-tinder bark spiral up tall trees; some are designed as swings. Locally, flat-needled hemlocks blacken the sun. Ordinarily, considerable effort is required to sort and transport the gravel used in road building. For this road, however, coarse gravel was prepared and delivered by glaciers more than 10,000

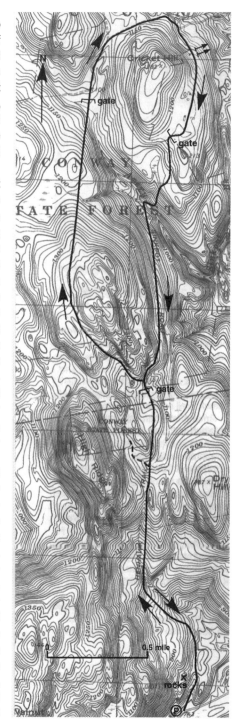

years ago. Continue straight where a road leads right near a large hemlock and a prominent glacial erratic boulder. You now begin a long, gradual climb through woods of red maple trees, mountain laurel bushes, and small chestnut shoots struggling futilely against the chestnut blight. The rocks in the road are bigger here, so most vehicles will not continue past this point.

At the crest of the grade, the forest is bright and serene, needing only a few deer to complete the postcard-perfect picture. The road forks just beyond the crest, by a small brook. Bear right. Annoying mud holes and ruts form a record of the infrequent passage of motorized vehicles. Turn left at the fork just inside an aging wooden gate marking the Conway State Forest boundary. A badly eroded uphill stretch ahead confirms your path. (You will return to this junction on the right fork when you complete the 4.1-mile circuit of Cricket Hill, the northern cornerstone of this patch of state land.)

A large black bear was sighted here by one of us in 1991. Initially, the bear was unaware of its human companion, due to the noise and direction of the wind and to the noise of its own footfalls in the leaves. Because bears are most dangerous when surprised at close range, a quiet retreat down the trail and a noisy return seemed prudent. The second approach prompted a dash for cover by the bear that was reassuring to a solo hiker. With a western Massachusetts bear population now numbering in the hundreds and growing, bear sightings are becoming more common. Hope for a chance to see one, to sense its untamed power. But respect these wild animals, especially females with cubs. Be aware of their presence and the possible danger. Don't get too close, feed, taunt, or challenge them.

Perhaps the stone walls remember the pioneers who once cleared these hills to till and graze the land, but they are not saying. Only the birds, the wind, the mosquitoes, and your footsteps break the silence. This sense of wilderness may be somewhat shaken when, at the crest of the next rise, your path becomes an "improved" forest road. Both recent and older bulldozer work has made the next section of road passable—although it is seldom used—by mere automobiles coming from the north. The road was developed here to permit selective cutting of competing trees for firewood, making possible the maturation of the best trees. Permits to cut the marked trees on plots containing as much as 20 cords were sold by the state in 1982 to the highest bidders for about $10 per cord. Although strict regulations govern the removal of trees in these plots, the forest and land suffer some trauma in the process. In 1998, the 1982 woodlots were crowded with an impenetrable growth of green-striped maple and beech trees filling the openings created among the taller trees left uncut. Is this a proper use of public land? Should state forests serve as tree farms, or stand as carefully guarded wilderness areas, or is there a satisfactory middle ground? Perhaps by viewing the results of cutting, first from 1982 and then from earlier years farther along the road, you will be better prepared to consider these issues.

Walking mainly downhill, you will eventually come to Avery Brook, where tall, pink joe-pye weed and spotted touch-me-not thrive in the moist soil. On the dark downhill stretch leading to Avery Brook, a road enters on the right. (A hard right turn to follow this road will shorten your hike by 1.3 miles, joining the full route at the second crossing of Avery Brook, mentioned in the next paragraph.) Walk past another wooden gate and straight along a stand of planted spruce,

An ancient sugar maple

Conway State Forest

where a road enters from the left. Time has significantly smoothed the wounds of thinning in the woodlots you are about to pass. At a fork, go right with the main road. Hemlocks will shade you as you descend to an intersection with a well-used gravel road. Turn right onto Cricket Hill Road and walk uphill to the south along a fenced pasture. A lovely white house and traditional red barn with roofs of Vermont slate, set among large sugar maples and black-eyed Susans, look over the pasture and across the Connecticut Valley lowland to Mount Toby (Hike 21). Old apple trees, stone walls, and several more pastures decorated with cows line the road as you continue uphill back to the state forest. Please respect the private land here in its timeless beauty.

Another wooden gate and a stand of spruce mark your reentry into Conway State Forest. Walk downhill through a mixed forest to meet Avery Brook again. Folded schist just downstream from the crossing is a reminder of the collision of two "drifting" continents. Just across the brook, turn left at the fork beneath some hemlocks. A long, gradual climb takes you up a path labeled SINKPOT ROAD on the USGS topographic map. Stone walls abound here, too, in spite of the rather steep slope. Again the forest is quiet. A few outcrops, similar to the one described earlier, are on the uphill side of the trail. Eventually you will reach the junction you passed earlier. Keep to the left and retrace your steps through the wooden gate and back over Henhawk Trail to your car.

23

High Ledges Wildlife Sanctuary

Total distance: 2.5 miles (4.0 km)

Hiking time: 2 hours

Maximum elevation: 1,406 feet (428 meters)

Vertical rise: 610 feet (186 meters)

Map: USGS Greenfield (7½' x 15')

Trailhead. 42°37'01" N, 72°42'55" W

"There is a spot along the crest of the ridge that, in the town of Shelburne, forms the steep eastern slope of the Deerfield River valley, where a rock fall in some distant past has left an overhanging cliff known locally as the High Ledges. Traditionally, this was a favorite destination for hikers from the nearby town of Shelburne Falls . . . Indeed, though 'breathtaking' is a trite term, many first-time visitors have found it accurate." With this passage, Ellsworth Barnard begins his delightful book *In a Wild Place, A Natural History of High Ledges,* published by the Massachusetts Audubon Society. But more than the view, it is the diversity of habitat, birds, wildflowers, mushrooms, ferns, and trees that attracts and sustains those who get to know High Ledges, as richly documented in Barnard's book and Charles Joslin's wood engravings. You will surely agree if you get a chance to explore this naturalist's haven. Barnard should know a lot about the area because he grew up on a small farm that adjoins High Ledges and has spent at least part of his summers there for most of his 92 years. Indeed, because of their love for these woods, Barnard and his wife, Mary, created the wildlife sanctuary by donating some 400 acres of land to the Massachusetts Audubon Society in 1970. Additional land purchases since then have expanded the sanctuary to nearly a square mile today.

To reach High Ledges from the junction of I-91 and MA 2 in Greenfield, drive 5.2 miles west on MA 2 to Shelburne and turn right, north, onto Little Mohawk Road. Keep to the right at the Shelburne Volunteer Fire

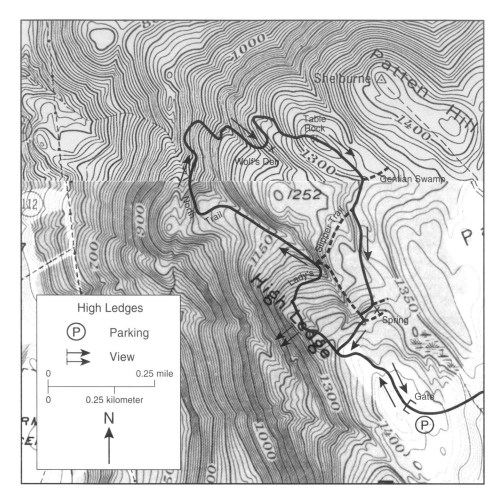

Department building, continuing north on Little Mohawk Road for a total of 1.5 miles. A sign displaying a road map of the area marks your turn left onto Patten Road. Follow Patten Road as it bends left past Reynolds Road in 0.5 mile and turn right with Patten Road in another 0.1 mile where Tower Road goes straight. (Tower Road will take you to a dead end and short trail to an old stone lookout tower in Shelburne State Forest.) The asphalt of Patten Road is replaced by gravel 0.2 mile after the turn, and in another 0.5 mile you come to the High Ledges entrance road and sign. Turn left

and travel 0.5 mile to a parking area where the road is blocked by a metal gate. (In winter, when more of the road is closed, park on the left 0.1 mile after the turn.)

To begin your hike, follow the continuation of the entrance road past the brown metal gate to the northwest through a narrow field thick with hay-scented fern. As the road starts downhill, you will pass a wonderful white oak on your right with a low horizontal branch that evokes the image of a swing. Near the bottom of the downhill stretch, a blue-blazed trail enters from the right and jogs across the road. This will be your return route. Continue northwest with the road, past moss-covered schist outcrops with layers tilted to the northeast, past the Barnard summer cabin, and down to the overlook at the ledges. The view is west up the Deerfield River valley over Shelburne Falls toward Charlemont and the Hoosac Range on the skyline. On a clear day, you can see Mount Greylock (Hikes 8, 9, and 10) still farther west (about 30 miles away). The river is about 1,000 feet below you in a very impressive valley. The depth of the valley reflects its geologic youth (a few million years), and the steepness of its sides reflects the erosive power of the continental glaciers that recently covered the region. Upstream, the bottom of the river valley is fairly flat due to sediments from a glacial lake. Downstream and mostly invisible from High Ledges, the Deerfield River has cut a gorge into the valley with the huge water flows from melting glaciers. It was this much enlarged Deerfield River that scoured the large potholes in the rocks at Shelburne Falls.

Perhaps most surprising is the unusual bend in the river just north of Shelburne Falls, reminiscent of the oxbow-shaped bends followed by rivers in flat terrain like the Housatonic (see Hike 3) and the Connecticut (see Hike 18). However, in this case the path followed by the Deerfield River has been strongly controlled by the hardness of the underlying rock rather than a river's uncertainty regarding which direction is downhill. Shelburne Falls is built on a group of gneisses and amphibolites that began their life as lava flows. The black, amphibole-rich rocks are more easily eroded than are the lighter gneisses, and this may have influenced the river's path. Also, it appears that the river used to take the more direct path now followed by MA 2, but was "captured" and redirected by the North River.

From the overlook, continue northwest along the ledges, populated with red and white pine trees, following a trail labeled with blue dots. In less than 100 yards you will come to a trail junction with signs indicating that Lady's Slipper Trail bears right and Westbrook Trail bears left downhill. Stay on the ridge with Lady's Slipper Trail. During a recent sanctuary census, Ellsworth Barnard counted more than 500 pink lady's slipper plants and 140 yellow lady's slipper plants in bloom. The pink variety especially likes the drier ground of the ledges, whereas the yellow variety, with its more slipperlike blossoms, prefers wetter ground. Blossoms of both orchids have a unique shape that appears to ensure good pollination of the single flower from any visiting bee. Lady's Slipper Trail leads you north across tilted layers of rock containing mica, which sparkles in the sun; red garnet crystals; and veins of pure quartz. The schists are the metamorphic version of muddy, ocean sediments deposited on the edge of North America in the Devonian period more than 400 million years ago. On the other side of the broad ridge, the trail descends to the edge of a ravine that guides Spring Brook. If you look across the ravine, you will see a small version of the High Ledges you just left. Because the rock layers are tilted to the northeast, cliffs are more likely to form on the southwest side.

The trail bears left along the ravine and in about 100 yards comes to a junction where three trails meet (Lady's Slipper, Spring Brook, and North). Continue straight, initially along the ravine, on North Trail, which is marked with blue-plastic disks. The woods are dark here in the shadow of northern hemlock trees, although witch hazel and sarsaparilla find enough light to grow. Among low outcroppings of schist, the trail crosses a stone wall that must have served

Pitcher plant

as a fence when this area was a pasture. Soon the trail drops into a north-trending valley that starts broad but becomes narrow between moss-covered schist outcrops. Scan the rock faces for the small, delicate ferns that grow best here, polypody and rusty woodsia, as well as for maidenhair spleenwort, with its ebony stems. Spring Brook cascades down a slope on your right to join the stream you are following, which itself originated in springs that you passed. Blue-plastic blazes guide you back and forth across the brook (right, left, right) to avoid rocks and fallen trees. The third crossing marks the topographic low point of your hike and takes you to the base of the impressive rock face that has arisen on the east side of the valley. The blue blazes mark a steep ascent up this face that begins around the exposed roots of a tall oak tree. Although you have quite a bit of climbing to do, the very steep section is short and ends at a switchback. When the leaves are off the

trees, you will have a view to the west here while you catch your breath.

On up the hill, the trail passes a cluster of trees that appear to have fallen victim to a burst of wind in a recent storm. As the grade lessens, you will cross a small stream and bear right to follow it along the base of another southwest-facing cliff. The trail crosses the stream to the right and then back again to the left to run close to the cliff, which is overhanging here. If you look in the recesses beneath the overhang, you will find a layer of rock that looks different from the schist so common elsewhere in the sanctuary. This is a layer of impure marble containing calcite, a mineral that dissolves more easily in rainwater than do the quartz and muscovite of the schist. A deep hole here, possibly a cave in the marble layer, is believed to have been the home of the last wolves in this part of Massachusetts. Several stories survive of the sheep owners who killed the wolf family living here in the late

18th century. In one story, the wolves were chased to the den and one hunter crawled into the den to shoot the wolves. In another, the trapped wolves were killed by putting sulfur on a fire built outside the den and the hunter crawled into the den to retrieve the wolves.

Turn left onto the Wolf's Den Trail just past the first overhanging rock and before the sign that says WOLF'S DEN. Climb uphill through a break in the cliff and bear left along a slope covered with mountain laurel. The trail soon bends around to the right in a broad switchback. Yellow blazes mark the route along smaller overhanging outcrops (more marble) and then left to climb steeply to the fairly level top of the ridge. Table rock occupies the high point of land, once clearly visible from the open fields around it. Walking is very easy here, where the path slowly descends through more thriving laurel bushes. In a hemlock grove, a path leads left to a boardwalk across Gentian Swamp. Take a short side trip here to see more interesting flora, like the carnivorous pitcher plants slowly digesting hapless insects caught in their water-filled, pitcher-shaped leaves. Smooth pitcher sides with downward-pointing bristles prevent escape from drowning.

Return to Wolf's Den Trail from the swamp, turn left, and walk downhill. At the next junction in more open woods, turn left again, staying with the yellow blazes but now on Lady's Slipper Trail. You will climb gradually up and across a more level area filled with mountain laurel bushes and in places trailing arbutus on the ground planning for April blooming. Bear right at a T-junction marked by a 30-foot-high American chestnut tree and walk left along a swamp that feeds the spring of Spring Brook. Turn left just past the spring and pump, following the yellow blazes, and then right at the next junction. Climb over a small, rocky saddle to the entrance road. Turn left and walk uphill to your car.

24

Mount Grace State Forest

Total distance: 3.9 miles (6.3 km)

Hiking time: 3 hours

Maximum elevation: 1,616 feet (493 meters)

Vertical rise: 1,138 feet (347 meters)

Map: USGS Northfield (7½' x 15')

Trailhead: 42°41'20" N, 72°20'29" W

This hike through a working forest affords extensive, panoramic views from a sturdy tower at the summit of Mount Grace, other views from the top of Little Mount Grace, as well as the opportunity to do some experiments with tree-ring counting. To reach the trailhead, drive north on MA 78 from its intersection with MA 2A, for 6.5 miles to Warwick Center. Continue north on MA 78 for another 0.5 mile until you reach the large parking area for the Oscar N. Ohlsen Memorial Field on the left (west) side of the road. Just up the grassy hill to the left you will find some pleasant picnic tables, and beyond that a clean, well-maintained portable rest room.

To begin your hike, walk south through hemlocks and pines alongside MA 78 past the Mount Grace State Forest office. Just beyond the next brown building, turn right onto a trail marked MT. GRACE SUMMIT and head west into the woods. The trail passes through tall pines and soon swings left to a southwesterly course. The trail rises gently uphill and in about 300 feet reaches a broad trail at a T-junction. Here you go right and continue gently uphill in a westerly direction. Your way goes through mostly tall pines with an understory of small deciduous trees: predominantly beech but also scattered oak and black birch. You should stay straight ahead where short side trails branch off right to a small clearing. You soon reach a trail fork by a twin-trunked black birch tree, where a sign on a pine tree tells you that either way will take you to the summit. On your ascent you will take the right branch, but later in your hike you will de-

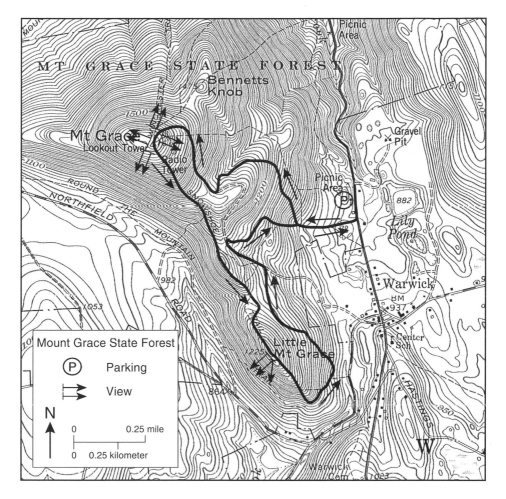

scend by the other path. Your route now heads generally a little west of north and climbs moderately steeply through a more varied forest, which becomes dominantly deciduous in nature. Scattered through the forest hereabouts rest large glacial erratics, mostly large boulders of granite, although thick lichens obscure most of their lithologic characteristics. More elusive inhabitants of the forest include nuthatches, chickadees, and kinglets. To obtain close-up views of these attractive birds, you might want to try the old birder's trick of "pishing." By calling out *pish, pish, pish* a few times, you may arouse the curiosity of the birds and draw them to your vicinity to check you out. This can be a fun activity and will really impress your companions if it works, but it can also make you quite breathless, so you may be thankful that the trail eases off a bit before swinging to a more westerly course. After meandering for a while in a generally south-westerly direction, your trail brings you to a T-junction with the service road that leads to the radio tower on the upper slopes of Mount Grace.

You should take careful note of this turn, marked by a small cairn, as it can serve as an alternative way down if you miss the turn described later. You should go right and follow the wide, gravelly road as it winds moderately uphill in a northwesterly direction. You will pass by some large beech trees and then through a grove of hemlocks where the trail levels off a bit. It soon steepens again and shortly begins to bend left to a more westerly direction. At the next junction the service road goes left (south) toward the radio tower, but your route goes straight ahead. After another 250 feet or so of uphill going, the trail flattens and is here joined by the white-blazed M & M Trail, which comes up from the right. You now follow the M & M Trail to the base of the lookout tower, visible through the trees ahead. Although the summit of Mount Grace affords no views from ground level, it's a different story if you climb the tall and sturdy fire tower! As you gingerly climb higher and higher, you will emerge above the screening trees to be richly rewarded with ever-expanding views. To the northeast in New Hampshire, Mount Monadnock rises prominently, while farther to the northwest the Green Mountains of Vermont can be seen dotted with ski areas. Mount Greylock (Hikes 8, 9, and 10) lies directly west and Wachusett Mountain (Hike 30) to the southeast, while parts of Quabbin Reservoir sparkle in the sunlight to the south. Certainly, this 360-degree panorama encompasses a treasure trove of hiking possibilities. Once safely down, you might want to examine the large glacial erratic near the base of the tower, with its many faded inscriptions and the mold where a plaque used to be. Or perhaps one of the sunny openings will be appealing as a restful lunch spot.

To continue, follow the M & M Trail (white blazes) as it heads southeast past two large white pines and follow the utility lines downhill. Near the start of this next section of your hike, you will pass through thickets of scrub oak. Look for a shrubby oak with hairy twigs and small leaves that are conspicuously white and woolly beneath. The trail heads moderately downhill generally following the utility-line cut, with a couple of diversions off into the adjacent woods. Some limited views of wooded hills and Hastings Pond appear, and you will pass a good variety of oak species as you go, including red, black, white, and mossy-cup. Lower down you will reach an area with large hemlock trees. Here you might want to examine the tree rings revealed in a sawn-down former forest giant that has been exposed to years of weathering, which accentuates the rings. Scientists use the growth rings as clues to past years' temperature and rainfall during the growing season with the advantage of a built-in calendar. In this way information is gained about climates of the past that may help us to make useful predictions about future climate trends. A less ambitious goal for the curious hiker would be to try to figure out the age of some of the logged trees that you may see on your way, by counting the tree rings. In some cases, you may be able to identify the growth ring for the year that you were born.

As you continue on your hike you will begin to have glimpses of views through the trees to the south and southwest. Looking down at the trail, you should be able to find small outcrops of dark, sparkly, micaceous schists. Continue along the utility-line route through a maze of logging roads down to a level col, which, in 1998, was the locus of logging in this area. You also will be very close to the service road at this point. Here you need to stay on the M & M Trail, which, in 1998 at least, was somewhat obscured by logging activity. You need to head southeasterly toward a small knoll. You'll find lots of opportunities for tree-ring counting here

A split glacial erratic

in the stumps of logged trees. Notice again how those trees that have been felled the longest show the best-defined rings. Once you reach the top of the knoll, the M & M Trail becomes more clearly outlined as it follows the top of a ridge with a very steep slope to its western (right) side. Beyond the knoll, the trail heads gently downhill along the ridge crest through predominantly coniferous woodlands. Eventually you will begin to climb easily on a needle-carpeted path to the northeast ridge of Little Mount Grace—your next objective. Upward the ridge narrows, the trail steepens, and views reveal themselves through the trees to the west. Shortly you will reach the rather flat summit of Little Mount Grace. This small mountaintop provides your last opportunity on this hike to enjoy extensive views. You can take a lunch or rest break here while sitting on the top of a small cliff and admiring the views of Moores Pond to the south and the flanking wooded hills.

Your hike route continues along the M & M Trail, which heads down the southeast ridge of Little Mount Grace. Soon after leaving the summit, the slope steepens and you walk down through a forest that slowly and progressively changes from one dominated by hemlocks to a deciduous woods of oaks, beech, and maples. Just after the steep trail begins to level off, you will reach a trail junction. Here it is time to say goodbye to the M & M Trail, which goes right; your route goes left to head gently downhill in a northeasterly direction. At the bottom of this descent you reach a trail fork near a large white pine. Should you need an escape route, a right turn takes you to nearby Northfield Road; traffic noise may confirm its proximity. However, to continue on the hike route, go left and gently uphill toward the north-northwest. Along the upcoming stretch you will find opportunities to study four species of birch tree: gray, white, black, and yellow. After about 600 feet of gentle ascent, the path steepens and swings sharply left to take you deeper into the state forest and away from the wire fence that marks its boundary. The trail soon resumes its more gentle slope and begins to contour around the hillside, and even drops a little to eventually reach the service road—recognizable by its lining of utility poles. Turn left here and head to the northwest. A few minutes of steady, moderately uphill walking brings you to the "logging col" where you were earlier in your hike.

Continue beyond the col on the service road as it winds moderately uphill. Here you need to keep a sharp lookout for a trail that leaves the road to the right just before the second curve. The trail angles back sharply and heads downhill. If you reach the top of this stretch of road, you have missed the turnoff. Either retrace your steps to find it or continue along the service road until you reach the roadside cairn that marked your ascent route—mentioned earlier as an alternative way down. Your downward path winds through an area that contains tree stumps of various ages, showing that here trees have has been harvested in the past as well as in the present. Forests can be a renewable and useful resource, provided they are exploited with care and understanding. Many opportunities for tree-ring counting occur along this stretch. The logging has created a more open, better-illuminated forest floor, permitting a greater diversity of plants to take advantage of the increased opportunity for photosynthesis. You will pass a giant glacial erratic that has been split into two pieces, perhaps by frost wedging along a plane of weakness. Eventually your meandering path will bring you to a familiar junction and your upward route. Go right here and follow your outward route back to the starting point, which you should reach in about 5 minutes.

25

Northfield Mountain

Total distance: 5.9 miles (9.5 km)

Hiking time: 4¼ hours

Maximum elevation: 1,100 feet (335 meters)

Vertical rise: 1,250 feet (381 meters)

Map: USGS Orange (7½' x 15')

Trailhead: 42°36'38" N, 72°28'16" W

Northfield Mountain Recreation Area is a successful compromise among industrial, recreational, and environmental interests in Massachusetts. Developed by Northeast Utilities as a pumped-storage hydroelectric generating station, Northfield Mountain also boasts 25 miles of trails for ski touring, hiking, and trail biking. Indeed, few places in Massachusetts offer such a well-groomed, year-round trail system. Most of the trails are wide, grassy roads for easy walking and skiing, but narrow footpaths traverse the more rugged terrain. Although well known as a ski touring center, the trails are surprisingly empty during snowless months and well worth a visit. The circuit hike described here thoroughly samples the terrain and trails, from the visitors center to the top of the mountain.

Demand for electric power peaks each day, sometime late in the afternoon. To avoid "brownouts," the electric utility companies must have sufficient power-generating capacity to meet the maximum demand. Because the minimum electric power consumption, which occurs in the early morning, is less than half the maximum, power plants must be able to turn on and off, or at least up and down, each day. Shutdowns and slowdowns are particularly difficult and inefficient for nuclear power plants. Pumped-storage facilities such as Northfield Mountain were conceived to allow nuclear power plants to run continuously at full capacity and maximum efficiency. Electric power generated during nights and weekends in excess of demand is used to pump water from the Connecticut River to a reservoir on the top of Northfield

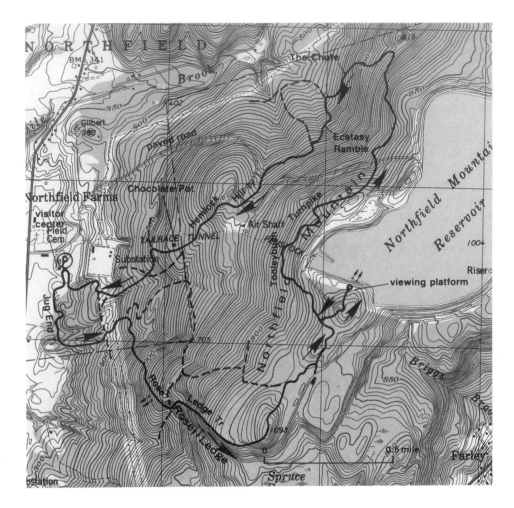

Mountain. The process is reversed, turning the enormous pumps into electric generators, during daytime peak-use hours. Only 3 kilowatt-hours are recovered from every 4 used to pump the water up, however, so the energy cost of meeting peak demand is considerable.

Northeast Utilities maintains and staffs a visitors center at Northfield Mountain to provide information, organize educational programs, and coordinate recreation (hours are 9 AM to 5 PM, Wednesday through Sunday, year-round). Tours of the power-generating facility and an interpretive boat ride on the Connecticut River are available during summer months (reservations recommended; call 413-659-3714). Although hiking in summer is free, you must purchase tickets to ski the groomed cross-country trails in winter. Trail bikers must register prior to their first tour. The visitors center and large parking area are prominently located on the east side of MA 63, 2.1 miles north of MA 2 in Millers Falls. Trail maps are available inside the center, which also sells precision topographic maps of Northfield Mountain, designed for use in orienteering meets. An extensive, inexpensive interpretive guidebook is also available.

A rest stop near Rose Ledge Trail

To begin your hike, look for a large, painted trail map posted between a small pond and the visitors center. From the map, walk south along a rail fence and the exceptionally clear, cattail-lined pond toward Jug End and the Instructional Area. When you come to an open field, bear right and follow the edge of the field. Low mounds on the sides of the field provide the "slopes" for instruction in cross-country skiing. These mounds are actually fossil dunes of wind-blown sand extracted from sandy sediment that was exposed and dried by the draining of glacial Lake Hitchcock. During the waning stages of the Wisconsin Ice Age, 15,000 to 12,000 years ago, Lake Hitchcock was ponded behind a dam of glacial deposits in Connecticut, filling the Connecticut Valley lowland to the north. Sand and clay carried into this lake, which was once 100 feet deep at this spot, settled to form the flat valley bottom so productively farmed today.

After crossing the open Instructional Area, the path runs along a stand of young white pine growing happily in the well-sorted dune sand. Follow the Jug End sign, bearing slightly left past a metal gate and into a lovely open woods populated by older white pine. The red squirrels objecting to your passage clearly do not need to use the fitness stations that may be found along the trail. Mats of hay-scented fern where there is light and Canada mayflower where there is not serve as attractive ground covers.

The Jug End path glides down across a stream, up to a left turn at a junction, then on up through woods to cross under an array of 345,000-volt power lines leading south from the hydroelectric facility. Look for low, flat outcrops of a well-layered gneiss on the southeast corner of the trail junction at the power lines. Black crystals of hornblende define thin, dark layers among whitish feldspar and quartz crystals. This Precambrian Dry Hill gneiss forms the bedrock throughout the Northfield Mountain area. You may want to taste the blackberries under the power line if they're ripe, or crush and smell a leaf of the woody-stemmed sweet fern.

Fifty yards past the power-line cut, watch for the sign and red-diamond blazes that mark Rose Ledge Trail. Turn right onto this narrow path into mixed woods of oak, hemlock, maple, hickory, and black birch. Twigs from the black birch emit a delightful wintergreen fragrance when broken. Mountain laurel bouquets garland this path in June, while blueberry snacks await you in August. Witch hazel, sassafras, and chestnut grow as tall shrubs along the route. Shortly after you cross the first stream gully, you will come to a junction sign marking a right turn for Lower Rose Ledge Trail. Do not take this turn. Your route is straight ahead with the red diamonds.

As you climb to higher ground, numerous outcrops of gneiss stand like monuments beside the trail. The planes of black hornblende and brown biotite mica in this gneiss, inclined to the northwest here, systematically change their tilt to delineate a large, dome-shaped structure when traced throughout the region. This "gneiss dome" was formed 380 million years ago when the hot, plastic gneiss was buoyed up into the denser overlying rocks, much as a balloon would push upward if submerged in water.

Stay on the footpath when it crosses a wider path. The trail soon skirts some impressive ledges carved in the gneiss. Several side paths lead to good lunch spots on the ledges with views west across the Connecticut Valley. Use caution near these cliffs; the drop-off is quite precipitous. You will be near ledges until the trail levels out and heads northeast along the tree-covered ridge of Northfield Mountain. Trail-lining blueberries give way to sarsaparilla in the darker woods on top. When the path ends at a grassy road, turn right. Tall fronds of interrupted fern congregate in clusters on damp ground near this junction, while huckleberries and bracken fern populate the drier sections. Continue straight, bearing slightly left as another grassy road enters from the right.

Turn right at the next wide path for a short walk to the summit of Northfield Mountain (a sign announces that you are now 1,100.49 feet above sea level), around a paved cul-de-sac, and down a path to a wooden viewing platform that overlooks the fenced storage reservoir. The reservoir was created by excavating and damming a natural depression on the mountain to hold more than 5 billion gallons of water, enough to generate over 10 million kilowatt-hours of electric energy. That's a 10-hour supply at maximum output of 1 million kilowatts. The hydroelectric pump/turbine-motor/generators are located in a cavern carved in the gneiss about 800 feet below the west end of the reservoir. You can see the northwesterly tilted gneiss layers, crosscut by vertical drill holes, in the rock face across from the viewing platform. Crag Mountain is visible to the north; southeastern Vermont is to the northwest.

From the viewing stand, walk back across the cul-de-sac and down to the intersection of your last turn (number 32). Turn right (west) onto the Tooleybush Turnpike and walk downhill and around the reservoir in a forest dominated by red oaks. Because red oaks are typically rather tall, it may be difficult to reach a leaf to confirm an identification. Chestnut oak bark, which is coarse, blocky, and angular, provides a marked contrast to the red oak bark, which has wide, vertical, slightly reddish furrows. Soon, as you climb from a low point, you'll come to a large, rounded boulder, dropped by a melting glacier, resting beside the grassy road. Prominent, white, rectangular feldspar crystals are set among gray quartz crystals and large, black "books" of biotite mica in this erratic from some point north.

Still on the Tooleybush Turnpike heading northwest, you eventually cross a paved road. (You can shorten the hike by more than a mile at this point by turning left and following the pavement downhill. Rejoin the described path by turning left onto Hemlock Hill Trail at the apex of a tight bend in the road.) The next section of trail was widened and smoothed by a bulldozer in 1982, presumably for the benefit of skiers. Soon the path bends sharply to the south and heads downhill into The Chute. Imagine yourself on cross-country skis, rushing downhill among the trees. As the trail levels out again, turn left onto Ecstasy Ramble, a wide path leading uphill to the east. The forest floor is barren of plant life here where hemlocks darken the sun. At the next junction, turn left and continue to climb, now on Hemlock Hill Trail, past hobblebush and striped maple to cross the paved road again. Four large wild turkeys were seen here on one visit.

Although you stay mostly on Hemlock Hill Trail, walking generally west and downhill from the paved road back to the visitors center, the many intersections are sources of potential confusion. Just past the paved road, turn right and continue straight at each junction on the main path. You traverse downhill past the Chocolate Pot winter warming spot and soon come to a T-junction, where you should turn left. Warblers, chickadees, and thrushes may be among the birds singing along your route. Ignore all cross trails until you reach the power lines. Bear right at the fork between the two sets of power lines and then right again just past them. The grassy road bends left to avoid a fenced area and leads you downhill to the open Instructional Area, where a right turn returns you to your car.

26

Northeast Quabbin

Total distance: 4.2 miles (6.7 km)

Hiking time: 2½ hours

Maximum elevation: 700 feet (213 meters)

Vertical rise: 340 feet (104 meters)

Map: USGS Shutesbury (7½' x 15')

Trailhead: 42°09'14" N, 72°15'24" W

Quabbin Reservoir, in west-central Massachusetts, holds more than 400 billion gallons of water and supplies the needs of Boston and neighboring communities. Construction of the reservoir gained final approval in the Massachusetts legislature in 1927, after many years of indecision, and the dams to impound the reservoir were finally completed in 1939, when ponded water began to flood the valleys of the Swift River. By 1946 the reservoir had filled, and a huge lake covered the sites of former farms and small towns. Humans made this lake to fulfill needs for water, but in the process created an "accidental wilderness" where many birds and other animals can live and thrive in peace.

You can explore some parts of the Quabbin Watershed, although access to others is restricted, and the hike described here represents only one of many possibilities. You begin and end your explorations in the Federated Women's Clubs State Forest, but much of the route crosses land owned by the Metropolitan District Commission, the body that runs Quabbin Reservoir. Along the way, you can enjoy extensive views of the island-studded, man-made lake and compare it with beaver-dammed ponds that conveniently lie close to the trail. As you encounter considerable evidence of the former homes of people who had to abandon their land to make way for the reservoir, you might ask yourself whether such a project would be approved today.

To reach the state forest, drive east on MA 122 for 3.6 miles from its intersection with MA 202 south of Orange, or west on

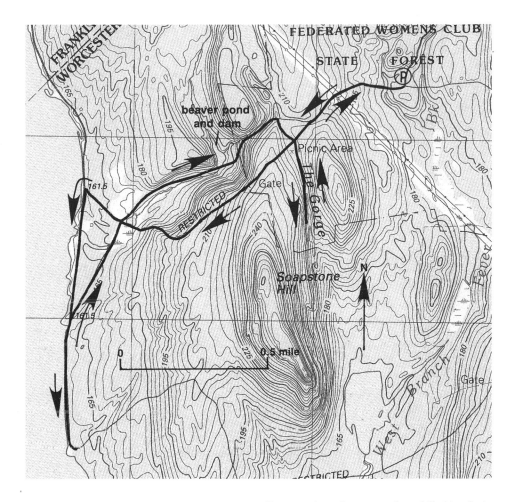

MA 122 for 4.7 miles from its intersection with MA 32 in Petersham. A sign directs you south along a paved road into the state forest. In 1.8 miles you will reach a parking area on the right just before a T-junction. There is no entrance or parking fee, nor are there any facilities.

To begin your hike, turn right (west) at the T-junction and walk along a dirt road through hemlocks and white pines. After traversing a damp area with a pond on the left where joe-pye weed, goldenrod, and asters grow, the trail rises gently through mixed woodlands, passes under power lines, and continues easily uphill. At a fork, stay left on the more prominent dirt road that will take you in about 200 feet to a picnic area. Amid the white and red pines on the south side of the picnic area, you will find a trail that will take you easily downhill in a southerly direction for a half-mile-long side trip. The trail soon reaches a more mixed woodland, where oak, maple, and black birch outnumber the scattered pines, passes through a stone wall, and in another 350 feet arrives at a fork. Mature white pines mark this turn, and your new route to the right heads down toward a large boulder

---

and then bears left alongside a small stream for 200 feet. You have entered a ravine called The Gorge. On the right (west) side of the stream, large jumbled boulders and rocky outcrops dot a slope that plunges steeply to the stream. You can have fun scrambling about the rocks and exploring the small caves formed in the spaces between the piles of large angular blocks. A profusion of plants grows in The Gorge, creating attractive rock gardens, but poison ivy lurks here too, so be careful where you put your feet and hands. Where the rocks have no cover of polypody ferns, mosses, or boulder lichens, you can see the alternating thin layers of light-colored quartz and feldspar and dark biotite mica that identify gneiss, a type of metamorphic rock. On a hot day you may want to linger in this cool, shady valley and try your hand at identifying some of the ferns and flowering plants.

When you run out of unidentified plants, or patience, return to the picnic area and continue your hike by walking southwest (left) down the dirt road. Shortly you will pass a pond on your right, followed by camping and picnic sites on both sides (rest rooms are here), and then will climb a short, moderately steep hill. At the top of Old Crow Hill you will enter Quabbin Watershed through Gate 36B. Remnants of stone walls line the wide trail, which soon begins to drop easily through white pine, hemlock, yellow and white birch, and maple to a stream valley that has been modified by both beaver and human activity. The trail crosses an active beaver dam that has a veneer of human-deposited sand and gravel on its top. Upstream many dead tree trunks stand starkly in the ponded waters that drowned them, and a beaver lodge reminds you of the busy animals that live here. You could not ask for a more conveniently located beaver dam to study than this one. If you stand quietly here on the trail, within a few feet of the dam, or walk along the banks of the pond, you may see the busy animals at work or hear the noisy flap of their tails if you frighten them. You will have your best chance of spotting a beaver in the hour or so before dark. Downstream from the dam, cattails dot a marsh, and spotted joe-pye weed, jewelweed, blue vervain, Virginia bower, and sweet fern brighten its edge. Just beyond the dam, the trail crosses a former road, passes between stone walls and large oak and white pine, and in 800 feet reaches a junction.

Turn left (south) onto the road, which was once blacktopped, and follow it alongside Quabbin Reservoir. For the next mile you will have many beautiful views across the water to wooded hills and islands. You also will see much evidence that this was once an inhabited valley. Apart from a few hikers and fishermen, the people—many of whom no doubt loved the land—have been forced out, but bald eagles, ravens, white-tailed deer, coyotes, and perhaps even mountain lions find homes in the man-made wilderness. This drowned valley now fulfills the water needs of far more people than it supported prior to the making of the reservoir, which raises other questions to ponder as you hike along the Quabbin shore. Sometimes, when you look out over the water, you may find yourself forgetting that human engineering built this beautiful lake. On your left you soon pass an inaccessible, disused fire tower and then a grove of large white pines, old stone walls, and cellar holes that mark a former homesite. On your right a narrow strip of shrubs and small trees separates you from the open water for a while and then, farther along, are rows of planted white pine. You soon pass them and your route is again bordered by shrubs, including buttonbush and abundant groundnut, which

The waters of Quabbin Reservoir

is easily recognized by its creeping habit and brown, pealike flowers. Out in the water, you can see new islands formed where sandbars emerged and were colonized by reed grass. If you keep walking straight ahead, you will reach a place where the former road and adjacent stone wall plunge under the water—graphic proof that the land was flooded by the rising waters of the reservoir. From here, too, you can enjoy fine views of the island-dotted lake.

Your forward progress blocked by the lake, you should turn around and walk back along the road for 0.5 mile to a fork, where you follow a grassy road to the right. The wide trail passes many stone walls, foundations, and large trees showing where homes once existed. Soon the road reaches a marsh—a layer of sand and gravel keeps the path itself high and dry—and a little farther you arrive at a familiar spot, the beaver dam you crossed earlier in your hike. Here you continue straight ahead along the beautiful,

now grassy road, lined by stone walls and majestic old oak and maple. On your right, the beaver pond merges upstream into a cattail marsh, where dead trees provide nesting cavities for birds. On your left, you will pass a former meadow, now thick with second growth, especially white pine, and then a wooded hill. A little farther uphill the trail crosses a stream that flows out of a former beaver dam.

Beyond the dam, swing right as the trail rises moderately past many large yellow birches and a small stream valley on your left. Down through the trees you can see a less accessible former beaver pond. Where the trail flattens, you will leave Quabbin Watershed through Gate 36. In 50 feet you should turn right onto a level trail through pine woods. In 400 feet you will reach the camping and picnic areas that you passed through early in your hike. Turn left along the dirt road and a few minutes of steady walking will bring you back to the parking area.

27

Harvard Forest

Total distance: 4.4 miles (7.1 km)

Hiking time: 2¾ hours

Maximum elevation: 1,383 feet (421 meters)

Vertical rise: 470 feet (143 meters)

Map: USGS Athol (7½' x 15')

Trailhead: 42°31'52" N, 72°11'28" W

At the Harvard Forest you have the opportunity to compress a lifetime into an afternoon and see what newly planted trees will look like in 50 years. Because trees mature at a rate that is slow in human terms, good detective work and long-term experiments are needed to learn about forest development and succession. The Harvard Forest was established in 1907 to provide a sanctuary for such experiments. At that time some 2,000 acres of land were donated to Harvard University by a group of Petersham residents, led by J. W. Brooks. Subsequently, data have been gathered, interpreted, and reported on forest growth, forest management, and the structure and function of trees. With a database spanning most of a century, Harvard Forest is already a scientific treasure that will become even more valuable with time.

Harvard Forest is divided into several separate tracts, each with its own points of interest. The hike described here is in the Prospect Hill tract located on MA 32 in Petersham, 2.8 miles south of the junction of MA 2 and MA 32 in Athol. On the east side of the road, a modest sign with red lettering signals the entrance to a parking lot in front of a large redbrick building that houses the Richard T. Fisher Museum as well as offices and laboratories. Try to include time for a visit to the Fisher Museum (open Monday through Friday from 9 AM to 5 PM all year, and on weekends from 10 AM to 4 PM May through October). On the first floor, intricate dioramas illustrate the history of New England land use and the principles of forest management and growth. Upstairs

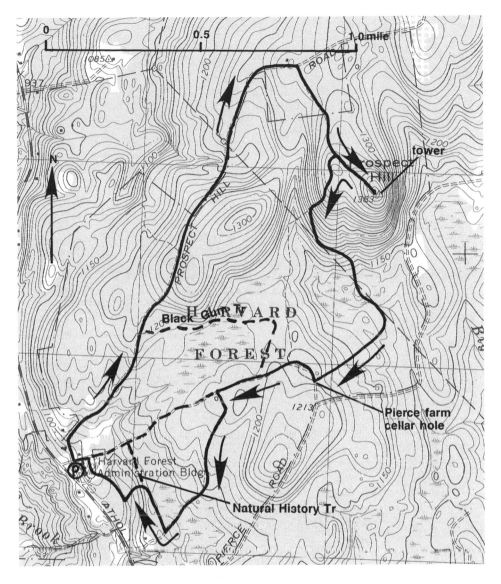

a potpourri of exhibits provide instruction on topics ranging from tree roots, to tree parasites, to the effects of the 1938 hurricane, when 70 percent of the trees were blown down in central Massachusetts.

Two nature trails are maintained for the benefit of the general public in the vicinity of the Fisher Museum. Both begin and end at the north end of the parking lot on a woods road leading east. Trail guides are available near the door to the museum, although both trails are well marked with numbered stations, yellow or red blazes, and typewritten, plastic-coated plaques mounted on wooden posts serving as silent instructors. After admiring the stately Sanderson farmhouse, built "sometime after 1763," you may find out how big an acre is or learn that the 2½

---

miles of stone walls on the farm are composed of 12 million pounds of rock.

The hike described here takes you on a 4.4-mile loop through thick woods to the top of Prospect Hill, where a fire tower offers magnificent views over the trees. Almost all the walking is on old woods roads with only gentle grades. From the parking lot, go north past the Sanderson house on unpaved Prospect Hill Road, a sugar maple–lined avenue that used to be the main Petersham–Athol road. Turn right with the gravel in about 150 yards and begin climbing a long, subtle incline, bearing right at the end of the cow pasture. Less used roads lead off to the northwest and southeast, but stay on the main route with its border of stone walls. Prospect Hill Road, although dirt, is a Petersham town road and open to motorized traffic, but you're not likely to see any.

As you pass through the forest, you can look for evidence of the forest history described at the museum and on the nature trails. The stone walls are monuments to a time when there was no forest here. From about 1750 to 1850 much of the land was cleared of the original trees to permit cultivation, hay fields, and pasture. More than 60 percent of the region was open in the mid-19th century when the size of the local population started to decline. The promise of rich, stone-free soil in places such as New York and Ohio must have been a powerful call to the thousands who had struggled to subsist on New England's rocky ground. As farms were abandoned, the fields were naturally seeded, typically by white pine. Early in the 20th century, the maturing pines were cut to be turned into items such as matches, barrels, and boxes by concerns such as the New England Box Company. Hardwoods, which can survive in the shade of the pine forests, were already present as small trees when the pines were cut. Because white pine depends on seedlings and cannot sprout from stumps, the growth of hardwoods advanced rapidly to dominate the Massachusetts forests you see today.

Unwilling merely to speculate on the subject of forest recovery and succession, Harvard Forest researchers created their own blowdown during September 1989. You will pass the 60-tree "pulldown" surrounded by a high electric fence on your right approximately one-half mile along Prospect Hill Road. The acre of forest was disrupted to simulate the effects of a hurricane like one that passed here in 1938. Keeping deer out with the fence, researchers hope to document the details of forest recovery from natural disasters. The first 0.5 mile of Prospect Hill Road is also the last 0.5 mile of Black Gum Trail. A yellow arrow indicates where Black Gum Trail enters from Swamp Road on the right. Stay on Prospect Hill Road, however, as it takes you up and down past conifer plantations, which stand in striking contrast to the naturally seeded hardwood sections. After passing a white sign marking the Phillipston town line, the road climbs steadily, bends right (east), passes a cabin on the left, and meets the road that leads to the Prospect Hill fire tower. At this junction, turn right. Here the route passes on public roads through private land for about 0.2 mile. The boundary will be clear as you reenter the Harvard Forest, not only because of the green metal gate, but also because you pass from mixed hardwoods into stands of spruce and white pine.

Watch for a trail leading off to the right through the spruce as you near the top of the first rise after reentering Harvard Forest. You will take this trail home after climbing the fire tower, which is about 0.2 mile farther up the hill. The view from the tower is

Strolling in Harvard Forest

impressive: To the northeast lies Mount Monadnock; to the southeast, Wachusett Mountain; to the southwest, Quabbin Reservoir and the Quabbin Tower; to the west, the Pelham Hills; and to the northwest, Mount Grace. The planted tracts of dark green conifers contrast with the hardwoods in the forest below, yellow-green in summer and brilliant red-orange in fall.

When you are ready to leave, retrace your steps to the trail you passed on the way up. You will find it on the left where the road starts downhill, 100 yards past the first conifers you encounter on the right side of the trail. Although this side trail is not blazed, it is well traveled and clear among the ferns. When the trail ends at a woods road, turn left. The woods road leads you up and down through a swampy section, past another fenced research area, and eventually to a T-junction with another old woods road. Turn right here, but not before exploring the cellar hole of the old Pierce farm on the right.

The road runs past a much overgrown clear-cut area on the right bounded by a stone wall, then a road, also on the right, and into more planted conifers. You meet Black Gum Trail where it sends hikers to the north (right) with a yellow arrow. Do not turn, but note the intersection because it will help you find the next one. Continue straight to the next woods road on the left (south); turn and follow it through a stand of tall, majestic red pine planted in 1926. Stay on this woods road as it leads downhill and bends right across a swampy section. You want to turn right onto a woods road just past the swamp. It is only a few hundred yards to a red arrow indicating a left turn onto the last portion of the Natural History Trail. An open area resulting from the clear-cutting of red pines, complete with Natural History Trail interpretive signs, is just beyond this junction. Follow this trail with its red blazes a short distance back to the Fisher Museum and your car.

28

Mount Watatic

Total distance: 2.8 miles (4.5 km)

Hiking time: 2¼ hours

Maximum elevation: 1,832 feet (558 meters)

Vertical rise: 800 feet (244 meters)

Map: USGS Ashburnham (7½' x 15')

Trailhead: 42°41'47" N, 71°54'18" W

In early fall, thousands of broad-winged hawks drift out of New Hampshire and gather in great kettles over Mount Watatic before gliding toward Wachusett Mountain, the next landmark on their southward wandering. What a view they must have as they spiral lazily upward hundreds of feet on columns of rising warm air. You too can have similar spectacular views, although less easily attained, from the summit of Mount Watatic, located in north-central Massachusetts at the south end of the Wapack Trail.

Your hike up Mount Watatic starts on an old road off MA 119, 1.7 miles south of the Massachusetts–New Hampshire border. Approaching from the south, drive northwest 1.5 miles from the junction of MA 101 and MA 119, located 4.1 miles north of Ashburnham, and turn right into a parking area adjacent to the road (free, but no facilities).

Your route, the Mid-State Trail, marked by yellow triangular blazes, starts at the north end of the parking area. Bordered by stone walls, it leads you steadily but easily downhill through mixed woods of white pine, hemlock, black oak, yellow and gray birch, black cherry, and red maple. Soon you will reach an attractive pond on the right, which sometimes overflows onto the trail, making a short stretch of wet going. Small birches, hemlocks, and white pines ring the pond and shelter green frogs that sit on its banks. After leaving the pond, the trail climbs moderately steeply, reaching a trail intersection where the Mid-State/Wapack Trail goes right and on which you will return later. You should continue straight ahead, staying on the blue-blazed State Line Trail. Alongside

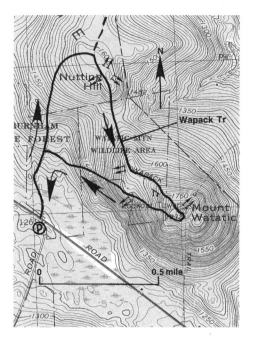

which crosses from New Hampshire into Massachusetts 0.4 mile to the north (left). Stay right. You will walk through meadowsweet and sweet cherry for about 100 yards to the rocky, open top of Nutting Hill. Views north extend across the Pack Monadnock region of New Hampshire, but they are being progressively restricted by tree growth. To the southeast you will have your first view of the goal of your hike, the tree-covered round bulk of Mount Watatic. At your feet, micas glistening in the sun draw your eyes to exposures of gneiss and schist. Shrubby thickets of sheep laurel, with its summerlong clusters of deep pink flowers and poisonous foliage, flourish in the poor soil and open sunshine of this rocky hilltop. The trail continues through trees for another 100 feet before emerging again into an opening, where views encompass Wachusett Mountain to the south (Hike 30). The gneisses here are cut by lighter granite bands called pegmatite dikes, which contain large crystals of quartz, feldspar, and mica.

To continue your hike, walk to the far end of the rocky pavement at the highest part of the ridge and then descend over bouldery ledges. Follow the yellow-blazed trail, heading directly toward Mount Watatic, and passing to the left of a white spruce and the right of a red maple. Beyond these two guides the trail tunnels through low trees, becoming well defined as it drops first through white spruce and then into hemlocks. The trail winds steadily down through mixed woods, levels, passing through a hemlock grove, and then rises again moderately steeply, with an attractive stone wall on your right, to a clearing in the hemlocks and white spruce that predominate here. From this clearing, look northwest for glimpses of Mount Monadnock, framed by the nearby conifers.

the trail, you will find a fine white birch, which you can distinguish from other birch species by its peeling bark and rounded leaves, and an intergrown beech and white pine. Just beyond the embracing pair, the trail flattens to cross a small stream and then begins another moderately steep climb up a bouldery slope. Hemlock and yellow birch predominate along here, although there are scatterings of gray birch, beech, and oak. The trail narrows, but bordering stone walls still identify it as an old road. Trees of similar age grow along the old road and in the adjacent woods, suggesting simultaneous abandonment of the road and the cleared land it traversed.

Some 0.8 mile into your hike, another segment of the Mid-State Trail leaves to the left and your path, the State Line Trail, continues ahead, now marked by yellow triangular blazes. Shortly thereafter the slope eases, and the now grassy trail swings right in a more easterly direction. Soon you join the prominent Wapack/Mid-State Trail,

The view north from the summit of Mount Watatic

Beyond the clearing the trail leaves the stone wall, crosses a ridge, and drops to cross a lower, muddy stretch. The trail now follows the moderately steep northwest ridge of Mount Watatic through woods dominated by hemlocks. The obvious route should cause no difficulties, but occasional yellow blazes will confirm your navigation. Soon you should reach a stone wall where the trail turns south (right), parallel to the wall. Just before the end of the stone wall, a rather obscure blue-blazed path, also marked by a small rock cairn, leaves on the right to a well-constructed shelter, built in 1981 by the Young Adult Conservation Corps, Camp Gardner, in a pleasant spot about 100 yards from the main trail. Unfortunately, this shelter has deteriorated in its years of use, abuse, and vandalism, although it still retains its sturdy roof. Continue on your yellow-blazed route as it heads southeast across rocky outcrops of an abandoned ski area and enjoy the good northerly views down the former ski slope.

After passing the wreckage of the old chairlift, turn right for a moderately steep climb to Mount Watatic's summit, topped by a large rock cairn. A well-defined trail takes you southeast to an open, rocky second peak.

From this mountaintop, unobstructed views extend in all directions: to Boston in the east, across much of central and western Massachusetts, and around to the Green Mountains of Vermont and the mountains of southern New Hampshire to the northwest and north. The countryside looks wild and sparsely inhabited, and it would be quite a project to climb all the hills and mountains visible from here on a clear day.

From this airy perch you will have something resembling a hawk's-eye view of the surrounding countryside. Perhaps you can imagine yourself soaring on outstretched wings as you feel for the rising air currents and circle in them, ever higher into the blue sky. Once you reach the top of the thermal and your elevator ride ends, you begin a long gliding descent to find another free lift. So it

Central Massachusetts

goes, for thousands of miles. You might wonder how it feels to be so free and, perhaps, whether hawks are ever afraid of heights.

To begin your descent, climb back up to the north summit and locate the yellow and blue triangles on the rocks. Walk down the rocky steps to a flatter, grassy patch and enjoy the fine views of Mount Monadnock directly ahead of you. Your route, marked by yellow blazes, curves left around the base of the former fire tower. Look for a narrow trail, not the wide one that heads off right toward the abandoned ski area. Where the trail enters the woods, stay right in the confusion of small paths and in 100 feet yellow blazes will confirm your navigation. The trail soon enters a cool woodland of spruce and hemlock. Following a sharp descent to the west, the way flattens as you reach the damaged shelter mentioned earlier. Look for yellow and blue triangles on tree trunks to guide you steadily downhill as you angle across a steep slope through hemlocks and occasional white birch. After 200 feet, the trail levels again and even heads north uphill for a short distance before turning west and winding down a steep, rocky stretch. The hesitant trail flattens once again and rises over a small craggy knoll before once again plunging down a moderately steep rocky slope. At the bottom, you leave the hemlock forest as the trail winds easily down through mixed hemlock and maple woods, crosses a stone wall, and eventually reaches a look-out.

You may wish to sit in this rocky clearing to enjoy the views, which range from Wachusett Mountain to the southeast all the way around to Mount Greylock in the western part of Massachusetts. To the south, and much closer, the forested dome of Little Watatic Mountain rises prominently before you. When you feel ready to continue, you will find a more or less level trail that shortly will bring you to another rocky clearing, where you will see less expansive views to the south. After paralleling a stone wall for a while, the trail turns left and drops sharply down over rocky ledges where the open aspect affords fine views of sharp-peaked Mount Monadnock directly ahead. Your path soon reenters the hemlock-rich woodland and edges steeply downhill before swinging sharply left to a southerly course. The needle-carpeted trail soon swings westerly again through a hemlock grove and there follows a few hundred feet of steady downhill hiking of variable trail steepness and short bouldery reaches, before you pass between two large granite boulders dumped here by the last ice sheet to traverse this region. The gradient eases along here as you travel through mainly deciduous woodlands, and soon you will cross a prominent stream on a rather dilapidated log bridge. The trail continues westerly, crosses a small ridge, then bends more northwesterly. In a few minutes you will reach the State Line Trail, your original ascent route, where a left turn will take you the 1,500 feet to the parking area.

29

Crow Hills

Total distance: 4.4 miles (7.1 km)

Hiking time: 3 hours

Maximum elevation: 1,230 feet (375 meters)

Vertical rise: 1,070 feet (326 meters)

Map: USGS Fitchburg (7½' x 15')

Trailhead: 42°30'23" N, 71°52'11" W

If you think you would enjoy a crow's-nest view of eastern Massachusetts perched at the top of a 100-foot-high cliff, this hike is for you. The Crow Hills are the high point, literally and figuratively, of Leominster State Forest near Fitchburg and Leominster. This hike ascends the twin peaks of the Crow Hills by way of the Mid-State Trail from Redemption Rock in Princeton. Although this route is not the shortest means of reaching the airy perches atop the cliffs, it may be the most pleasant.

To reach Redemption Rock from the north, drive to the traffic light at the junction of MA 2 and MA 31 in Fitchburg and turn south toward Princeton on MA 31. In 3.7 miles you'll reach a flashing red light and MA 140. Turn right onto MA 140 and travel 0.9 mile to the narrow driveway for the unobtrusive parking area for Redemption Rock on the left. (From the south, take MA 31 or MA 140 north to their second junction just north of East Princeton. Redemption Rock is 0.9 mile north on MA 140 from the yellow flashing light that marks this junction.) According to legend, Redemption Rock, now a property of the Trustees of Reservations, is the site where Mary White Rowlandson was ransomed in 1676 from Indians who had held her captive for 11 weeks. You may enjoy reading "A narrative of the captivity and restauration *[sic]* of Mrs. Mary Rowlandson" in *The Portable North American Indian Reader* (F. W. Turner, ed. New York: Penguin, 1973). An impressive, flat-topped outcrop of gneiss, Redemption Rock is covered with white pine needles, mosses, lichen, and Canada mayflower.

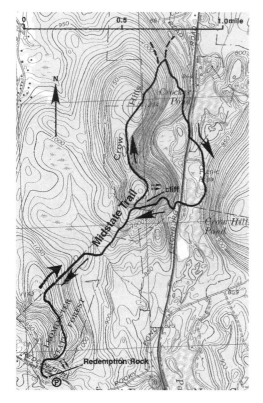

scape and even the stone walls are influenced by the strong layering in the gneiss. Look closely at the rock and you will see that the gneissic banding is due to the planar alignment of minerals, which crystallized at high temperatures (650 degrees C) and pressures (6 kilobars) when this rock was metamorphosed deep in the crust.

The Mid-State Trail has been relocated since the last edition of this book to follow a ridge and the western boundary of Leominster State Forest. The new trail is clear and the yellow blazes are easy to see. When you reach the ridge, the path levels out for easy walking on pine needles or gneiss outcrops. A sparkling lake can be spotted downhill to the west. Stately red oaks share the high ground with the white pine. Stone walls cross the hill, remembering a time when this was open pastureland. You will follow one of the stone walls downhill to the northeast, passing an open area where there has been logging. Mountain laurel decorates the landscape and becomes quite thick as you drop to cross a small stream. Climbing again, you will shortly reach a sort of terrace that leads to a cliff face of the Crow Hills.

As you near the cliff, look for folded rock layers outlined in relief on the cliff face on your left. These folds confirm that the gneiss, which traveled to this spot as magma (molten rock), had solidified prior to the end of the metamorphism and deformation of this region roughly 380 million years ago. Just past the folds, at a fork in the trail, turn left as directed by an arrow painted on a low rock, and scramble steeply up through a break in the cliff. Near the top, the trail bears right and becomes a nearly level path along the eastern scarp of the Crow Hills. Stay on the yellow-blazed trail and keep back from the edge, for the drop is precipitous! You will have plenty of opportunities to

From the parking area, walk northwest past the rock and look for the yellow triangular blazes of the Mid-State Trail painted on white pines. Follow the trail across MA 140 and uphill to the north alongside a stone wall. The yellow blazes will guide your ascent through mountain laurel and steeply up gneiss outcrops that have the same horizontal layering that is visible in Redemption Rock. A large granite boulder with prominent white, blocky feldspar crystals may be found where the melting glacier left it some 50 yards to your left along a side trail. Pause at the top of this first hill to look over a cliff toward Wachusett Mountain (Hike 30) and to snack on tall huckleberries in August. Continue northeast with the trail as it winds over rocky knobs of gneiss through an open forest of oak and maple. Details of the land-

---

Crow Hills Pond from the ledges

satisfy your curiosity about what lies over the edge when you walk along the base of the cliff on your return. You may be surprised to see climbers emerging over the cliff edge. The area is popular with technical rock climbers, who must obtain a permit from a Leominster State Forest ranger to scale a cliff. Find a comfortable spot at one of the overlooks to enjoy the view across Leominster State Forest to Boston in the east and around to Wachusett Mountain in the southwest. Rocks beneath you sport blocky alkali feldspar crystals and more complex folds.

Much of the topography that stretches before you has been strongly influenced by the underlying rocks. Hills remain where the rocks, because of their mineralogical makeup, have resisted erosion more successfully than other rocks in the valley bottoms. The lowland to the east sits on granite that is less resistant than the gneiss beneath you. Wachusett Mountain is capped by the same tough schist that caps Mount Monadnock and Mount Washington in New Hampshire. Rock structure, specifically the horizontal gneissic layering, is also responsible for the fairly level tops of the Crow Hills, Redemption Rock, and other features you may see.

After enjoying the view, continue north through the mountain laurel along the top of the Crow Hills. You may see fern-leaved false foxglove, which has yellow bell-shaped flowers on tall stalks with fernlike leaves, as well as purple-stemmed yellow false foxglove, a similar plant that lacks the lacy leaves. Red oaks, blueberries in open sections, and a view of a landfill to the northwest also figure in this ridge walk. Don't be surprised if you scare a hidden partridge into flight.

At the north end of the hills, descend a rough stone staircase, and where the slope becomes less steep, watch for a fork marked by double blue blazes on a tree. Bear right, leaving the yellow blazes, and in about 100 yards turn right again at a less prominent junction next to a large rock. Blue blazes mark this trail as it wends downhill to the southeast through young white pines looking for light beneath the canopy of much taller hardwoods. You eventually cross MA 31 by a small parking area; walk south along the shoulder for about 50 yards and then turn left onto a blue-blazed trail leading into the woods, just past a highway sign for Leominster State Forest. After crossing a small stream in a boggy fern garden, you'll enter an open white pine wood where you may spot some delicate white Indian pipe poking up through the pine needles and surrounded by plentiful ground cedar and Canada mayflower. The trail will lead you to a paved parking lot for the picnic and swimming area at Crow Hills Pond. Walk south past (or visit!) the new rest rooms to a wide path on the pond's east side, which leads you to a causeway between the two parts of the pond. Turn right and cross the causeway leading to MA 31. Just before the highway, turn left into a parking lot and walk south 100 yards to the middle of the parking area. Turn right and cross MA 31 to climb stone steps up a steep bank. At the top of the stairs, turn left and follow a prominent path south along a stone wall as far as the first major trail to the right, which leads uphill on some log steps.

The cliff face of the Crow Hills will soon loom above you, much higher here than when you met it earlier. Turn left and walk along the base of the cliff, but be sure to avoid straying beneath any rock climbers. They should be well attached to the cliff with their ropes, but they might drop some of their gear or accidentally dislodge a rock. Among the interesting features displayed in the cliff face are folds in the gneissic layering that record the ductile character of this rock when subjected to high temperature and pressure. Some less ductile, quartz-rich layers have been stretched into sausage-shaped "boudins" (from a French word for sausage). Mica-rich layers may be pieces of schist that fell into or were surrounded by this rock when it was molten, 400 million years ago. Follow the cliff around to the west and up to the point where you ascended it earlier. At the trail junction, turn left and follow the yellow blazes for a half-hour walk back to your car on the Mid-State Trail.

30

Wachusett Mountain

Total distance: 2.8 miles (4.5 km)

Hiking time: 4 hours

Maximum elevation: 2,006 feet
(611 meters)

Vertical rise: 920 feet (280 meters)

Map: USGS Sterling (7½' x 15')

Trailhead: 42°28'27" N, 71°53'40" W

Rising high above the surrounding country-side, Wachusett Mountain provides views over much of Massachusetts and the southern mountains of neighboring New Hampshire and Vermont. Trails past sparkling streams and through a variety of woodlands in the Wachusett Mountain State Reservation take you to the 2,006-foot-high summit, where you can enjoy this vast panorama.

Before your first hike in the reservation, you should obtain an accurate map to its more than 17 miles of trails and a guide to the views from the summit of Wachusett Mountain. Both are available free at the reservation's visitors center, located on Mountain Road 3.8 miles north of the intersection of MA 31 and MA 62 at the square in Princeton. The center is open year-round daily from 9 AM to 4 PM.

The loop hike described here is designed to avoid as much as possible the paved Summit Road and to give you a real feeling of climbing to the top of a significant mountain. Later you may wish to explore other trails on the mountain.

To reach this hike's starting point, retrace your route from the visitors center 2.4 miles on Mountain Road to Westminster Road, on your right. Follow this road 0.8 mile to a small parking area on your right next to a pond; the now closed Administration Road is just beyond. You begin your hike on the wide, blue-blazed Stage Coach Trail, which enters the woods between Westminster Road and Administration Road. The trail, bordered on the left by a stone wall, leads you into mixed woods of white pine and oak. When a fork goes left through this wall to a

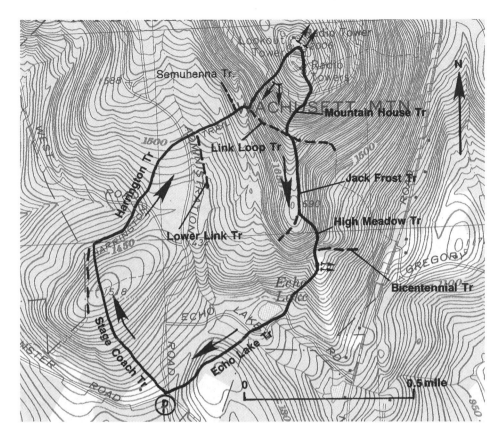

windpower-generating facility, stay to the right, keeping the wall on your left. You will climb 240 feet in the first 0.4 mile of hiking, but just when you are beginning to wonder about your physical condition, the trail levels and then begins dropping through a forest composed mainly of beech and oak. Look also for striped maple, which has large three-lobed leaves and characteristic vertical white stripes on a green trunk. In May and June you should find Indian cucumber root in bloom—its yellowish green flowers hang from the center of a three-leaved whorl. Later in summer this 2-foot-tall plant has dark purple berries. Its root tastes like cucumber and was used as food by Native Americans, but this plant species is now scarce and should not be disturbed.

After 200 yards of moderately steep descent, you reach a T-junction. Turn right onto Harrington Trail, your route to the summit of Wachusett Mountain. Initially the trail, which is marked by both yellow and blue triangles, leads you through hardwoods, but you soon enter a cool hemlock grove traversed by a small stream. After dropping to cross the small wooden bridge, the trail climbs a short slope to West Road. Cross the gravel road and continue uphill 400 yards through mixed woods to Administration Road. The trail crosses this road, too, and then within quick succession two small streams. Just beyond the second, you will pass Lower Link Trail on your right. Continue on Harrington Trail, which rises steeply for 200 feet but flattens again to cross another stream.

Beyond this crossing, the trail angles steeply right and then left as it continues climbing through mixed woodland. At the top of this rise Semuhenna Trail goes off to the left. Thirty yards beyond, you cross a south-flowing stream and then ascend a steep, rocky stairway to Link Loop Trail, on your right. The way is a little confusing here, but look for blue triangles on the rocks to guide you sharply left onto Harrington Trail. Your route climbs steeply uphill over rocky ledges. With a vertical rise of 250 feet in just 600 feet of trail, this section is the steepest and most testing ascent you will have on your way to the summit. The trail is distinctly blazed and, after the initial sharp left turn, easy to follow to Summit Road. Take whatever time you need to enjoy this rocky climb and experience the feeling of being on a real mountain. You will relish a quiet satisfaction when you reach the top and a secret pride in your achievement in getting there on foot while others around you have driven there in cars. A short side trail to the right provides a welcome respite and takes you to a lookout with views extending from Little Wachusett Mountain to the south, the windmills that you passed earlier straight ahead, and Bickford Pond to the west.

Cross the Summit Road and continue upward over steep rocky steps and ledges. The beech, mountain ash, and oaks here are noticeably smaller than those on the lower, less exposed part of the mountain. About 500 feet beyond Summit Road, Harrington Trail emerges from the woods to cross flat exposures of rock. The pale gray rocks with alternating layers of light and dark minerals are gneisses, and those with thinner layers rich in shining micas are schists. Cutting across these metamorphic rocks are veins of paler granite, with large crystals of quartz and feldspar. Muds and sands that accumu-lated in some ancient ocean were buried deep in the earth's crust, where they were warmed and changed to metamorphic rocks. Some were heated enough to melt them so that they could flow into the metamorphic rocks, where they cooled slowly to crystallize into granite veins. Take a look at these rocks as you walk over them and think how they formed at a depth of several miles in the earth's crust. Now they form the summit of a 2,000-foot-high mountain. What immense geologic processes must have brought them to their present location? Many geologists believe that such rocks are pushed to the earth's surface to form high mountains when two drifting continents collide. Bear right over these rocks to find the last stretch of the Harrington Trail, which you follow straight ahead for a few yards to the top of the mountain.

For your hard work, you are rewarded with a magnificent panorama over much of Massachusetts and adjacent states. Sixty-five miles to the west, in the far northwestern corner of Massachusetts, rises 3,487-foot-high Mount Greylock, the highest peak in the state (see Hikes 8, 9, and 10), and on a clear day the high-rise buildings of Boston, almost 50 miles to the east, are visible. Stretching invitingly across the northern horizon, the peaks of southern New Hampshire, including most prominently Mount Monadnock, and the Green Mountains of Vermont stir the dreams of mountain hikers.

When you are ready to begin your descent, walk 60 yards along the paved road from the parking area to Mountain House Trail (also labeled as part of the Mid-State Trail), a wide path with yellow and blue blazes entering the woods to the left of the radio towers. In 100 yards it crosses Summit Road. With one trail sign nailed to a tree and another carved into a boulder of gneiss at the roadside, you should have no problem

A rocky stairway on the High Meadow Trail

heading in the proper direction. The trail descends moderately steeply over rocky steps through a hardwood forest of small oaks and beeches. Some 700 feet beyond Summit Road, you reach Link Loop Trail, where an inviting flat rock makes a fine uncrowded rest or lunch spot, sheltered by trees from the winds that frequently cool the open summit. At this intersection bear left for only 20 yards on Mountain House Trail, and then turn right onto Jack Frost Trail. This route, marked by blue triangular blazes, is moderately steep, dropping through a predominantly oak wood into hemlocks, where it angles left across a slope with scattered outcrops of schist. Here you have a stretch of fairly level going as the trail follows close to the crest of a ridge. It soon crosses the crest to continue through oaks just below the ridgeline on the other side. Dropping easily on this route, you soon reach the narrow High Meadow Trail, which you should take to the left.

This trail is somewhat obscure in places, but blue triangular blazes show occasionally as you now drop quite steeply in a generally southeasterly direction. After crossing a stone wall, watch for the blue blazes to keep you on the narrow but discernible path over steep rocky ledges and across a bouldery slope. The very large old oaks here were spared the lumberman's saw because of their inaccessible location. The trail eventually flattens out and passes through a tunnel of shrubs before reaching a more open area by Dicentennial Trail. Here you go right into a former meadow that is reverting to woodland. It's a pleasant place to rest and enjoy the extensive views of Little Wachusett Mountain and Worcester to the south and distant Boston to the east. You can find meadowsweet and succulent blackberries growing here, and in early summer lots of striking orange hawkweed. The trail runs southwest across the meadow toward the woods, at the edge of which you may find a porcupine or hear a rufous-sided towhee giving its *cup-of-tea* call from a nearby tree.

Again the trail drops steeply, crosses a streambed that is dry much of the year, and then passes through yet another stone wall. Beyond, you find yourself walking through an open woodland of oaks, maples, beech, and hickory. On either side sit large boulders that were carried here by an enormous glacier during the last ice age, which ended some 12,000 to 15,000 years ago. After passing under a power line, you soon reach the northeast corner of Echo Lake and a small picnic area with a stone fireplace. Turn left and then right to follow the gravel road alongside Echo Lake to the lake's south end, where there is a pleasant view across the water to the mountain you have just descended.

Continue along the road as it rises toward a pine plantation on the left. Blue triangular blazes at the road crest direct you left onto Echo Lake Trail. Follow this trail downhill across East Wachusett Brook and then uphill through mixed woods. The trail parallels a stone wall up the steep hill, then crosses it near the top of the rise. From here the trail is well marked, dropping downhill in a southwesterly direction, mostly in conifers. Soon a pond appears through the trees, and in a few moments you will be back at your starting point.

31

Wachusett Meadows Wildlife Sanctuary

Total distance: 2.3 miles (3.7 km)

Hiking time: 2 hours

Maximum elevation: 1,312 feet (400 meters)

Vertical rise: 440 feet (134 meters)

Map: USGS Sterling (7½' x 15')

Trailhead: 42°27'19" N, 71°54'20" W

Standing on the summit of Brown Hill, you can look out over the swamps, meadows, wooded hills, and old ponds of a complex landscape where abandoned farmland is reverting to forest. Hiking through Wachusett Meadows Wildlife Sanctuary, you can explore these different habitats and look for the many plants, birds, and other animals that live in them. You will wander paths strewn with inviting benches near a beaver swamp to a rocky hilltop, passing meadows, a huge sugar maple, stone walls that date back to the old farming days, and giant glacial boulders that remember the even older ice age.

To reach this Massachusetts Audubon Society property, drive west on MA 62 from its intersection with MA 31 in Princeton center for 0.6 mile to Goodnow Road, on the right (sanctuary sign at the corner). Follow Goodnow Road for 1.0 mile to the sanctuary parking area. The sanctuary is open Tuesday through Sunday dawn to dusk. Admission is free to members of the Massachusetts Audubon Society, otherwise $3 for adults and $2 for children and senior citizens (in 1998). This hike only samples what the sanctuary has to offer, and after walking the two loops described here, you may wish to explore other trails. To guide you, obtain a trail map from the information board adjacent to the parking lot.

Map in hand, follow the South Meadow Trail, which begins at the east end of the parking lot next to the information booth. The route starts southeasterly past a barn on the left and then swings right (southerly) and descends gently through meadows brightened in early summer by buttercups,

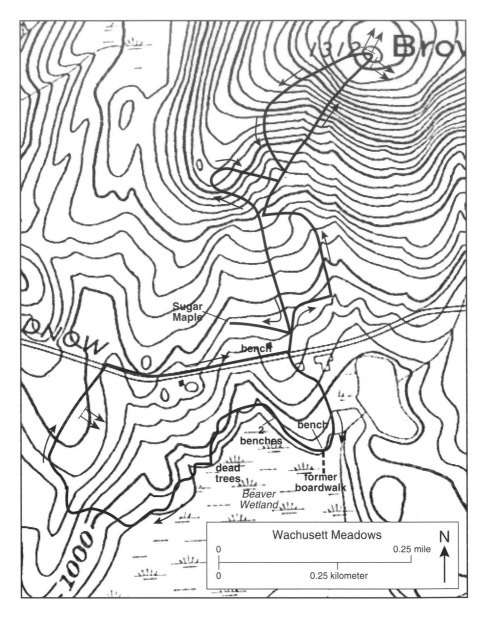

vetch, clovers, hawkweed, and oxeye daisies. Many birds, including bobolinks, nest in
the meadows, and from April through July
you must stay on the trail to avoid disturbing
them. Shortly you will reach a fork in the trail.
Your route goes straight ahead, but you may
wish to take a short spur to the right, which
brings you to a bench shaded by a large oak
tree. Return to your main route and walk
easily downhill past a stone wall lined with
large oak and hickory trees on the left. The
trail swings around to a southwesterly direction and shortly brings you to a wooden
bench. A former boardwalk goes left, but

Shagbark hickory

your route turns right along the edge of the meadow skirting the wetland to your left. Shortly after passing another wooden bench, a short side trail brings you right next to the swamp where two benches invite you to stop, look, and listen.

To resume your hike, return to the trail and follow it into a shady woodland of maple trees. In 70 feet you reach a trail junction where you leave the South Meadow Trail and follow the blue-blazed Beaver Bend Trail through a stone wall. Numerous benches have been placed alongside the next stretch of the trail to encourage visitors to slow down and really explore the sights, sounds, and serenity of this lovely place. Your path meanders at first through deciduous woods where colorful warblers may decorate the trees during spring migration. Abundant glacial erratics dot the hillsides, and some of the smaller ones have been arranged into stone walls by industrious former inhabitants. Angling downhill now through a needle-carpeted pine forest, the trail brings you to the edge of Beaver Wetland. Here a short boardwalk brings you to another pair of inviting benches, affording views over the open water. Many skeletons of drowned red maple trees and the heads of partly submerged glacial erratics protrude from the water. Duckweed dots the water surface like green confetti and beautiful dragonflies skim over it. Listen for the excited *wichity-wichity-wichity* song of the common yellowthroat, and look in the shrubs for this small warbler with a black mask over its yellow face. If it fails to perform, you will at least be sure to hear a chorus of frogs.

The trail continues alongside the swamp for a while, with short diversions to avoid wet areas but seemingly reluctant to leave the wetland edge. Eventually, though, the path begins to wind uphill to drier terrain, where you will note the change from red maples to mixed deciduous woodlands as you pass from swamp to hillside. On the forest floor you may see American toads in among the partridgeberry, Canada mayflower, and starflowers. Continue up a moderate slope on bouldery paths past more wooden benches until you reach the edge of a meadow. Out in the meadow you will see bluebird nest boxes, and a convenient bench allows you to sit and watch some of these beloved and breathtakingly colorful birds. The bordering stone walls remind us of the farming heritage of this land. A few steps beyond the birder's bench, you will reach a trail intersection where a right turn will quickly bring you to the mown path of Beaver Bend Trail, which takes you across the meadow.

Viewed from the meadow, you can't miss Little Wachusett Mountain rising prominently about 1 mile away to the northeast. Continue past Hemlock Seep Trail, on your left, and reenter woodland. Shortly you will reach an intersection with Pasture Trail (left) and your route, which continues to the right. Walk past stone walls and beautiful, tall shagbark hickory, beech, and oak that border the old road. In 500 feet the Mid-State Trail goes left, but you go ahead to pass a gate to the paved portion of Goodnow Road, which soon dips to cross a stream valley. As you walk along here, listen for the songs of house wrens, blue-winged warblers, and chestnut-sided warblers. Soon you will reach the parking area on your right and the sanctuary headquarters on your left. In this vicinity, listen for the raucous call of a great crested flycatcher, a bird with a chestnut tail and yellow underparts, which you may see sitting on top of the old barn just beyond the parking area.

To continue your hike on the second loop, pass the parking lot and in 100 feet turn left on the mown North Meadow Trail through a meadow and then left again on a short spur to view one of the largest sugar maple trees in the United States. This amazing giant, the Crocker Maple, has grown here for more than 300 years, has branches thicker than most tree trunks, and measures 15½ feet around its trunk. You may wonder why this maple was spared when the land was cleared for farming in the 1780s; perhaps it provided maple sugar, welcome shade, and a touch of beauty for the farm family.

Return to the trail intersection and turn left up a gentle slope, then bear right past a spruce to Farm Pond. A yellow warbler uses the spruce as a favorite singing perch, and many goldfish live in the pond. You may hear the croaking call of bullfrogs, and in early summer look for large tadpoles in the water. Continue easterly across the meadow and then turn sharply left at an intersection just before the woodlands. The path follows an ecological edge as it skirts the boundary between woodlands to the right and the meadow to the left. Pass a trail that goes off right between two benches and you soon will reach Chapman Trail, where you exit right from the northwest corner of the meadow.

The trail exits the grassy field and crosses a stone wall before continuing as a grassy path through a grove of large shagbark hickories. You will pass many fine examples of this species, which you can identify by its compound leaves with five leaflets; thick-hulled, edible nuts; and the unmistakable long strips of peeling bark for which it is named. After crossing a stone wall, the Chapman Trail joins the Mid-State Trail. Stay right as the trail, here prominently blazed in blue, winds up a moderate slope through mixed woods of white pine, maple, and oak. Along here mountain laurel puts on a spectacular display in June, with masses of pale pink flowers set against dark evergreen leaves, but look also for the more re-

tiring pink lady's slipper that blooms at the same time.

The trail crosses yet another stone wall and then divides. Chapman Trail goes left, but you should turn right onto Glacial Boulder Trail toward a small cluster of huge rocks that you can easily see perched on the hillside about 40 yards away. The trail to these boulders crosses rocky outcrops of schist and gneiss, ancient rocks formed at high temperatures and pressures deep within the earth's crust by a process known as metamorphism. The giant boulders are made of granite and therefore differ from the metamorphic rocks on which they rest. These chunks of rock were scraped off some northern outcrop, carried here by an enormous ice sheet, and dumped when the ice melted, around 12,000 to 15,000 years ago. Try to imagine how this area looked during the last ice age, when there was no vegetation and a thick layer of ice lay upon the land. The trail, marked by yellow blazes, crests the hill just beyond the glacial boulder and drops down alongside a stone wall over more ledges of schist and gneiss. In about 100 yards you'll reach the corner of a small, partly overgrown meadow. Here you turn left onto Summit Trail. The route now swings left and climbs easily through the small meadow and into the woods at its northern margin.

Just inside the woods you intersect Brown Hill Loop; bear left and after 25 yards pass through a stone wall and encounter another trail intersection. Go right here onto Summit Trail (unmarked in 1998), which is heading toward Brown Hill where fine views will be your reward at the end of the next and most strenuous part of the hike. Climb up some rocky ledges, staying close to a stone wall on your right. Blue blazes and arrows on the rocks pointing toward the summit will guide you over a rocky step and steeply uphill alongside the wall. As you reach the more open upper part of Brown Hill, you may feel the stirring of the wind or the warmth of the sun through the scattered shrubs and small trees. The trail eases off finally, and you can catch your breath and enjoy extensive views to the south over woods, meadows, and the sanctuary buildings. At the cairn that marks the summit of this 1,312-foot-high hill, you can sit and admire Wachusett Mountain (Hike 30), which dominates the view to the northeast, and Little Wachusett Mountain to the east.

After enjoying the views and a well-earned rest, leave the summit in a north-westerly direction on Summit Trail, following yellow arrows and blazes. The trail circles left around the summit area and then drops toward the southwest on a rocky path. Upon entering the woods the trail steepens, but it soon levels off. When you reach an intersection on Brown Hill Loop turn left, following the yellow blazes steadily downhill past white pines on your right. You will pass Glacial Boulder Trail on your right and soon will be flanked by pines on each side of the trail. The path circles around to the left and then goes to the right through a wall to rejoin the trail you hiked uphill. Retrace your earlier route on yellow-blazed Summit Trail and as you pass through the small meadow, listen for the distinctive *cup-of-tea* call of a male rufous-sided towhee. This bird, with a black V-shaped bib, white belly, and chestnut sides, perches on small trees, throwing back his head as he calls. The trail leaves the small meadow and passes through a narrow band of trees into the larger meadow. Here a mown trail will take you either way back to the parking area.

Eastern Massachusetts

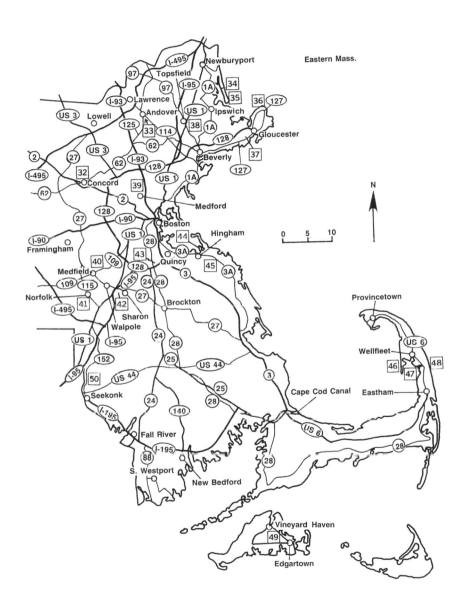

32

Great Meadows National Wildlife Refuge

Total distance: 1.5 miles (2.4 km)

Hiking time: 1 hour

Maximum elevation: 120 feet (37 meters)

Vertical rise: 30 feet (9 meters)

Map: USGS Maynard (7½' x 15')

Trailhead: 42°28'29" N; 71°19'48" W

Something in the call of wild geese as they thread their way across the sky in great V-shaped skeins stirs the human soul. But if future generations of our species are to hearken to their call, these wonderful birds need safe stopping places on their great migrations. When you stand on the top of the observation tower at the Great Meadows National Wildlife Refuge, you look out over such a place. But not only the geese benefit; many plants, birds, and other animals also take advantage of this sanctuary on the Concord River in the busy, historic town of Concord. You, too, may take some peace here as you wander along easy trails amid the marshes and ponds, briefly sharing this place with its many inhabitants.

To reach the refuge, drive east on MA 62, 1.8 miles from MA 2A in Concord, or west on MA 62, 2.6 miles from MA 225 in Bedford. Then turn north onto Monsen Road and follow the refuge signs for 0.4 mile to the parking area at the end of the dirt road. Entrance is free, and the refuge is open daily from sunrise to sunset.

Before you begin exploring Great Meadows, climb the observation tower located at the northwest corner of the parking area for a preview of your hike, aided perhaps by the permanently mounted telescope. Immediately before you lies the extensive open water of Upper Pond, fringed by red maples that become more scattered pondward as they mingle with marsh plants. To the right, marshy Lower Pond is separated from Upper Pond by a narrow dike, along which you will soon be hiking. You will notice many nest boxes out in the pond and marshes,

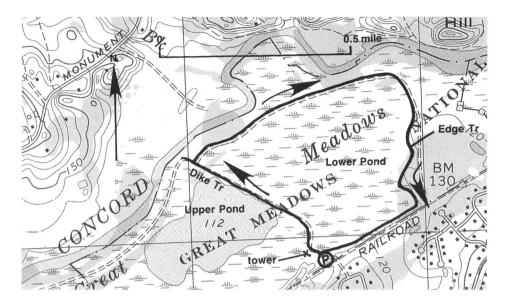

reminding you that this refuge was established to provide a habitat for waterbirds. Since that time, in 1944, more than 200 species of birds have been recorded here.

After descending from the tower, begin your hike by taking the Dike Trail from the northeast corner of the parking area. Follow the wide gravel path past the red maples and take a little time to study the displays and trail map located there. Continue through the shorter shrubbery of willows, smooth alder, round-leaved dogwood, raspberries, and grape that lines your route. All around you, in season, you will hear the calls of frogs and red-winged blackbirds and the songs of common yellowthroats and yellow warblers. A wooden bench amid the trees soon appears on your right; it's an excellent place to observe pond vistas and undisturbed wildlife, at least until the summer growth of tall vegetation obscures the view. From here, in summer, you may see families of black ducks, mallards, and Canada geese; if you are a patient photographer, you may also take some memorable pictures. Beyond the bench, Dike Trail has no bordering

shrubs blocking your view of the marsh, and you can observe cattails, arrowhead, and purple loosestrife, as well as buttonbush, identified by its shiny green leaves and white, ball-like flowers on long branchlets. About halfway along the dike, benches invite you to sit and watch birds or just enjoy the peace and sunshine. A solitary common cottonwood stands a little forlornly near the benches, as though looking for human company to compensate for its isolation; out on the water float yellow water lilies. Walk to the end of the dike and beyond, past a trail to the right, to the banks of the Concord River.

During high-flow periods, the Concord River spills over its banks into the adjacent low-lying floodplain. Silver maples, which typically grow on floodplains, line the levee of the river and can be identified by their flaking gray bark and the whitened undersides of their deeply notched leaves, which in fall turn brilliant red and yellow. Retrace your steps for about 200 feet and turn left at the first intersection, which you walked through recently. To the left a number of

Great blue heron

different habitats form narrow zones parallel to the trail. Many large silver maples grow alongside the trail, and beyond them a swamp extends toward the Concord River, from which it is separated by the tree-lined levee. On the right, buttonbushes fringe the marshes of Lower Pond. Farther along, the Concord River and the trail diverge, and you may hear the rattling twitter of marsh wrens that nest in the cattails to your right.

Soon the Concord River wanders back toward the trail and you recognize once again the row of silver maples marking the levee. Among the cattails on your right, the bloom of more purple loosestrife will probably catch your eye; look also for pickerelweed. This emergent aquatic plant has large, glossy, heart-shaped green leaves and pretty blue flowers on a cluster at the end of a short stem. The trail swings right, passes a stand of willows on the left, crosses a culvert that drains Lower Pond, and in 80 yards reaches the edge of the marsh. Just inside the woods, turn right onto the wide, signposted Edge Trail into a grassy, open area. In the woods to the left you will see a workshop and other buildings. Walk past a large red maple on your left to a slope down to the marsh. On the slope rests a large granite boulder that was probably dumped by a melting ice sheet. The trail continues beyond the large red maple, passes a pair of benches, and enters the woods. In 100 feet you will reach a more open area with some fine views out over Lower Pond to some hills beyond, and more glacially transported boulders nearby.

Toward the end of the last ice age, this area was covered by a lake filled by meltwater from the ice sheet. The low hill behind you, and those beyond the pond, consists of sediments deposited in this ancient lake by meltwater streams that drained from the ice front. While standing here quietly enjoying the pond scenery, you may become aware of a pair of phoebes that nests hereabouts.

Apart from a white throat and underparts, this sparrow-sized flycatcher has a mostly gray plumage. You will recognize this species by its tail-bobbing and by its habit of flitting out from a perch in a shrub to snare passing insects. During the summer your identification will be confirmed by the bird itself, as it calls its own name over and over again: *phee-bee-phee-bee*.

The trail meanders through mixed woods of white pine, red maple, and black oak, over a forest floor brightened by blueberry, sarsaparilla, pink lady's slipper, Canada mayflower, and club moss. The trail stays close to the marsh for a while, but as it begins to move away from it, bear right onto a wide, easy trail. You pass many boulders of schist and granite, also brought here by the ice sheets, and then cross a small stream and wet area on a short boardwalk. Soon the trail curves around a knoll and crosses small outcrops of dark gray gneiss cut by irregular quartz veins. Just beyond, you climb a few steps and then turn right onto an old railroad bed. This raised, straight track forms the refuge boundary and through the trees affords views out over the marshes. In about 1,000 feet, just beyond a bench, the trail descends a short wooden stairway and continues into mixed woods of red maples, black oak, white birch, and white pines. Catbirds haunt this damp woodland in summer, and you may catch sight of one as it flits like a dark gray ghost among the shrubbery. Often catbirds will hide in the shelter of bushes and sing their strange mixture of sweet and hoarse squeaky notes, but if you hear their catlike mewing calls, you will understand the origin of the name catbird. Shortly you reach a gravel road, where you should turn right to end your hike at the parking area.

33

Charles W. Ward Reservation

Total distance: 4.0 miles (6.4 km)

Hiking time: 2½ hours

Maximum elevation: 420 feet (128 meters)

Vertical rise: 600 feet (183 meters)

Map: USGS Lawrence (7½' x 15')

Trailhead: 42°08'25" N, 42°06'44" W

This loop hike along the trails and former roads of the Charles W. Ward Reservation in Andover takes you over two hilltops, through sunny meadows and mixed woodlands, and past luxuriant swamps. This land, now largely reforested, was settled in 1646 and farmed until late in the 19th century. You will see many stone walls on your way—silent witnesses to the farming era. From the unforested slopes of Boston Hill, you can enjoy wide panoramas, including fine views of the Boston skyline. As an added treat, a short detour will bring you to a boardwalk that extends deep into a marvelous northern bog, permitting you to examine its many unusual plants close at hand.

To reach the Ward Reservation, owned by the Trustees of Reservations, take exit 41 from I-93 and travel east on MA 125 toward Andover. Stay on MA 125 at the 2.5-mile mark, where MA 28 goes north to Andover, and in another 2.6 miles turn east onto Prospect Road (there's a sign for the reservation at the corner) and drive 0.4 mile through a residential area to the parking area on the right. The reservation is open daily until sunset, and admission is free. An unmanned information booth at the parking area is the only facility. Here you may borrow or purchase a trail map for $2 (honor system).

Start your visit to the Ward Reservation with a short 0.4-mile excursion on the Bog Nature Trail to Pine Hole Pond. From the east end of the parking lot near the information booth, walk downhill diagonally left to the southeast corner of a small meadow and then enter the woods on an obvious path.

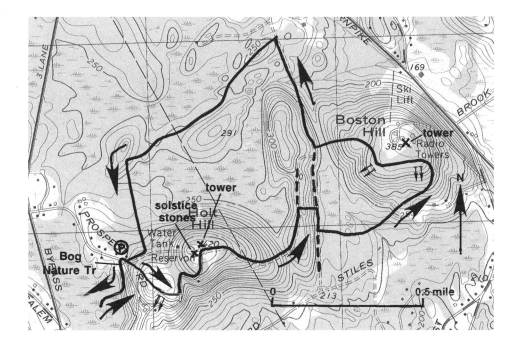

Bear right at a fork 100 feet into the woods and in 500 feet turn right onto a boardwalk that will take you to the heart of the bog. Among the many unusual plants that live in this swampy area is wild calla, which has a distinctive, macelike fruit. You'll find it growing alongside the boardwalk. Just beyond a row of four red maples on the right, a solitary sour gum stands on the left. This swamp-dwelling tree has dark, rough, furrowed bark, bitter although edible fruits, and rather sparse pale green leaves.

After two sharp left turns, the boardwalk ends with attractive views over the open water of Pine Hole Pond. Here, close to the water, you can compare tamarack, which loses its rather scant needles in fall, and black spruce, which retains its dense foliage year-round. It takes only a little imagination to pretend you're deep in the muskeg of Canada, hundreds of miles to the north. The bog sits in a kettle hole (see Moose Hill, Hike 42, for an explanation of the origin of

kettle holes), and the depression acts as a frost hollow, effectively shortening the growing season by almost a month, thus permitting only a more northerly flora to exist here. Near the boardwalk's end you can also find the insect-eating pitcher plant growing atop the quaking layer of sphagnum moss. This amazing plant traps insects in its water-filled, pitcherlike leaves and digests them by using enzymes dissolved in the water. Some insects (for example, the pitcher plant mosquito) have adapted to living in the pitcher plant leaves. After your tour of this northern bog, retrace your route to the parking area to continue your hike.

From the parking lot entrance, turn right onto Prospect Road and walk uphill to an intersection. Here a private road continues straight ahead and another road goes at right angles to the left. Your path splits the angle between these roads, passes by a bronze tablet to Nicholas Holt, and heads diagonally uphill through a mixed woodland.

Solstice stones

In about 150 feet you will emerge into an orchard with scattered fruit trees. Stroll across the orchard for about 500 feet and exit through a fringe of hemlocks on a path here marked with orange blazes. Continue gently downhill along a tree-lined path. In about 500 feet you reach a prominent, wide trail near a large sugar maple. Bear left on the well-defined trail, marked by white rectangular blazes, that rises steadily but not steeply to a meadow where soon you will see the radio tower on the top of Holt Hill ahead of you. The broad track through the meadow will head you directly to the tower. You will also run smack into the Solstice Stones. These large, flat stones were assembled in a compasslike pattern by Mabel Brace Ward, who established the reservation in 1940 as a memorial to her husband, Charles W. Ward. The four larger stones point to the cardinal points of the compass; north is marked. The smaller stones point to the sunrise and sunset, respectively, in the

northeast and northwest quadrants at the summer solstice, and in the southeast and southwest quadrants at the winter solstice. Splendid views extend to the southeast and south, with the high-rise buildings of Boston clearly visible.

Proceed east—try using the Solstice Stones to orient yourself—downhill through a meadow that affords extensive southerly views. Although the path may be indistinct, you can find the trail into the woods by heading toward a prominent clump of white birches. Stay on the main trail as it descends easily through mixed woodlands, swings around to the left, crosses a small valley, and winds uphill to a broad, pine-covered ridge. You need to keep a sharp lookout for a trail that leaves the main trail on the right, just before a stone wall, at a trail fork guarded by a large white pine. Turn right alongside a stone wall onto this path, which takes you about 300 feet down a moderate slope to an overgrown old road flanked by stone walls. Again turn right (south), walk about 500 feet, and turn left at a break in the stone wall. The trail, flanked by lots of fragrant-flowering pepperbush, passes through a pleasant, level, open woodland of maple and oak. It crosses a stone wall just before joining another overgrown road, also lined with stone walls. Turning left here, you will drop to a stream, angle easily uphill, then cross to the left side of a stone wall. Following a stretch through smaller trees, you will reach a grove of pitch pines, identified by their three-needled clusters and reddish bark.

From the pitch pines the trail circles up a grassy, boulder-strewn hillside, heading toward a radio tower. The granite boulders rest where they were dropped by the ice sheet that was carrying them when the ice melted perhaps 15,000 years ago. One of the flatter of these glacial erratics provides a good rest and lunch spot, where you can also enjoy panoramic views from the east around to the west, with Boston again clearly visible to the south.

To resume your hike, follow the trail almost to the top of Boston Hill, where it enters a woodland of shrubby trees that are replacing former meadows. The wide grassy trail, bounded on the right by a stone wall, soon bends sharply to the right. Before making this right turn you can walk ahead a short distance to obtain views south to Boston and west to Holt Hill, which you climbed earlier. Return to the trail, which soon drops downhill among birch scrub and crosses a stone wall. You easily could miss the next turn, so you should navigate carefully along here, beginning where the trail starts to parallel a stone wall and wire fence. Where the fence and the stone wall part company, swing left and then immediately right on the main path. Follow this trail as it descends to a stream, passes a trail on the right, then winds steadily downhill past a number of stone walls and many glacial erratics. After dipping past a small pond in a glacial kettle hole, the trail rises to be joined by another trail from the right—it's the one you passed on your right a few minutes ago. Shortly you will reconnect with the former road on which you hiked earlier.

Turn right (north) along the old road, which drops into a small stream valley and then rises easily. Notice the sharp contrast in woodlands along here, with hardwoods on the left but white pines to the right; the pines indicate natural reforestation of a former meadow. You should turn left at the second well-defined trail, which appears 1,000 feet beyond the stream, and then left again at the fork 30 feet farther on. This trail heads southwest for 0.8 mile, soon crossing a ski trail while skirting a small hill with many rocky outcrops of granite. The path gently undulates along the lower slopes of a rocky hill on the left and adjacent to a swamp on the right. Soon the trail edges away from the hill to meander across a flatter, wetter area for a while, then climbs to the top of a ridge and a trail intersection. Here your route back to the parking lot goes downhill to the left. In 250 feet the trail crosses a small stream on stepping-stones and a short wooden bridge in a wet-bottomed valley, and then begins to climb through an open, mixed woodland of white pine, hemlock, oak, maple, birch, and pignut hickory. The narrow but distinct trail continues steadily uphill for what may seem longer than the actual 0.3-mile distance. However, it eventually intersects a narrow, paved road. Turn right, walk to Prospect Road, and turn right again to reach the parking area.

34

Hellcat Swamp Nature Trail

Total distance: 1.9 miles (3.0 km)

Hiking time: 1 hour

Maximum elevation: 45 feet (14 meters)

Vertical rise: 140 feet (43 meters)

Map: USGS Ipswich (7½' x 15')

Trailhead: 42°44'29" N, 70°47'44" W

How delightful the sea breeze feels on a hot summer day as it ruffles your hair and cools your skin. You are standing on the high point of the Hellcat Swamp Nature Trail, exploring with your senses the sights, sounds, and smells of this coastal wild spot. Before you extend salt marsh, freshwater swamp, sand dunes, and coastal thickets. Behind you, beyond the restless sand dunes, the mighty Atlantic rolls and surges in endless rhythm. Humans have abused wetlands, thinking them damp and miserable at best, places fit only to hunt and kill or more commonly to drain and fill, denying them their life-giving wetness. But here in the middle of Plum Island a different choice has been made. The wet places are nurtured, and a boardwalk carries you, dry of foot, to the heart of their beauty and wildness.

To reach this coastal sanctuary, drive east from US 1 in the center of Newburyport on Walter Street (farther along it is grandly called the Plum Island Turnpike). In 3.3 miles you will cross the bridge over Plum Island River to Plum Island. In another 0.3 mile, follow the sign for the Parker River National Wildlife Refuge and turn right along the road that skirts cottages on the left and salt marshes on the right. In 0.5 mile you will reach the sanctuary entrance. The refuge is open dawn to dusk year-round, and entrance is $5. To increase your enjoyment of what you'll see on your hike, make sure you obtain a Hellcat Swamp Nature Trail guide, available at the entrance station (it may also be available from a box at the start of the trail if the supply has been replenished at the time of your visit). There is

Dunes by the Hellcat Swamp Trail

Hellcat Swamp Nature Trail

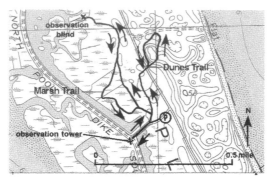

a limit to the number of cars admitted each day, so on sunny summer days arrive early to avoid disappointment. Once through the entrance, drive south on the refuge road for 3.8 miles to Lot 4, the parking area for Hellcat Swamp Nature Trail. There are also rest rooms here.

Begin your hike by walking westerly from Lot 4 along a shrub-lined trail that soon brings you onto a narrow dike. This artificially constructed ridge separates two freshwater pools, North Pool and Bill Forward Pool. The wide path leads to an observation tower that you should ascend for a fine overview of several different zones of the Plum Island barrier island complex.

In the distance to the west are the low hills of the mainland and to the south the rounded hills of Great Neck. The open water of Plum Island Sound separates Plum Island from the salt-marsh-fringed mainland. The sound is connected to the ocean by a narrow tidal inlet at the south end of Plum Island. Salt marshes, threaded by tidal creeks, extend from the dike immediately in front of the observation tower out to the sound's edge. You may see a variety of birds feeding in the marshes and creeks, including snowy egrets, green herons, and Canada geese. The dikes you see were built to protect some of the marshland from the twice-daily tidal invasion of seawater. The resulting freshwater ponds and marshes contain a much greater diversity of plants than the salt marshes and in turn support a wider variety of birds and other animals. From the tower you often can spot deer and muskrats in North Pool, as well as many ducks, geese, herons, and other wading birds. In late summer you may be lucky enough to sight peregrine falcons, which visit Plum Island on their southward migration. Swirling groups of waterbirds taking suddenly to panicky flight may be a sign that one of these magnificent birds has arrived. Eastward from the tower extend some of the partly wooded sand dunes that form the backbone of Plum Island. In the distance shines the Atlantic Ocean, and if strong onshore winds are blowing, you will hear the low roar of waves crashing on the beach.

Following this overview you should be ready for a closer look at some of the different environments of the Parker River refuge. Retrace your steps past the ponds and through some shrubs to the boardwalk of the Hellcat Swamp Nature Trail. Start down the boardwalk and bear right at the first fork (later you will visit the observation blind and Marsh Trail to the left) onto Dunes Trail, which initially leads you through shrubs and small trees including wild rose, honeysuckle, raspberry, bayberry, chokecherry, black cherry, northern arrowwood, birch, oak, red maple, bigtooth aspen, and quaking aspen. If you crush a leaf from one of the bayberry bushes at trailside, you'll release a beautiful scent. Many birds find homes in this dense thicket, and you may hear some of them scurrying or scratching in the underbrush or singing from a more lofty perch. After passing a sign for the Ralph H. Goodno Woods, you drop slightly into a moister area with many red maples and pignut hickories. A conveniently located bench encourages you to sit and enjoy the singing birds and scolding red squirrels. This spot is good for seeing migrating warblers, as well as catbirds and rufous-sided towhees. The trail then rises toward the refuge road, passing on the right a sassafras tree, whose leaves exhibit strange and varied shapes.

Cross the road to pick up the trail again; at the intersection a few steps in, bear right. This area has many dunes—great piles of sand that are moved and redeposited by the strong northeast and northwest winds that accompany coastal storms (nor'easters). The winds also erode sand and scoop out hollows known as blowouts, creating a very irregular landscape. Some of these blowouts are deep enough to reach the fresh groundwater table that normally lies at some depth below the surface layer of dry sand. The availability of this water allows a wide variety of shrubs and small trees to fill these depressions. Many of these plants grew from seeds eaten and later excreted by birds—a form of natural gardening that ensures a food supply for the many birds that frequent these hollows. The shrubs, trees, and creepers growing along here include raspberry, northern arrowwood, greenbrier, Virginia creeper, black cherry, Tartarian honeysuckle, and fire cherry. See how many different ones you can identify on this outing.

Soon the boardwalk reaches a stairway leading up a dune. In some cases, growing plants stabilize the dunes so that they withstand the wind's buffeting, but sometimes the winds continue to move the dunes into vegetated areas, where they overwhelm even the trees. Both stabilized and mobile dunes occur on Plum Island. The stairway climbs the face of a moving dune that is slowly burying the plants before it. At the top of this high dune you will find a platform and a seat; it's a delightful place to spend some time, perhaps enjoying a cool sea breeze on a hot day or a warm sun on a cold, still day. From this vantage point, spectacular views extend in all directions. North and south along the length of Plum Island stretches the hummocky terrain of dunes and hollows. Beyond the dunes the dynamic energy of the ocean impinges on this outermost fringe of land to create beautiful sandy beaches. The endangered piping plover struggles to survive along these sandy shores, which are off-limits to humans until the nesting season ends. To maintain summer access to this delightful trail, please respect this restriction and stay on the boardwalk! Westerly lie the salt- and freshwater marshes, the narrow sound, and the distant rise of the mainland. Only at the complex margin of land and sea do so many disparate environments occur in such close proximity.

When you are ready to leave this airy spot, follow the boardwalk down through the dunes toward a clump of black pines, specially planted here because they can thrive in this dry and windy place. Note the yellow-flowering beach, or false, heather growing in patchy carpets that help to hold down the shifting sand. Beware, however, of the shiny three-leaved poison ivy. This plant grows abundantly on Plum Island, where it helps to immobilize the sand and provides cover and food for many animals and birds, but it is best left alone by humans and serves as an inducement for you to stay on the boardwalk. The boardwalk circles to the left and shortly you will reach a trailside memorial to

Ludlow Griscom, a well-known ornithologist who fought for the preservation of Plum Island and studied its bird life. The granite gneiss memorial stone was carried to the Plum Island vicinity by a large ice sheet sometime during the last ice age, perhaps 20,000 years ago; it was moved to this spot in 1965.

Beyond the memorial stone, the trail enters a woodland dominated by red cedar, black cherry, and honeysuckle. Watch out for the thorny, dark green barberry, whose clusters of small yellow flowers turn to red berries in late summer. Summer hikes through here are made more delightful by an accompaniment of birdsong, especially that of the colorful purple finches. In the cool shade of black cherries and red cedars, you will find a seat and a small platform where you can sit peacefully and look out over the shrub-filled swamp. Waiting quietly here, you may even see young red foxes walk by on the boardwalk and be visited by red-breasted nuthatches.

Refreshed by your pause, continue down through a swamp dominated by northern arrowhead, which is draped by creeping greenbrier, willows, and red maple. Nesting catbirds skulk among the shrubbery in summer, and you often can hear their song of mixed sweet and rasping notes and their characteristic mewing cat imitation calls. Climb a few steps past two large red cedars and in 10 yards you will complete the dune loop. Cross the road and retrace your path to the boardwalk junction and turn sharply right onto the Marsh Trail. Walk for 200 feet along an up-and-down boardwalk through woodlands to an intersection. Take the right fork and continue north to another junction, where you should again go right for another 700 feet of meandering, but generally north-northwesterly tending boardwalk that will bring you to the observation blind.

From the blind you can observe closely the freshwater marsh without being seen by its inhabitants, which will continue with their business undisturbed if you are quiet enough. The marsh has both open water and areas filled with cattails, reed grass, and purple loosestrife. Look for the red-winged blackbirds, ducks, and Canada geese that frequent the marsh and the mourning doves and squirrels that are attracted to the grassy patches to the right. Muskrats live in the marsh, too, and they are often seen near the blind, busily feeding on marsh vegetation or swimming through the water.

When you are ready to stretch your muscles again, go back along the boardwalk to the first trail junction and turn right. In 30 yards you'll pass from shrubbery into the freshwater marsh. The boardwalk provides a wonderful opportunity to explore this wetlands area while keeping your feet dry. You will have close-up views of the cattails and reed grass that tower above you. By early August the marsh is colored vividly with masses of flowering purple loosestrife. The beauty of this plant adds much to the appeal of the late-summer scene, but its prolific spread may pose serious threats to the long-term viability of the marsh. Introduced accidentally from Europe perhaps 100 years ago, purple loosestrife is well established in much of the Northeast and is rapidly expanding north into Canada and west as far as Wisconsin. This plant forms elevated clumps of decay-resistant stalks, roots, and debris that shade out native plants such as cattails and eventually form impenetrable tangles that also exclude many birds and other animals.

After circuiting the marsh, the boardwalk returns to the main trail. Go right here and also at the next junction, and you will soon arrive at Lot 4.

35

South Plum Island

Total distance: 3.0 miles (4.8 km)

Hiking time: 1½ hours

Maximum elevation: 44 feet (13 meters)

Vertical rise: 60 feet (18 meters)

Map: USGS Ipswich (7½' x 15')

Trailhead: 42°42'25" N, 70°46'24" W

As the great ice sheets moved south over this area more than 20,000 years ago, they brought with them mud, sand, and boulders they had scraped from more northerly lands. When the ice melted, this glacial debris was, quite simply, dropped. The melting ice poured water back into the oceans, causing the rising sea to flood the land. At the edge of the ocean, winds and waves sorted and redistributed the dropped sediments to form beaches, dunes, and muddy marshes. Many plants and animals colonized this new-formed land, and later humans called it Plum Island. The waves and winds have not finished their work, and this land still changes, usually slowly, but when buffeted by storms, sometimes quite rapidly. On this hike at the south end of Plum Island, you can see some of the landscapes formed by these events and walk on splendid beaches to observe geologic processes still at work. Some of the hike extends along soft sand beaches and you are reminded to bring along a good supply of drinking water, especially on hot summer days.

To reach the south end of Plum Island, follow the directions given in Hike 34 for the Hellcat Swamp Nature Trail. From the entrance to the Parker River Wildlife Refuge, drive south 6.5 miles to Lot 7. During the bird-nesting season, parking in Lot 7 may be time limited and you may need to use the Sandy Point State Reservation parking area, another 1,000 feet south along the road.

After you've parked, cross the road and head toward the observation tower, which affords an excellent view of the southern part of Plum Island and surroundings. Immediately before you to the west spreads a

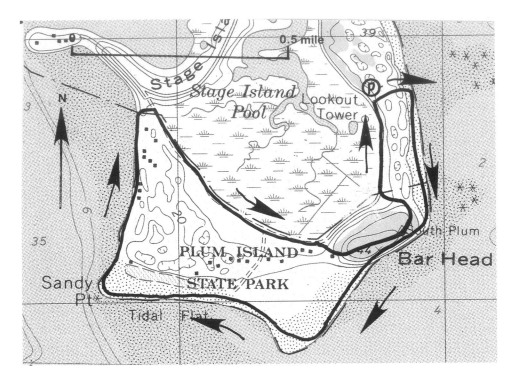

freshwater marsh whose open pools are being replaced gradually by expanding stands of cattails, reed grass, and purple loosestrife. The amount of open water depends on rainfall and varies considerably from season to season and year to year. The tower makes an outstanding spot for bird-watching, especially in the morning hours when the sunlight comes from behind you and illuminates bird plumages. In the summer months cormorants, Canada geese, herons, egrets, gallinules, kingfishers, red-winged blackbirds, terns, gulls, and ducks all spend time here. You may well find yourself standing next to experienced bird-watchers scanning the marsh for rarities that sometimes visit this refuge, or others just enjoying the regular inhabitants. Many birders will willingly share their expertise with you, and they may let you peek through their telescopes at some particularly beautiful or interesting bird.

If you look to the east, you'll note the narrow stretch of low dunes separating you from the open Atlantic Ocean. A short distance offshore, Emerson's Rocks protrude through the surging water, unless it's high tide, when they usually are submerged. To the south lies the rounded, shrub-covered hill known as Bar Head. These views eastward and southward give you a preliminary look at features you will see in more detail as you hike.

Now return to the parking lot and follow a boardwalk toward the beach. If the boardwalk is closed to protect nesting birds, you can access the beach and study its features via a short trail from the Sandy Point State Reservation parking area mentioned above. The trail crosses low sandy dunes spotted with bayberry bushes and poison ivy, as well as beach heather, beach goldenrod, beach grass, and dusty miller, which stores water in its silvery-colored leaves. When you reach the wave-lapped beach, turn right and walk along the shore. Beaches can undergo rapid changes in their profile, being eroded in a few hours by storm waves and rebuilt in a matter of days during calmer weather. Usually the beach profile has a high point, known as the berm crest, which runs roughly parallel to the shoreline. From this crest the sand slopes quite steeply to the water and more gently down to the dunes. Walking along the berm, you may find ridges and depressions alternating on the sloping beach face. These are beach cusps, and they channel the water of each breaking wave into complex patterns as it surges up the beach face. You soon will reach the end of the Parker River refuge and the start of Sandy Point State Reservation. This boundary is marked by a line of rocks across the shore, a wire fence over the dunes, and refuge signs.

Not far beyond the boundary the terrain changes abruptly. Instead of the sandy shore there are many boulders, and in place of the low dunes there is a 40-foot-high cliff. This cliff is the seaward edge of Bar Head, a hill composed of materials carried here by an ice sheet during the last ice age some 20,000 years ago. The glacial deposits were molded into a streamlined elliptical shape by the movement of the overriding ice sheet to produce a landform known as a drumlin. The drumlin is composed of sediments ranging in size from boulders several feet across to material as fine as flour. This mixture is called glacial till, and examples are exposed in the sea cliffs along Bar Head. This area is a good outdoor laboratory for observing the results of geologic processes that are operating today. Waves attack and erode the drumlin, especially during storms, slowly wearing it away and separating out the different-sized components of the till. The fine floury material is suspended in the turbulent water and car-

ried offshore; sand grains are moved a shorter distance to form beaches and dunes; and the larger, heavier boulders remain behind to produce the rock-strewn foreshore you can see stretching out into the ocean. Erosion has considerably reduced the size of the drumlin; it once extended seaward several hundred feet. After looking at this area, can you explain the origin of Emerson's Rocks? On a warm summer's day an ice age seems far away, but come here in January with a sharp winter wind and it will feel a lot closer!

At low tide a wide expanse of sand, boulders, and small pools is exposed and awaits your exploration. A thin veneer of purple garnets often coats the sand, creating an attractive and rather exotic appearance. The garnets are heavier than most of the sand grains and become concentrated by the swirling waters—a form of natural panning similar to that used by old-time gold miners. If you examine the boulders closely, you will find a wide variety of sizes, shapes, colors, and rock types. These boulders were probably plucked from many different New Hampshire hills and carried south by the ice sheet.

Beyond the eroding drumlin, the beach is once more sandy and backed by low dunes. On those summer afternoons when the tide is rising and water floods back over the wide, exposed sand flats warmed by the sun, this beach is a most tempting place to interrupt your hike for a swim and a little sunbathing.

Resuming your hike, you approach the summer home of at least one family of nesting piping plovers, an endangered species now gradually pulling back from the brink of extinction. It is truly a struggle for beach-nesting birds to raise their young in such a vulnerable location, where they are subject to flooding by exceptionally high tides and

The view north toward Emerson's Rocks from Bar Head

storm waves, predation by gulls and other animals, and interference from humankind. In this case, at least, human activity is helping these birds in their fight, and you are urged to do your part by not trespassing onto their homes on the beach. If you keep a sharp lookout, you may spot these small shorebirds as they run across the sand with rapid leg movement. With white underparts and backs the color of the beach sand, you could easily miss them, but their black necklace and orange bill and legs will give them away. You might be alerted to a bird's presence by the soft two-syllable piping calls that give the plover its name.

Leaving the plovers in peace, continue walking along the beach, now in a westerly direction, with the fast-flowing currents of the tidal inlet on your left. Across the inlet, in Ipswich, rise the hills of Great Neck, Little Neck, and Castle Neck, all composed of ground moraine-glacial sediments depos-

ited by the same ice sheet that formed Bar Head. Turning at Sandy Point, you head north on a long sandy beach. This stretch might feel like a bit of a slog on a hot summer day, but you can always plunge into the clear, inviting ocean—guaranteed to cool and refresh you at any time of the year! When you reach the fence that forms the refuge boundary, turn right; in 100 feet, turn right again onto an old road, now becoming very overgrown in places. You may need to make a diversion and use a winding trail that you will find at the seaward edge of the encroaching vegetation, including poison ivy, so watch out! Soon this informal trail rejoins the former road and you will walk along the southern edge of the freshwater marsh you saw from the observation tower. Cattails, reed grass, and purple loosestrife are close at hand, and you may see raccoons and muskrats as well as some of the many birds that inhabit the marsh. The shrubs to your right include wild rose, blackberry, bayberry, arrowwood, honeysuckle, and poison ivy. About 0.5 mile after leaving the beach, you'll pass through a gate into a parking area for the state reservation. Here you will find rest rooms and a display about piping plovers.

Now you have a choice. You can walk along the gravel road directly back to the parking area or you can follow a more adventurous way over the drumlin. To do that, walk to the end of the parking area and find the trail up the wooded slope of Bar Head. You can follow the path safely, although it is narrow and squeezed by shrubbery and some poison ivy. Several short side trails lead to the cliff edge, where there are good views out over the restless ocean and south toward Castle Neck and Cape Ann. After a few more yards, the trail reaches a clearing with fine views over the ocean, to Emerson's Rocks, and along the length of Plum Island.

From this viewpoint the trail descends to the beach and then turns left alongside the wildlife refuge boundary. A last push through soft sand brings you to the reservation parking area, where you will find a rest room and an information board but no water. If you parked in Lot 7, follow the dirt road into the wildlife refuge, and in 300 yards or so you'll reach your car.

36

Halibut Point

Total distance: 1.5 miles (2.4 km)

Hiking time: 1 hour

Maximum elevation: 105 feet (32 meters)

Vertical rise: 170 feet (52 meters)

Map: USGS Rockport (7½' x 15')

Trailhead: 42°41'11" N, 70°37'54" W

Halibut Point State Park and the adjacent Trustees of Reservations Halibut Point Reservation provide an uncommon island of public access where you can explore the human history and richly varied natural environment of a stretch of the rugged, rocky northern coast of Cape Ann. Here you can study the relationship of plant distribution to proximity to the ocean, scramble among granite outcrops and marvel at the ingenuity and fortitude of the former quarry workers, stand on a large heap of discarded rock slabs and admire the view, or search for unusual seabirds.

To reach the start of the hike, drive north out of Rockport along MA 127. In Pigeon Cove you will pass the Ralph Waldo Emerson Inn on the right (east) side of the road, and in another 0.6 mile you will reach a turnoff to the right that in 0.1 mile will bring you to the parking area. This side road is located on a downhill curve and you should keep a sharp lookout for the small HALIBUT STATE PARK sign on the corner. The park is open daily during daylight hours year-round. There is a parking fee of $2, and an informative trail map is available from a box near the information board.

To begin your hike, cross Gott Avenue from the northeast corner of the parking area. A board displaying a map of the trails marks the entrance to a wide path and the starting point for your exploration of this combined state park and Trustees of Reservations site. You also will learn here that Halibut Point is a corruption of Haul About Point, a geographic location from the era of sailing ships. The level trail tunnels north for

650 feet through a great variety of overarching trees that line both sides of your way—good practice here for a review of your tree identification. You can expect to find apple trees copiously draped with greenbrier and wild grape, wild cherries, dogwoods, hickories, white birch, red cedar, various oaks, and mountain ash, complete with its brilliant red berries in late summer. In contrast to what you will see later in your hike, the trees are quite tall here in this relatively sheltered spot.

As you reach the end of the botany tunnel, you will see on the right side of the trail a large block of coarse-grained granite. Switch gears from botany to geology and see if you can find the three principal minerals of the granite: shiny, glassy quartz; and the two feldspars, one milky white and the other bright pink. This plutonic rock cooled slowly from molten magma formed deep in the earth's crust, thus allowing ample time for the slow growth of the large crystals that make up this granite and others that you will see on your hike. Later, powerful geologic forces bought these rocks to the surface, where they are now exposed to your view and made accessible to human quarrying and use. Nearby you will see a mooring stone—an example of one of the first such human uses of Cape Ann granite. You will learn from the explanatory sign that these large, heavy granite blocks were used to anchor oak posts to the seafloor so that their above-water extensions could be used as moorings for fishermen's boats. If you look carefully at this granite, you will notice that it contains no pink feldspar, which may cause you to wonder about the source of the granite that you looked at earlier.

Just beyond the mooring stone you will reach a trail rotary. Go straight ahead here to the water-filled former Babson Farm Quarry. This large hole was created by hu-

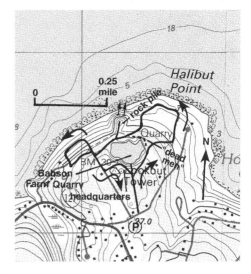

mans during 90 years of quarrying operations, some of which you will learn about as your walk continues. Keeping the quarry free of water was a constant problem during the period when granite was being removed from here, and once the continuous pumping was terminated—when the quarry was abandoned some 60 years ago—the quarry soon filled with accumulated rainwater. On a hot summer day you may be tempted to swim here, but notices will remind you that this is forbidden. After contemplating the human effort and ingenuity that were required to carve this large hole in the tough rock, retrace your steps to the rotary and turn left toward the ocean. Just beyond this turn you will pass a pond on the right in which wild rice and purple loosestrife grow. In 200 feet you will reach a grove of small black locust trees near the edge of the quarry. To solve the problem of retrieving the heavy granite from the quarry floor, steam-driven derricks were built to hoist up the rock. To keep the derricks from toppling into the quarry, they were bolted to large blocks of granite such as the one still standing here in mute testimony.

Granite exposures along the Atlantic shore

Continue along the wide trail as it skirts the quarry from which it is separated by a fringe of shrubs that are noticeably smaller than the trees that you passed earlier in your hike. You are beginning to see the effects of the strong, salt-laden winds that blow in off the Atlantic Ocean. Shortly you will reach a jumble of large granite blocks. These are worth searching for evidence of both human activities and geologic phenomena. The difficult task of splitting this hard, unlayered rock was accomplished by drilling a row of holes and then wedging the rock apart. Larger holes were made in the granite blocks to aid in attaching them to the derrick chains when they were being hoisted out of the quarry. A little searching will reveal examples of these blocks in the vicinity. As you study the rocks, you may find patches of darker rock enclosed in the light-colored granite. These are known as xenoliths, and they represent pieces of preexisting rock that were incorporated into the molten granite magma as it was forcing its way into the surrounding rocks.

The main trail continues to hug the quarry edge, but about 200 feet beyond the granite blocks that you studied, look for a narrow trail that goes off to the right from the main path. Follow this trail through a short, shrubby tunnel onto Trustees of Reservations land, keeping a sharp lookout for poison ivy as you go. Shortly after emerging from the bushes, you will reach a trail intersection marked by two iron staples protruding from the granite. Such staples were known as dead men, and they were used to attach the hoisting derricks to their granite base. Go right here and head in an easterly direction across a coastal heathland. Prominent among the many plants growing here you will pass sumac, sweet fern, goldenrod, lowbush blueberry, greenbrier, and bayberry. Follow the narrow, rather overgrown trail over occasional low exposures of granite. You need to be persistent here and wait to turn left (north) until you find a much more prominent trail. In another 300 feet you will reach a junction of several trails: to the right the reservation boundary and private land, straight ahead the ocean, and your route to the left, a narrow trail through the heath. Soon the slender path rises slightly and brings you to the top of a promontory of large, rounded outcrops of granite. This is a good place to scramble around and explore among the boulders, to observe the growth of seaweeds, and to notice the darkening of the granite in the intertidal zone at the edge of the sea. You will also see ahead of you to the west a giant rock pile of angular granite slabs.

When you are ready to continue your hike, you should head toward the rock pile, choosing from several trail options: Some scramble over the coastal exposures, others through the shrubby heath. As you proceed, you will see a sign that warns of the dangers of swimming along this stretch of rocky coast. From this sign, a more obvious trail swings left onto a wide gravel path past a small former quarry on the right. Follow this trail as it rises moderately for a short distance, then levels off and swings west, before climbing again through an arch of trees to reach a major trail intersection. Turn right here on a spur trail, which will take you to the top of the rock pile that you earlier used as a navigation marker. Here granite slabs have been made into unusual picnic tables that resemble a miniature Stonehenge. This is a good spot for lunch. A painted information panel on a granite slab identifies landscape features visible to the west on a clear day. These range from Hog Island in the south to the Isles of Shoals in the north and include Plum Island (Hikes 34 and 35) and the Seabrook nuclear power plant. The lookout that you stand on consists of the discarded, unused, or unusable blocks of granite from the quarry workings.

The pile now affords a prominent perch from which to search for the marine birds that frequent the offshore areas; in winter, hopeful birders must sometimes brave biting winds that blow in from the ocean. Wintering sea ducks, including buffleheads, red-breasted mergansers, common eiders, and white-winged scoters, congregate close inshore along the rocky sea margin. More eagerly sought, however, are the occasional king eiders and small groups of harlequin ducks that relocate here for the colder winter months. Farther offshore, more pelagic species may be observed, including the elegant gannets—large, black-and-white marine birds that may be described as being pointed at both ends. Training binoculars or a telescope on the pack of gulls that commonly trails incoming fishing boats may reveal a gannet or two mixed in with the crowd. You may be lucky enough to see them perform their spectacular dive as they plunge vertically headfirst into the water in search of food.

When ready to leave this viewing point, walk back along the spur trail to rejoin the main path and turn to the right. In about 200 feet you will reach a trail junction where the left option goes toward the quarry, but your route continues to the right along the wide path. Your way will be lined by small red cedars, sumac, and northern arrowwood and will take you 350 feet to a T-junction. Turn right here past two gnarled black cherry trees, identified by their rough dark bark and narrow pointed leaves. Heading downhill on the Bayside Trail toward the sea, you soon will pass into heathland with only scattered shrubs. Ahead you will see the rock-fringed ocean, populated in the summer months by gulls and cormorants but the wintering place of many sea ducks. Before reaching the water, the trail swings left and heads southwesterly parallel to the coastline and affords you views of the maritime environment. In about 500 feet, the trail turns sharply to the left and heads uphill to regain the height that you recently lost. The trees become noticeably taller as the distance from the stunting salty winds increases, and in 150 feet your route turns left once again and heads back toward the intersection guarded by the black cherry trees. On your way you will pass through woods that include fire cherry and oaks. When you reach the intersection, go right and easily uphill. On the left side of the trail, just beyond a closed path to the right, there are large rounded outcrops of granite that have been polished and striated by an ice sheet that ground over them from north to south. Near the top of the hill you can make a short detour out to the right to study the granite bollards on display here. These hand-carved granite posts were used for tying up ships at wharves and docks. To complete your loop hike, walk up to the prominent building on the hilltop that serves as the park headquarters and visitors center. Here you will find a museum with natural history and historical displays, as well as rest rooms. A short trail beyond the building will bring you back to the trail rotary that you passed earlier, and from there a short walk down the tree-lined path will bring you back to the starting point of your hike.

37

Ravenswood Park

Total distance: 3.5 miles (5.6 km)

Hiking time: 2 hours

Maximum elevation: 215 feet (65 meters)

Vertical rise: 390 feet (119 meters)

Map: USGS Gloucester (7½' x 15')

Trailhead: 42°35'30" N, 70°41'56" W

It will take you only a few minutes to see why Mason A. Walton, the "Hermit of Gloucester (and lover of nature)," lived for 33 years in Ravenswood Park. Towering oaks, lacy ferns, elegant stone walls, giant boulder gardens, lush wetlands, and thick blueberry patches are just a few of the many attractions of this park endowed by Samuel E. Sawyer in 1889. Sawyer, who loved walking over these hills as a boy, gradually acquired the property from parcels held as woodlots. His original bequest of 300 acres has been increased to almost 500 acres by subsequent gifts. Ownership passed to the Trustees of Reservations in 1993, ensuring good management in perpetuity.

To find Ravenswood from the junction of MA 133 and MA 127 in Gloucester, drive 1.9 miles south on MA 127 to a parking area on the right behind the Ravenswood Community Chapel. A glass-protected trail map stands for your inspection near the gated entrance to the park at the north end of the small parking area. Proceed past the gate to begin the hike on the wide, boulder- and wood-aster-lined Valley Road, a woods road protected by dark, angular gravel. There are lots of trails and few blazes in Ravenswood Park, but it is difficult to get lost. We will guide you on a counterclockwise circuit, so the center of the park and this road will generally be to your left.

Red oaks rule over this mature, predominantly hardwood forest whose inhabitants also include American beech, white birch, and white pine. At the first opportunity, turn right onto a wide footpath marked by small granite boulders and labeled LEDGE HILL TRAIL.

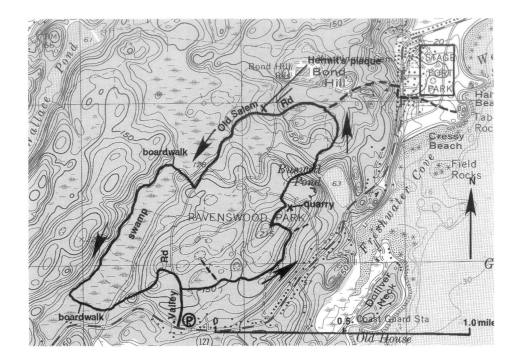

Volunteers have lined the first part of this path with piles of rocks, separating it from Canada mayflower, various mosses, and occasional mushrooms. Your route curves left, crosses another path, and follows an old stone wall that stands as a monument to the hard work of those who once cleared this land. Evidently there was no shortage of boulders here, most of which are Cape Ann granite. An unusual toad-skin lichen has colonized the wall, confirming its antiquity. Here many small hardwoods are competing against each other and a few large white pines. Red oak generally wins the growth race, because its growth rate, unlike that of other hardwoods, does not decrease after the tree reaches a moderate height.

You will soon see a paved road and a red house off to the right, just outside the park. The path starts downhill, jogs sharply left to avoid some very impressive, large boulders, and scrambles uphill past low ledges. The

ledges are outcrops of Cape Ann granite, the bedrock that underlies the whole park and most of Cape Ann. The boulders you just passed, and those resting on the ledges, are samples of the same rock type, carried a short distance and dropped by passing glacial ice. Both contain black pyroxene and amphibole, gray quartz, as well as alkali feldspar crystals that can have a coating of chalky white clay.

Just over the crest of a rise near the top of a hill, the path meets another at a T-junction. Your route is right, but if you want a view of the coast, turn left and walk 50 yards to an opening through a cleared area. Don't forget to return to the T-junction and continue with the trail. The fine, crunchy gravel that paves this path consists of angular feldspar crystals that have accumulated from granite that has disaggregated due to chemical reaction and frost wedging. Soon the trail winds past an old, water-filled quarry. Vertical half-cylinder grooves in the rock are the drill holes used by quarry workers to break out rectangular granite blocks for use in construction. White pine needles and thick *Polytrichum commune* moss make cushions for a comfortable rest or for taking a close look at the even-textured granite. Keep to the left at the quarry and you will soon cross a woods road to a level area where witch hazel and then hemlock grow beneath maples and oaks.

With a switchback around granite ledges, the trail drops into a moist valley, turns right, then ascends to another flat area through a tunnel of young hemlocks. Side trails right lead down to a large pond supporting a population of lily pads. After stopping to nibble some blueberries (if it's August), you will cross a long rib of granite and come to a woods road called Old Salem Road. (If you wish, you can take a 1.2-mile round-trip detour to the ocean by turning right; at MA 127, turn right again and then take the first left, Tolman Avenue, down to Stage Fort Park.) To continue your explorations of the hermit's woods, turn left to cross a low, glacially smoothed outcrop and walk among more blueberries, solitary fronds of bracken fern, sassafras saplings, and, in a wet section, cinnamon fern and curtains of greenbrier. After bearing right to join a gravel road, look for violet creeping bellflowers on tall spikes guarding a plaque to Mason Walton on the right. Walton lived Thoreau-like in a cabin near this spot, enjoying nature and entertaining occasional visitors from Gloucester, from 1884 until his death in 1917. Some of Walton's experiences are recorded in his 1903 book, *A Hermit's Wild Friends*. Where the road climbs from a wet section, cuts in the hillside expose some of the fine-grained, rust-colored clay left by meltwater from the same ice that brought the giant boulders.

About 200 yards after passing a wide

The "Hermit" and his home.

road on the left, turn right and descend onto a cross trail labeled with a green sign for MAGNOLIA SWAMP. (Continue straight on the road to your car if you wish to shorten your walk.) Boardwalks built by the Trustees of Reservations have opened the swamp to all without requiring waterproof boots. Tall groups of cinnamon fern, interrupted fern, and in June magnolia blossoms line the boardwalk. On the far side, turn left to follow a needle-padded path decorated with partridgeberry carpets along the swamp's edge under large hemlocks and white pines. Listen for the beautiful song of the hermit thrush. This part of the park feels different, somehow wilder than the rest. Perhaps it is the mat of common polypody fern crowded on the flat top of a balanced rock. Maybe it is the scent of skunk in the air. Or possibly it is a sense that some large outcrops are trying to push the trail and you into the swamp. Whatever the cause, the effect is worth the price of wet feet. Eventually you reach another boardwalk crossing among fragrant-blossomed sweet pepperbush, blueberry bushes, and red maples. Climb with the trail across a wide path, through mountain laurel and more blueberries, and past a large erratic boulder perched on a smoothed outcrop. Turn right at the top of a small knob where there is another green MAGNOLIA SWAMP sign and head back to the wide gravel road on which you began this hike. Turn right for a short walk to your car.

38

Ipswich River Wildlife Sanctuary

Total distance: 3.3 miles (5.3 km)

Hiking time: 2 hours

Maximum elevation: 111 feet (34 meters)

Vertical rise: 240 feet (73 meters)

Map: USGS Ipswich (7½' x 15')

Trailhead: 42°37'53" N, 70°55'17" W

A rich treasury of delights awaits explorers in the Ipswich River Wildlife Sanctuary, located along the winding Ipswich River in Topsfield. This largest of Massachusetts Audubon Society sanctuaries comprises more than 2,500 acres of freshwater marshes, ponds, meadows, woodlands, and splendid glacial landforms. During the first half of this century, the previous owner, Thomas Proctor, imported many perennial plants to enrich the flora and beautify the woodland. He also hired a landscape architect to design a rockery and a Japanese garden. On this hike, in the northern and central parts of the sanctuary, you'll enjoy not only exploring the wealth of varied wildlife habitats, but also uncovering many relics of the bustling colonial communities that occupied the small hills between the inhospitable marshes. Later you may wish to explore some of the sanctuary's other trails, which lead to an observation tower, a gazebo, an arbor, and the Ipswich River itself.

To reach the Ipswich sanctuary, drive southeast on MA 97 from its intersection with US 1 in Topsfield. In 0.5 mile, turn left onto Perkins Row (sanctuary sign on the corner); in another mile you'll reach the sanctuary entrance on the right. The trails are open daily except Monday from dawn to dusk. The sanctuary office is open Tuesday through Friday from 9 AM to 4 PM. Admission is free for Massachusetts Audubon Society members, and $3 for adults and $2 for children and seniors who are not members (fees as of 1998). The sanctuary buildings and parking area sit atop Bradstreet Hill, a mound of mud, sand, and boulders deposited and

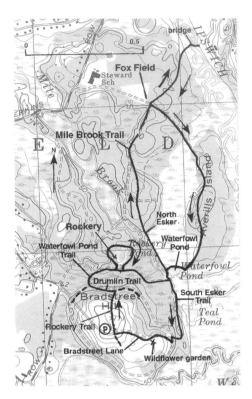

The Massachusetts Audubon Society bought this land from Proctor in 1951, using funds obtained from the sale of land on Plum Island to the federal government. In 1901 Proctor hired Shintare Anamete, a Japanese landscape architect, to design and supervise the construction of The Rockery. It took nine years to build the grottoes, stairways, and platforms, and many of the huge boulders you see were carried here by horse and cart from 10 miles or more away. You can have fun exploring here and in early summer thrill to the gorgeous color of the azaleas and rhododendrons, but stay on the cobble pathways (note that they can be quite slippery when wet). Winding side paths lead up to a platform with views out over Rockery Pond.

Beyond the grotto, the trail follows the pond's edge to a rock jetty, which offers unobstructed views over the water. A little farther along, a pondside seat is perfectly situated for listening to the foghorn calls of bullfrogs or the sweeter songs of yellowthroats. Around the north end of Rockery Pond, the narrowing trail passes lots of wild bleeding heart and red columbine and soon reaches a veritable forest of tall, many-colored rhododendrons. Beyond these walls of greenery you will cross a pretty bridge over one of the pond's inlets and then turn right onto a short boardwalk that connects to a trail. Just before a dip to a bridge, turn left onto a trail and boardwalk through a marsh, which will quickly bring you back to Waterfowl Pond Trail.

Turn left to continue your explorations. Here the path follows a road initially built in the late 18th century to connect a thriving community on Averill's Island to Perkins Row and thence to the town of Topsfield. The road was built across marshes or swamps in places and must have required many days of hard work for its construction.

molded by an overriding ice sheet perhaps 25,000 years ago to form a glacial landform called a drumlin. You begin your hike by walking north from the parking area and on down the slope of this drumlin. Follow Rockery Trail, guided by trail signs, across a meadow where bobolinks nest in early summer, past a grove of young spruce trees on your right, and then bear right into woods. At the bottom of a short hill, turn left onto Drumlin Trail and walk 0.1 mile to Waterfowl Pond Trail. The way here is brightened in early summer by colorful rhododendron, azalea, and mountain laurel. Turn right onto Waterfowl Pond Trail, then stay right at the next junction near a stone seat on the hemlock-lined road. In about 400 feet, a trail leaves on the left to begin a loop around Rockery Pond past The Rockery, which you must not miss.

Swamp azalea blooms along the trail's edge in early summer, and you may hear the beautiful, descending song of the veery rolling from a tree in the nearby wetland. In about 0.2 mile you intersect Mile Brook Trail, on which a left turn will bring you shortly to a stone-parapeted bridge over a stream connecting Waterfowl Pond on your right to the marsh on your left. Here you are likely to see chickadees, grackles, red-winged blackbirds, common yellowthroats, and northern orioles—and you may be lucky enough to see the waterfowl that give this pond its name. In summer, colorful dragonflies skim over the white blossoms of fragrant water lilies floating on the pond's surface.

Just north of the pond, Mile Brook Trail reaches a large pin oak, which you'll recognize by its down-pointing lower branches; near this tree you should bear right onto blue-blazed North Esker Trail, which climbs easily to the top of a narrow, sinuous ridge. This feature is a fine example of an esker (for more on these glacial landforms, see Moose Hill, Hike 42). Your route follows a stony path along the crest of North Esker through mixed woodlands of white pine, hemlock, beech, oak, and shagbark hickory. To the right is Hassocky Meadow, actually a marsh, and beyond it Averill's Island, which you will be exploring later. At a trail intersection with Hassocky Meadow Trail, stay left on North Esker Trail. As you walk northward, you will notice the esker becoming lower and more poorly defined. The trail then descends to shrubby, rather overgrown woods marking regeneration after an old forest fire, but it soon rises again to cross a small hill and rejoin Mile Brook Trail.

You should continue north, staying first right and then left at successive trail junctions to join the White Pine Loop. Soon you will reach an unmarked fork. Go left here. At the top of the next rise the wide, level trail passes through groves of large white pine, beech, and maple and soon reaches a junction, where you should bear left onto Bridge Trail. In another 50 yards, you'll come to a three-way junction; here you should bear right onto the main trail. In another 100 feet, bear right at a fork to begin a 0.6-mile spur to the Ipswich River and back.

Before taking this trail, however, you may wish to go left a short distance to an upland meadow, known as Fox Field, where gaily colored spring and summer flowers thrive in the sunshine and delight the eye. At first your path down to the river will take you through mixed woodlands, but you'll soon reach another meadow. Cross this open stretch on a shrub-lined trail that brings you to a wooden footbridge over the Ipswich River. This river nourishes a broad adjacent wetlands area where marsh plants flourish and red-winged blackbirds call from scattered shrubs. You have reached about the midpoint of your hike, and you may wish to sit here for a while and perhaps eat your lunch and watch for passing canoeists.

When you feel ready to resume your hike, walk back across the meadow and retrace your route through the woods to Fox Field. Go left at the junction near the meadow and left again at the three-way junction you entered earlier; in 50 yards, at yet another junction, stay straight on White Pine Loop toward Averill's Island (you came out on the trail from the right). At first the trail drops through mostly pines, but as you approach the wetter upper reach of Hassocky Meadow, red maple becomes dominant. At the next trail junction, you leave the White Pine Loop and follow the Averill's Island Loop. The trail crosses a stream that connects Hassocky Marsh to the Ipswich River wetlands and then rises slightly into a hemlock grove.

You have reached Averill's Island, where the Averill family developed a busy community and carpentry business in the late 17th century. They also printed a small newspaper and became so well known as sources of local news and information that the island came to be called The Colleges. Nowadays you can hike a network of trails here through cool woodlands of magnificent white pine, hemlock, and beech. Just inside the first hemlock grove you should bear right at a fork and follow the edge of the marsh for a while before passing a small pond on your left and then winding easily uphill. If you follow the wide trail and stay right at a trail intersection, you eventually will drop easily toward the marsh, pass through an archway of small trees, and intersect Stone Bridge Trail by Waterfowl Pond.

Turn left, cross the stone bridge, and in about 500 feet, go left again onto South Esker Trail, immediately beyond a wooden bridge. Your path wanders up and down along the spine of this marvelous esker, the second of your hike. You will have glimpses to your left (east) of a broad marsh as well as of Fox Island and the larger Pine Island. In about 800 feet, turn right to a log stairway

that will take you down the esker's side and in a short distance to a T-intersection. Look for the magnificent copper beech tree growing to the right by the intersection of Drumlin Trail and Stone Bridge Trail. You should go left here, however, onto the wide Drumlin Trail, and in 200 feet, right onto another wide trail, Bradstreet Lane, which will take you uphill past the Hemlock Trail on your left to a meadow on the south side of the road. One of the earliest roads built in the area, Bradstreet Lane was used as a route to Ipswich for 200 years or more before it was finally abandoned in 1899.

You should detour across the meadow to your left to visit Vernal Pond, which Shintare Anamete originally designed as a Japanese garden. Here a path takes you around a small shaded pond surrounded by bouldery slopes covered by flowering dogwood, mountain laurel, and a multitude of wildflowers—a botanist's delight. A trailside seat invites you to sit quietly for rest and reflection. To complete your hike, return to Bradstreet Lane, turn left along the stone wall, and in a few minutes you will reach the parking area.

Rockery Pond

Eastern Massachusetts

39

Middlesex Fells Reservation

Total distance: 7.4 miles (11.9 km)

Hiking time: 5½ hours

Maximum elevation: 311 feet (95 meters)

Vertical rise: 1,540 feet (469 meters)

Map: USGS Boston North (7½' x 15')

Trailhead: 42°25'50" N, 71°06'29" W

The city of Boston is located in a topographic basin 200 feet or more lower than the surrounding highlands. The traveler who approaches the city on MA 2 from the west or I-93 from the north will find the edge of the basin marked by steady downhill grades and good views of the Boston skyline. A special appreciation of the Boston Basin can be obtained by climbing Wright's Tower, situated near the summit of Pine Hill in the Middlesex Fells Reservation in Medford. Built during the Civil War, Wright's Tower presents a commanding view across the entire city.

Much of the topography of New England can be described as erosional, and the Boston Basin is no exception. Hard igneous and metamorphic rocks that comprise the surrounding hills are more resistant to the forces of erosion than are the softer sedimentary rocks that underlie the lowland of the city. The abrupt boundary to the basin visible to the southwest from the Pine Hill tower is unusual, however, and marks the location of a great fault, or break in the earth's surface. Rocks to the northwest of this fault have been raised by thousands of feet relative to the rocks of the Boston Basin, creating the sharp juxtaposition of hard and soft rocks that currently exists.

Although the view from Wright's Tower alone merits a trip to the Middlesex Fells Reservation, the park has many other attractions, including an extensive trail network. Just a few miles from downtown Boston, the reservation protects more than 1,000 acres of woodland. I-93 and MA 28 together physically divide the reservation

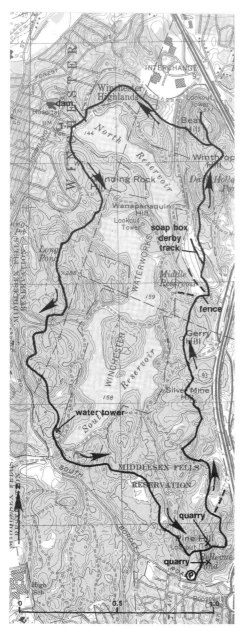

into distinct sections east and west. The Skyline Trail described here will lead you on a circuit directly over many of the hills in the western section and completely around three reservoirs. By the end of this hike you will have had a chance to view much of what the park has to offer as well as to get a pretty good workout for your feet.

The hike begins at a parking lot adjacent to Bellevue Pond in the southeast corner of the western section, which is easy to reach from exit 33 of I-93 (watch for signs for Route 28, Fellsway West and Winchester). The exit leads to a traffic circle. Head northwest from the circle on South Border Road for 0.2 mile to the parking area, on the right. A bulletin board near the parking area displays a map of the 50 miles of trails and gives other information about the reservation. Copies of the map may be purchased from Friends of the Middlesex Fells Reservation, Inc., P.O. Box 560057, West Medford, MA 02156 (telephone: 781-662-2340). Skyline Trail is surprisingly rugged, doggedly climbing many rocky knobs that could easily be avoided. The path is never very difficult, but its length and hilly character are factors to consider before you start. Because the hike will last several hours, be sure to carry along water and lunch or a snack. From late spring until late summer, mosquito repellent is a must here, as it is in most Massachusetts woods.

From the parking lot, follow the wide path (Quarry Road) along the east side of Bellevue Pond. In addition to providing a quiet home for mosquito larvae, the pond harbors a chorus of frogs to serenade you from among the water lilies. The woods road and pond are in a narrow northeast-trending valley some 50 to 100 feet below the surrounding hills. This valley marks the location of the Medford Dike, a vertical sheet of dark igneous rock called diorite that is less resistant to erosion than are the rocks (also igneous) that comprise the adjacent hills. You can see the diorite, with its long gray plagioclase crystals and shiny black biotite flakes, in a small quarry on your right just before and opposite a stone picnic table. Interestingly, this rock is one of the youngest in the Boston area, having arrived at its present location as a liquid, or magma, only some 200 million years ago; surrounding rocks are at least twice as old.

Ignore all side paths until you're past the pond, then look for a right turn onto Skyline Trail about 100 yards past the stone table, marked by a sign and white blazes. The trail climbs steeply up Pine Hill over glacially smoothed outcrops of the Medford Dike. A switchback redirects you toward the summit tower. Unfortunately, the top of Pine Hill has been desecrated by immature visitors who have taken pleasure in the sound of breaking glass—at your expense. The wooden roof of castlelike Wright's Tower is charred as the result of a fire built by vandals inside its base. Farther along the trail, blackened trees stand as monuments to carelessness or folly. Though minor irritations when compared with the splendor of the reservation as a whole, these scars serve as reminders that the quality of our parks may be more fragile than beer bottles. Step over the glass and climb the stone-and-concrete tower for a magnificent view across the Boston Basin to the sparkle of the Atlantic Ocean in the east and the dark silhouette of the Blue Hills in the south. Most of the low, elongated hills to the east in the built-up towns of Revere and Chelsea are drumlins left by glaciers during the last ice age (see World's End, Hike 44).

After descending the tower stairs, walk north to the actual summit of Pine Hill, which consists of light-colored rocks that were spewed from volcanoes in violent eruptions long ago. Geologists still dispute the age of these rocks, with estimates ranging from 450 to 650 million years. In sharp contrast to the light volcanics are interconnected dikes of rusty-weathering basalt, cooled magma squeezed into east–west trending cracks in the volcanics probably about the same time that the Medford Dike was intruded (200 million years ago). The magnetism of the rock is so strong here that your compass may not read correctly. For reference, a set of white stripes oriented north–south has been painted on the smooth outcrop. With these stripes as a guide, you can conclude from the parallel scratches on the rock that the glacier moved southeast across this hill.

The oaks on Pine Hill periodically struggle against a plague of gypsy moth caterpillars. These caterpillars were brought from Europe to Medford in 1869 by a researcher named Trouvelot in an effort to breed hardier silk producers. The large populations of gypsy moth larvae that defoliate several million acres of Massachusetts forest in bad years are apparently the descendants of the few individuals that escaped not far from Pine Hill just over 100 years ago. Surges in caterpillar population followed the end of DDT spraying, which kept the gypsy moths in check but at an unacceptable cost to the environment. The gypsy moth relies on enormous population growth to survive natural predators such as birds and wasps, although a fatal virus can infect the larvae in epidemic proportions if the population density becomes too high. It is likely that the rain of digested leaves, the tangle of fuzzy caterpillars rappelling on silk ropes, and the blizzards of buff-colored moths will be present in New England forests for years to come, offending the sensibility of most and provoking rash-producing sensitivity in some.

From the summit outcrops, follow the

white-blazed Skyline Trail to the north and downhill across Quarry Road. Although this trail follows a tortuous and occasionally illogical route through the reservation, crossing many other trails and woods roads, it is very well marked with white blazes. If ever you are in doubt about the trail, return to the last white blaze and the correct route should be apparent. The trail next climbs Little Pine Hill, where a fire in the early 1980s has spawned new growth of white pine and white birch. The theme of fire, new growth, and forest succession is repeated throughout the reservation. See if you can recognize it. Also along your route are pink lady's slippers in May and blueberries in July.

As the trail drops to cross one of the many old roads in the park, you cross from the light-colored volcanics into Precambrian granite rocks, with their coarse crystals of gray quartz, pink alkali feldspar, and white plagioclase. Look for more black dikes cutting through the granite as you climb the next hill. Your route now lies mostly in mixed hardwood forest dominated by oaks, but the vegetation varies considerably as you pass from moist low areas to rocky drier hills. When the Middlesex Fells Reservation was acquired by the newly created Metropolitan Park Commission (now the Metropolitan District Commission) in 1894, most of the area was in brush rather than forest. Being close to a center of population, the hills have received heavy use since colonial times. Timber was cut time and again, and some of the land was cleared for farming or pasture. Few trees are more than 100 years old.

When you reach the fairly level top of Gerry Hill, after coming quite close to I-93, you should consider whether you are prepared to walk three times farther than you already have traveled. If not, this is a good spot to reverse direction and retrace your steps to your car. Otherwise, descend with

the Skyline Trail to a T-junction at a fence around a wetland. The trail turns right onto a woods road, then left along the fence and across a paved road leading to a parking lot, Sheepfold Parking Area. (You could make your hike much shorter by leaving a second car in this lot, which is accessible from MA 28.) The white-blazed trail bears left and runs along the open hill above the parking area to the start of an old soapbox derby track adjacent to a large meadow. Continue north along the east side of the meadow and back into the woods.

Your next task is to climb steeply to the top of an unnamed hill, where you will jog left and get a good view of the North Reservoir of the Winchester waterworks, which was dammed in 1898 before the Middlesex Fells became a park. Glacially smoothed, light-colored volcanic rocks crop out at the top. Look for pieces of dark rocks in the light matrix to get a sense of the complexity of volcanic processes. Gray birch, quaking and bigtooth aspen, and poison ivy are reclaiming the land here following a fire. Soon the Skyline Trail will lead you partway up Bear Hill, only to sidle around the top and drop to the northwest. Before losing elevation, however, bear right at the first junction onto a blue-blazed trail for a 10-minute walk to the observation tower at the summit of Bear Hill. Climb the spiral staircase for a spectacular view of the entire reservation over the top of a large concrete water tower. To the east you can see the ocean and Graves Light over Revere. To the south is Boston in its basin. To the west you can see Mount Wachusett and, on a good day, Mount Monadnock.

When you tire of this perch, retrace your steps to the Skyline Trail, which you should rejoin on its downhill trek to the northwest. After crossing a dirt road, a stream, and a clearing, you will enter a wood of pine and then mixed hardwoods that covers the Win-

Frog with lily pads.

chester Highlands. The forest is carpeted here with mats of Canada mayflower. This ground-hugging lily spreads by underground runners in the acid soil of deep woods. Its whitish flowers of late May are replaced by small red berries by late summer. Walking is easier around this end of the park, where you will pass your halfway point. As you travel west away from I-93, the background hum of traffic softens considerably. It may be replaced by the clicks of derailleurs as the Skyline Trail runs close to or along cart paths, popular among mountain-bike enthusiasts.

As you leave the Winchester Highlands, the white blazes guide you down and across a brook to avoid the dam confining the North Reservoir. The Town of Winchester owns and maintains as its water supply the three lakes in the middle of the western section of the Middlesex Fells Reservation. Out of concern for water quality, the town forbids any recreation along their shores. Be sure to stay on the trail to avoid the tempting water and the possibility of a fine. The trail runs past the end of the earthen dam to a paved road, Hillcrest Parkway. (A second car might be parked on the street near this intersection if you wanted to cut the hike in half.) Turn left and walk about 100 yards along the pavement. White blazes will guide you to the left into the woods where the paved road starts uphill. Here the Skyline Trail leads you through an open forest of white pine and oak over a floor crowded with ferns and poison ivy. The western portion of the reservation seems to be less heavily used and evokes the feeling of wilderness more than the eastern portion.

The Skyline Trail, true to its name, crosses

the tops of many more glacially smoothed, rocky knobs as it meanders to the south. However, there are not as many vistas in this westernmost section of the Fells. Carefully follow the white blazes. After passing a water tower and nearing South Border Road at the entrance to a water treatment facility, the trail angles back into the woods, passing the south end of South Reservoir. In the next section you will see several swampy areas created when the receding glaciers indiscriminately dumped silt and rocks, which then blocked old drainage patterns. Watch the rocks again for changes from the even texture of the coarse granite to the chaotic texture of the fine-grained volcanic rocks. Eventually, Bellevue Pond will appear ahead through the trees, and you'll meet the woods road on which you started. Turn right to return to your car.

40

Rocky Woods

Total distance: 2.8 miles (4.5 km)	
Hiking time: 2 hours	
Maximum elevation: 435 feet (132 meters)	
Vertical rise: 485 feet (148 meters)	
Map: USGS Medfield (7½' x 15')	
Trailhead: 42°12'21" N, 71°16'38" W	

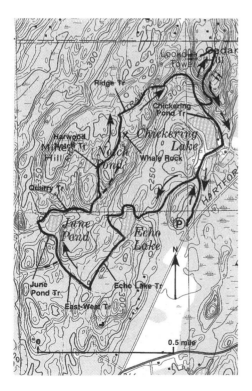

An extensive system of easy, wide hiking trails crisscrosses the 473-acre Rocky Woods Reservation in Medfield. Owned by the Trustees of Reservations and conveniently located less than 20 miles from downtown Boston, the reservation is well known for cross-country skiing on its many trails. Winter is not the only season for recreation in Rocky Woods, however; the hike described here, delightful in spring, summer, and fall, takes you to beautiful Echo Lake, has you scrambling around Whale Rock, and finally brings you to Cedar Hill, where views extend in several directions over southeastern Massachusetts.

To reach the reservation from the direction of Boston, exit from I-95 on MA 109 and drive southwest 2.1 miles to the Westwood end of Hartford Street. The reservation entrance is 3.3 miles along Hartford Street on the right. From the west, drive to the junction of MA 27 and MA 109 in the center of Medfield, turn east onto MA 109, and drive 1.7 miles to the Medfield end of Hartford Street, on the left. The reservation entrance is 0.6 mile along Hartford Street, on the left. A parking area for weekday use is located near the entrance (a second parking area can be accessed from 10 AM to 5 PM on weekends and holidays near Chickering Pond, 0.3 mile farther along the reservation road). The reservation opens daily year-round from sunrise to sunset and admission is free.

Begin your hike by walking along the trail that begins at the north end of the parking area near the reservation notice board and continues parallel to the paved road. In 600 feet you will reach a dark gravel road in a

A view of Echo Lake from the footbridge

dip. Turn left here. If you parked near Chickering Pond (Chickering Lake on the USGS topographic map), walk along the south shore of the pond through a picnic area shaded by oak and red maple. Leaving the lakeshore, drop down alongside a playing field and back into the woods. In 200 feet you will find the dark gravel road where you need to turn right. Your route, a wide gravel path, circles left between granite knolls covered with pin oak, gray, yellow, and white birch, and red maple and reaches an intersection posted Echo 16 and Loop 16 at the end of a straight southerly stretch. Turn right onto Echo Lake Trail. You'll traverse a swamp, brightened by summer-flowering swamp azalea, and then wind easily uphill through a mixed wood made colorful in early summer by blooming dogwood, mountain laurel, and rhododendron. At the top of the rise, the main trail bends left. Your route is on the small trail to the right, but first go straight ahead a few feet to the edge of Echo Lake. Standing amid the fringing pepperbush, honeysuckle, swamp azalea, and highbush blueberry, you can look out over the calm surface of the shallow lake and admire the fragrant water lilies and yellow water buttercups that decorate it.

To explore the Echo Lake section of the reservation, follow the small trail northwest through the mixed woods that surround the lake. Watch for the brown thrashers and colorful orioles that nest along here, and from openings in the forest look for iridescent dragonflies skimming over the water— or for the bullfrogs that you will hear calling. The trail crosses a small dam and the lake outlet before winding up a bouldery hill. As you climb, watch for downy false foxglove, which you can recognize from the cluster of butter-colored flowers growing at the end of a long downy stem. This species depends in part on a parasitic relationship with oak tree roots and sure enough, when you look up, you will find oak trees around you, including chestnut oak. After passing some large glacial erratics—granite boulders dropped by a melting ice sheet—the trail reaches a junction, where you should bear left. You'll drop easily to Echo Lake again and follow the water's edge briefly to a footbridge. Crossing this bridge, you will have clear views of the entire small lake and, perhaps, of the wood duck family that lives here in summer and of the fish and frogs that swim in the pond.

Across the bridge you will rejoin the main trail you left to loop around Echo Lake. Bear right and walk uphill to Intersection 15, where your route goes right onto the East–West Trail, and continue past Harwood Notch Trail, on the right at Intersection 14, to Intersection 13. Turn right here, too, onto June Pond Trail, which will lead you, logically enough, to June Pond. This pond represents a later stage in the pond-filling sequence than Echo Lake; note the many shrubs growing in it, especially buttonbush. In summer, noisy red-winged blackbirds will remind you that for them this pond means home. Just past the pond you should turn right at an intersection and, shortly, right again at Intersection 7 onto Quarry Trail. Your route crosses a small hill to Intersection 4 and there turns left onto Harwood Notch Trail. You will pass many outcrops and huge boulders of granite as you climb easily to the crest of a hill, where you look out over Notch Pond, which is covered by water lilies.

The trail swings northeast away from this small pond and climbs easily through white pine, beech, oak, and dogwood to a junction atop a rise. You should stay left on Harwood Notch Trail as it descends easily to Whale Rock—a huge outcrop of granite whose shape does resemble that of a whale. You may enjoy scrambling around on this stone monster—children especially find climbing it irresistible—but be careful not to trample the pink lady's slippers that grow around its base. You are now just past the midpoint of your hike, and the stone whale makes a fine rest or lunch spot. Please remember not to leave litter in this popular area.

Harwood Notch Trail continues past Whale Rock over a slight rise to Intersection 5. Turn right to follow Ridge Trail as it swings left and descends easily through a mixed wood to a stream valley, which may be dry during the summer. The trail rises out of the valley, passing massive outcrops of granite on the left, before circling right and dropping once again; here an intermittent stream flows during wet weather. The trail soon swings to a southerly course and descends easily through mixed woods. Look for the shagbark hickory, identified by its characteristic flaky bark. The trail bends southeast and shortly reaches Intersection 2, where Quarry Trail goes to the right. Stay straight ahead for 200 feet to a fork, where going right onto Chickering Pond Trail will take you on an easy path to the parking area should you wish to shorten your hike.

The left fork is your route to and from Cedar Hill. It swings to a generally northerly course, climbs steadily, and for a short stretch quite steeply, to a small col. Just beyond the col, turn left onto the short, wide, shingly road to the site of a former lookout tower on the top of Cedar Hill, where you will find limited views. For better views, retrace your route beyond the col to the top of the steep stretch you climbed not long ago. To your left (east), you will see a rocky knoll, which you can reach by following a narrow path that bears off here. Several openings present views toward the southeast, south, and west. On hot summer days you will welcome the cooling breezes that catch this hillock and the flat outcrops that provide good sunning ledges.

While enjoying these pleasures, notice how the vegetation around you differs from what you have seen elsewhere in the reservation. Although some white ash and red cedar grow here, scrub oak predominates in this dry habitat. You will recognize these shrubby trees by their small lobed leaves that have woolly, white undersides and their thicket-forming habit. The evergreen bearberry, growing here as a ground-covering creeper, has clusters of white bell-like flowers in early summer and edible, but not very tasty, bright red fruits in fall. It is common in the sandy areas on Cape Cod, but you will see it much less frequently in other Massachusetts woods.

When you are ready to leave, retrace your route down the steep hill to Chickering Pond Trail. Follow the wide trail left along the edge of the pond and shortly you will reach the weekend parking area. Rest rooms are available near the start of Bridle Trail, located behind the picnic area near the southwest corner of Chickering Pond. If you parked near the reservation entrance, you will need to continue along the pond's edge and pass through a picnic area and a playing field back into woodland. In 200 feet you will reach the dark gravel road, and you will have completed your long loop hike. The wide trail straight ahead will soon bring you to your starting point.

41

Stony Brook Wildlife Sanctuary

Total distance: 0.6 mile (1.0 km)

Hiking time: ½ hour

Maximum elevation: 180 feet (55 meters)

Vertical rise: 30 feet (9 meters)

Map: USGS Franklin (7½' x 15')

Trailhead: 42°06'26" N, 71°19'04" W

Perhaps the stream once flowed over glacial boulders through a sunlit meadow, but no one knows for sure the origin of its name: Stony Brook. Whatever its former nature, it was changed forever by the construction of a dam in the early 18th century, and for almost 250 years it was the site of much industrial activity. People still use the area, but now they come not as workers in the mills but as visitors to Stony Brook Wildlife Sanctuary. Following an easy trail, you can enjoy close-up views of the plants, birds, and animals that inhabit the ponds, marshes, and wooded knolls of this refuge southwest of the Boston suburbs. Here you can observe the relationship between plant distribution and small changes in topography and perhaps ponder the lives of 18th-century millworkers. What would they think of this area now?

To find this Massachusetts Audubon Society sanctuary, drive south on MA 115 for 1.0 mile from the traffic lights in Norfolk Center to a four-way intersection. Here turn right onto North Street; in 0.1 mile you will reach the sanctuary parking area, on the right. The trails are open daily from dawn to dusk. The office is open 9 AM to 5 PM Tuesday through Friday (and Mondays in July and August), 10 AM to 4 PM Saturday and Sunday. Admission is free to Massachusetts Audubon Society members, otherwise $3 for adults and $2 for children and seniors.

To begin your hike, walk west past the sanctuary buildings and turn right and then immediately left toward Pond Loop on a wide grassy trail bordered by stone walls. In earlier days, cows wandered down here on

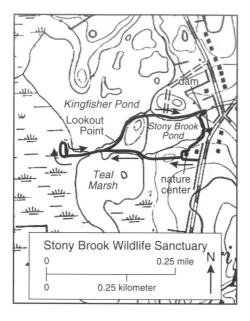

Stony Brook Wildlife Sanctuary

0   0.25 mile   N

0   0.25 kilometer

their way to pasture, and the walls kept them from straying into cultivated fields. On either side, open meadows provide homes for nesting birds, including tree swallows, which live in the nest boxes provided by the sanctuary. Shrubs and trees line the walls and in places overhang the trail to form a leafy arch for you to walk beneath. See if you can pick out the white birch, red maple, black cherry, and cedars along this route; among the shrubs look for arrowwood and winterberry. Virginia creeper clambers over the walls and bushes in places, but so does poison ivy; make sure that you are able to recognize the three shiny leaves that can spell an itchy end to a pleasant day. After passing a spruce grove on the right, the main trail curves right and reaches a small bridge over a stream that flows from Teal Marsh on the left to Stony Brook Pond.

This vantage point invites you to spend some time viewing and thinking about wetlands. You should quickly recognize the yellow and white pond lilies floating on the water and the cattails growing up through it. Green duckweed covers much of the water surface and provides a major food source for ducks and other birds. You may see turtles basking in the sun on the large rocks that protrude out of Stony Brook Pond, and brilliantly colored dragonflies skimming over its surface. Small islands covered with buttonbush and clumps of arrowhead, which has large, arrow-shaped leaves, break up the expanse of shining water in Teal Marsh. Wetlands provide food, shelter, and breeding places for many birds and animals, and these in turn attract human visitors to watch and study them. A marsh acts like a giant sponge, absorbing large quantities of water during rainy or snowmelt periods, thus reducing flooding in downstream areas. In dry spells water slowly drains from the marsh to help maintain flow downstream.

Beyond the bridge, the trail enters a woodland of red maples and then rises slightly into a drier area where white pine, oak, and white birch mingle with the maples. Alongside the trail and on the knoll to your right lie many granite boulders, known as glacial erratics because they were brought from elsewhere some 20,000 years ago by the great ice sheets of the last ice age. Stay left on Pond Loop, turn left again, and walk through shrubs to a boardwalk, which offers fine views over Teal Marsh and across Kingfisher Pond to your right. The wooded hills surrounding the wetlands are composed of glacial material, similar to the knoll that you passed earlier. Continuing along the boardwalk, you pass swamp azalea, pepperbush, highbush blueberry, and sweet gale, all growing at the margin of the marsh. The boardwalk ends where you reach the drier land of another knoll of glacial sediments, and the path continues, as a clockwise loop, through markedly different vegetation. The trees that grow here include

Eastern Massachusetts

Reflections on Stony Brook Pond

Stony Brook Wildlife Sanctuary

maple, white pine, oak, and beech; beneath these, mapleleaf viburnum, sarsaparilla, and Canada mayflower live on the forest floor. A seat at an observation platform provides a restful spot to look out over the marshes at the upper end of Kingfisher Pond, where Canada geese, black ducks, mallards, and wood ducks feed and swim. Sometimes, long-legged great blue herons stand motionless at the water's edge or stalk in the marsh for frogs, which they stab with sudden darting movements of their sharp bill.

After this watchful interlude, complete the loop through the woodland and recross the boardwalk to the intersection and onto Pond Loop again. Now turn left, and in 50 feet you will reach Lookout Point, a large pile of granite boulders, which provides another peaceful overlook across Kingfisher Pond. Notice the shrubby hummocks of alders, buttonbush, and sweet gale scattered in the pond. Leaving the rock pile and keeping Kingfisher Pond on your left and a knoll covered with white pine, maple, oak, and white birch on your right, follow the wide trail to a bridge over the stream connecting Kingfisher Pond with Stony Brook Pond. Here you may be tempted to sit in the sun for a while, as you enjoy the views northward over Kingfisher Pond or toward the nature center, which rests on the grassy hillside beyond Stony Brook Pond.

From the bridge, the trail takes you alongside Stony Brook Pond. On your left a hill covered by mixed woods rises out of the pond, reminding you once again that relatively small changes in topography strongly influence the distribution of trees and other plants. Also on your left you will pass a good exposure of the glacial sediments that make up the hillside. Known as glacial till, these sediments consist of large, angular-shaped boulders dispersed in finer sands and clays. Soon you will pass the dammed outlet of Stony Brook Pond, the site of several former enterprises, including a gristmill, sawmill, cotton mill, and finally a shoddy mill, which continued operation into the 20th century. The shoddy mill was an early recycling industry in which wool fibers were removed from the wool-and-cotton mixtures of old rags and clothes. The separation was incomplete and the product inferior to pure wool from a woolen mill, hence the connotation of cheapness and poorer quality associated with the term "shoddy." The trail bends left and drops into a moist woodland of red maple, white ash, and white pine traversed by a small stream that flows attractively over boulders and through little rapids. The trail passes the old concrete foundation of the former shoddy mill and then crosses a bridge over the outlet from Stony Brook Pond, where there is a view upstream of the dam spillway. Beyond the bridge, the trail continues right along the stream and past stone walls, and climbs a few steps to a view over Stony Brook Pond. Turn left along the grassy bank of the dam and pass between a red mulberry tree and a mountain ash; both trees have fruits in fall that are eaten by many birds. To complete your hike, walk up the gentle grassy slope to the sanctuary buildings and the parking lot.

42

Moose Hill Wildlife Sanctuary

Total distance: 3.5 miles (5.6 km)

Hiking time: 2½ hours

Maximum elevation: 534 feet (163 meters)

Vertical rise: 585 feet (178 meters)

Map: USGS Brockton (7½' x 15')

Trailhead: 42°07'22" N, 71°12'29" W

Quietness. Quietness broken, but not disturbed, by the song of a bird, the swish of the wind in the trees, the gentle gurgle of the flowing stream, the soft crunch of your footfall. Here in Moose Hill Wildlife Sanctuary, within a few miles of expanding, urban Boston, time seems to flow back, and formerly inhabited farmlands revert to wilder forests and swamps. Trails over rocky hills and through woodlands, old meadows, and swamps invite your explorations.

To reach this oldest, and recently greatly expanded, Massachusetts Audubon Society sanctuary, drive east toward Sharon on MA 27 for 0.5 mile from its intersection with US 1 in Walpole to Moose Hill Street, on your right (sanctuary sign on the corner). Follow this road 1.3 miles to the sanctuary parking area, on your left. The sanctuary office, gift shop, and rest rooms are across the road to the north. The sanctuary is open from 8 AM to 6 PM daily except Monday; admission is free to members of the Massachusetts Audubon Society, otherwise $3 for adults and $2 for children and senior citizens (in 1998). The sanctuary buildings are open Tuesday through Sunday 9 AM to 5 PM. Approximately 20 miles of trails crisscross the sanctuary. You can borrow trail maps and an information brochure at the office. The hike described here consists of two loops: the Moose Hill loop and the Hobbs Hill circuit. Both begin and end at the parking area, so you can hike either or both, as you wish.

To begin the 1.2-mile Moose Hill loop, turn right from the parking lot onto Moose Hill Street and then left between stone pillars onto Billings Loop, a wide, former road that quickly leads you to a right turn onto Summit Trail, marked by A blazes (blue heading away from the parking area, yellow returning toward it). Follow this path as it heads generally northwest through mixed woods of birch, oak, maple, white pine, and hemlock. You soon walk through an old stone wall that marks the former sanctuary boundary. Among the many flowering woodland plants growing here are the Canada mayflower, pink lady's slipper, sarsaparilla, Indian cucumber root, false Solomon's seal, starflower, yellow star grass, and mapleleaf viburnum. You may wish to see how many you can find. In early summer, birdcalls and songs will accompany you; listen for noisy crows, fussy blue jays, whistling cardinals, and the characteristic *teacher-teacher-teacher* of the elusive ovenbird. As you pass stone walls on the right and then cross a wide old road, remember that this area was once farmland and supported many people.

Beyond the road, the Summit Trail starts to rise quite steeply and becomes strewn with boulders. A little farther on, it jogs left to skirt some moss-covered rock ledges, which are quite slippery when wet. Continuing uphill through oaks and white pines, the trail crosses another stone wall, passes a small group of red cedars, and then enters a clearing. You may be tempted to linger awhile in this sunny spot and examine the rocks exposed here. Almost a billion years old, this igneous rock, called syenite, formed deep in the earth's crust when liquid magma cooled and then crystallized. If you look carefully, you should see the light feldspar and dark pyroxene minerals that characterize these rocks. From this vantage point you can see the fire tower on Moose Hill, which you will reach after a short walk though cedars and white ash. The view from the tower is reputed to be the best in southeastern Massachusetts; unfortunately, the tower is not open to the public, but there are views of the Boston skyline from ground level.

To continue your hike, pass right around the wire fence guarding the tower and over rocks northwest of the tower to find your trail, marked by white blazes on the rocks. Follow the trail downhill in a southwesterly direction, through white pine and white ash. Dip down, past stone walls on your left, then climb up to a partial opening, where more outcrops of syenite are exposed. The continuation of Summit Trail is almost hidden by small trees and departs the clearing from its southwest corner. Once through the obscuring trees, you will find the trail quite obvious. The trail takes you down a ridge through white pine, oak, and white ash. Pink lady's slipper pokes through last year's leaves in June. Turn left at the next junction and follow a narrow, rocky trail downhill another 150 feet to an abandoned woods road. You have reached Moose Hill Loop, where your route goes left gently downhill on a wide grassy trail toward the parking lot. A stone wall borders the trail on your right, and shortly another crosses the trail. Soon you pass an overgrown meadow on your right, a further sign that you are hiking former farmland. If you stay in the woods margin, you may catch sight of an indigo bunting, which has brilliant, unforgettable blue plumage. This scarce bird favors edges, such as this one, where trees border open meadows. The trail swings left downhill to intersect another trail, where you turn first right toward Billings Loop and then in a short distance left onto the broad Billings Loop. On your left at this corner human efforts are being made to prevent a meadow from reverting to woodland. Many flowers brighten the open area, including buttercups, oxeye daisies, yellow hawkweed, phlox, blue-eyed grass, and mouse-eared

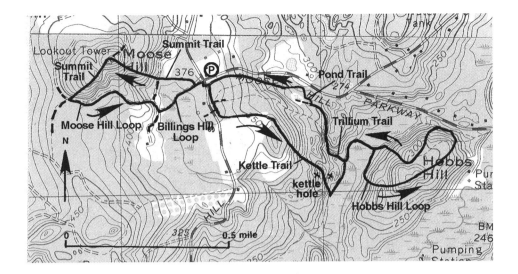

chickweed, but the pioneering red maple and white birch are making some incursions. Pass a red maple swamp on the right as you continue along your way back to Moose Hill Street and the parking area.

To begin the 2.3-mile Hobbs Hill circuit, turn left onto Trillium Trail (A blazes) just before the exit from the parking area to Moose Hill Street. In 300 feet you leave the wide, grassy Trillium Trail as it goes to the left and continue straight on the narrower Kettle Trail (K blazes), which is separated from the paved road only by a stone wall and a narrow fringe of trees. In another 250 feet the trail veers away from the road and winds gently downhill toward the east. Stay on Kettle Trail. After passing a meadow to the right beyond a stone wall, the trail parallels the wall for a while before crossing it and turning sharply right. The trail undulates through pine woods around the east side of an overgrown meadow and next crosses a stone wall and angles left, downhill, through a quite open woodland of hemlock, white pine, and oak. Suddenly the trail drops steeply into an enclosed basin filled with rhododendrons and mountain laurel—a

beautiful display when these shrubs are blooming in early summer.

You are standing in a kettle hole, a glacial landform from the last ice age, which ended some 12,000 to 15,000 years ago. Huge boulders of ice, like giant ice cubes, sometimes mixed in with the load of sand and boulders that dropped when the ice sheet melted. These blocks eventually thawed, too, and the resulting hollows were partially filled by sediments, thus leaving depressions in the landscape such as the one you are now exploring.

The trail climbs out of the kettle hole onto a narrow, steep-sided ridge—another glacial feature, called an esker. A meltwater stream flowed along a tunnel within the ice sheet, carrying sand and pebbles with it. As the sand and pebbles were deposited, the tunnel slowly filled. When the ice melted completely, the sediments were left behind as a long, sinuous pile to form the esker you can see extending through the woods. A comfortable spot on top of the ridge invites you to rest for a while and perhaps imagine this land covered by an ice sheet, when it looked more like present-day Greenland or Antarc-

Indian pipe

tica than the verdant Massachusetts we know today. Most geologists believe that in a few thousand years, this area once again will be buried in ice.

This forecast leaves ample time to complete your hike as you continue down the side of the edge of a swamp. Continue left on Kettle Trail. After passing through a level, damp stretch, you will rise slightly to drier terrain and pass the Trillium Trail on the left, where you continue across a small stream. The path curves right over a small rise and soon reaches a trail junction, where your route goes right onto Hobbs Hill Loop. The first part of the Hobbs Hill Loop crosses a low swamp, and you will push your way through tall ferns and much fragrant pepperbush and pass small pools of water. This can be a steamy spot on a hot August day, and you might feel like a jungle explorer, even though downtown Boston is less than 20 miles away. Just beyond the swamp, the land begins to rise and the trail

splits to begin the Hobbs Hill Loop. Go right here and head toward the southwest along the edge of the swamp for a while before making a sharp turn uphill to the left. Your route to the summit of Hobbs Hill heads generally southeast through maples, white pines, and oaks. You will find the hilltop marked by rocky outcrops and red cedar trees, but you will find no distant views. Leave the summit in an easterly direction along a broad ridge. After a short, steeper downhill section, the trail curves toward the left and soon passes a dense white pine grove to the right. The path turns more northerly and follows a straight course along the top of a steep, pine-covered slope. After flirting with the pine forest for a while, the trail eventually dips into the shady depths of the coniferous trees, where the shortage of sunlight greatly reduces the underbrush. Along here, in late May and June, you will find many lady's slippers glowing like elfin lanterns amid the brown-needled gloom.

The path angles across the steep slope through the pine woods and then briefly follows the top of a small cliff, from where you will see a paved road down through the trees that parallels your northerly hiking route for a short distance. Soon, though, you will be forced to make a sharp left turn as the Hobbs Hill Loop heads uphill to the west through mixed oak and white pine woodlands. Look for Indian pipe at trailside along here. The trail crosses a broad, flat-topped hill dotted with large glacial erratic boulders and then drops westerly downhill to the swamp and the trail fork where you began your loop of Hobbs Hill. Stay straight ahead to recross the swamp that you traversed earlier until you reach an intersection, where you should go left along the swamp margin. Notice how the red maples in the wet swamp contrast to the more diverse mixed woodland on the much drier hillside to the right. Just beyond the small stream that you crossed earlier, turn right at the trail junction and continue on Trillium Trail.

A very attractive stretch lies ahead as the trail climbs easily up a beautiful stream valley. Many flowers, including wild geraniums and jack-in-the-pulpit, brighten the scene, and the stream flows appealingly through a bouldery reach known as Rocky Glen. The trail crosses a stone wall and veers away from the stream before reaching another junction. You should go right onto Pond Trail, which soon swings left alongside a wire fence and then passes through mixed woods once again parallel to the stream. Soon you will reach a small, dammed pond with swamp margins lit by yellow iris. Pond Trail continues across the dam and sweeps left through pine woods to recross the stream on a wooden bridge. Turn right at the next trail junction and then sharply left to leave Pond Trail and proceed up a short, steep stretch and through a stone wall. Continue uphill to a junction with Trillium Trail. Go right and uphill through the pines and another stone wall and over a flatter stretch to an intersection, where you continue left on Trillium Trail. Climb gently uphill and follow the Trillium Trail, which, after one sharp turn to the right, will take you back to the parking area.

43

Blue Hills Reservation

Total distance: 4.1 miles (6.5 km)

Hiking time: 3 hours

Maximum elevation: 500 feet (152 meters)

Vertical rise: 1,370 feet (417 meters)

Map: USGS Norwood (7½' x 15')

Trailhead: 42°13'26" N, 71°04'12" W

Nearly everyone in Boston has heard of the Blue Hills, but most have not climbed them. Rugged topography, outstanding panoramas, deep woods, and an extensive network of trails provide the ingredients for many days of pleasant hiking in the Blue Hills. The circuit hike described here provides a good sample of what the eastern part of this Metropolitan District Commission (MDC) reservation has to offer. If you like what you see, many more trails await you in other sections of the park.

The start of this hike is easily located from the junction of MA 28 and I-93 (exit 5). Drive north 1.4 miles on MA 28 to a traffic light for the first cross street. Turn right onto Chickatawbut Road and park immediately in a small gravel lot on the right. Posted on a prominent bulletin board are various notices and regulations and a map of the reservation. Trail blazes were changed in 1988 and again in 1991, so it would be wise to check the posted map for any recent changes. You may obtain a trail map from the MDC headquarters located 1.7 miles west on Chickatawbut Road.

To begin your hike, walk south on Braintree Pass Path, a woods road that is blocked by a metal gate. Initially the woods are composed of mixed species—white pine, red oak, white oak, silver maple, and smaller chestnut and witch hazel, but beyond the open ground above a pipeline, you enter darker woods where solitary fronds of bracken fern stand in the shade of white pines. Look carefully on the hillside to your left and you may be able to detect signs of a 1981 fire, a memory fading beneath the

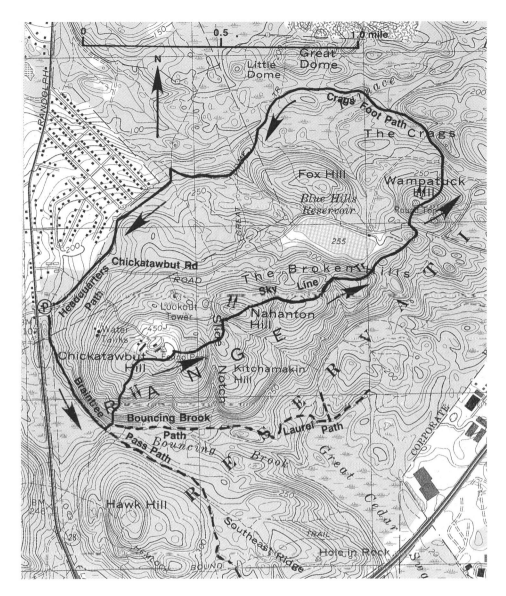

lush growth of white pines. Sweet pepperbush lines the wetland to your right. Where the road begins to rise into a grove of hemlocks, turn left to follow the blue blazes of the Skyline Trail. In about 100 yards, turn left again with the blue blazes at a sign for St. Moritz Pond, leaving the road for a steep climb up Chickatawbut Hill. Mapleleaf viburnum and chestnut seedlings grow along the road near this turn, the latter in youthful defiance of the chestnut blight.

When you stop to catch your breath during the climb, look at the rocks that make up the talus and, higher on the hill, the outcrops. Large crystals (white feldspar, gray quartz, and black amphibole) surrounded by a fine-grained matrix identify this igneous rock—which you will see many times on your hike—as a porphyry. The texture probably reflects a two-stage cooling history: slow cooling when the magma was deep in the crust of the earth, permitting the large crystals to grow, and more rapid cooling after the magma was intruded near the surface, causing the growth of many small crystals. Here and throughout the Blue Hills, the outcrops have been smoothed by the abrasive action of the mile-deep river of ice that covered Massachusetts for most of the last 100,000 years. Erratic boulders of other rock types have been dropped by the glacier at several spots along your route.

The trail leads you past wooden skeletons left by the 1981 fire to lovely southern vistas that grow behind you as you climb. Eventually you can see over Hawk Hill to Great Pond. Scrubby bear oak and coarse pitch pine trees dominate the summit. Where the trail turns to follow a chain-link fence around the Chickatawbut Hill Education Center of the Massachusetts Audubon Society, you can see a white pine tree that branches oddly about 6 feet above the ground, in memory of an encounter with a white pine weevil. Huckleberries and blueberries growing on the hilltop may provide you with an August snack. Clumps of sweet fern offer only the fragrance of their crushed leaves.

The Skyline Trail descends gradually to the northeast, its blue blazes guiding you up and down over porphyry outcrops, in places on stone steps. The longest staircase descends into an unusual rock-bounded col between Kitchamakin Hill and Nahanton Hill. Cross the woods road there in the shadow of an immense block of porphyry and climb the stone steps, bearing right with the blue blazes. At the top of the steps, take a short detour left to find wonderful panoramas along the top of Nahanton Hill. Views of the Boston skyline and the tall cranes of the Quincy shipyards to the north and west are blighted only by the scar in the foreground that marks the now closed Quincy landfill. Continue northeast and down a rocky slope modified by fire. You cross another pass and climb to more views from an unnamed hill. Stay with the blue blazes as the trail descends again, then rises to meet a chain-link fence that surrounds the Blue Hills reservoir.

Downhill to the northeast, the path climbs a small knob of porphyry containing dikes of lighter, buff to greenish granite. These dikes mark cracks along which molten granite was squeezed after the porphyry solidified. At the north end of this outcrop, the blue blazes lead you left and northwest to paved Chickatawbut Road. Just across the pavement, several large boulders block a woods road. From the boulders, blue blazes will direct you on a path up Wampatuck Hill. Partway up, look back for a view of the reservoir you have been skirting. Then continue for an unobstructed panorama of the Boston skyline and Boston Bay that is breathtaking on a clear day.

Rocks atop Wampatuck Hill are more fine-grained than the porphyry you saw earlier. The fine grain size suggests quickly cooled volcanic rocks, a hypothesis that is confirmed by the complex folding, produced by moving lava, displayed by similar rocks in an outcrop just downhill to the north. Following the blue blazes down, you can find the outcrop of flow-banded rhyolite where a trail enters from the right. Continue straight (north), eventually crossing a long mound protecting a pipeline, and then bear left onto a woods road at the base of The Crags (Crags Foot Path), staying on this road when the blue blazes follow a steep trail up The Crags. The Crags are made of yet a

Blue Hills porphyry

third variety of igneous rock, Quincy granite. This coarse-grained granite, once quarried in Quincy, is famous around New England for building stone and tombstones. Its even texture reflects a slow cooling and crystallization several miles below the earth's surface. All three rock types have the same chemical composition and mineralogy, but they look different because of their different cooling histories. It is likely that all three—granite, porphyry, and rhyolite—originated at the same site of melting deep in the crust, but each crystallized at a different rate, reflecting different depths of intrusion or extrusion. Subsequent faulting has brought the three rock types together for us to see some 450 million years after they were formed.

Continue straight with the woods road and its green blazes as other roads enter from the left and then the right. When you come to a fork, bear left with the green blazes past a shagbark hickory. Ignore the next road on the left, cross a wetland, ignore a road on the right, ignore the departure of the green (and orange and white!) blazes, and continue with the main gravel path. Fragrant pepperbush thrives in the wetlands along your route. Ignore another road on your left, but bear right when you meet a major road just past a granite outcrop. You will shortly come to a T-junction, where you should turn left. Turn left again at the next T-junction onto the wide, sandy Headquarters Path, which tracks the park boundary. This path is the least inviting part of the hike, but it completes the loop very efficiently. You may even find some ripe blackberries here during late summer. Eventually, the sound of passing cars alerts you that Chickatawbut Road and your car are near. Cross the road and turn right at the first opportunity, avoiding the poison ivy, to reach the parking area.

44

World's End

Total distance: 4.0 miles (6.4 km)

Hiking time: 2 hours

Maximum elevation: 110 feet (34 meters)

Vertical rise: 370 feet (113 meters)

Map: USGS Hull (7½' x 15')

Trailhead: 42°15'32" N, 70°52'23" W

Although most of Massachusetts shows some imprint of continental glaciation, World's End at the edge of Boston Harbor owes its very existence to the most recent of the great ice sheets. During the Wisconsin glacial period, which lasted from about 70,000 to 12,000 years ago, Massachusetts was covered by an ice sheet that probably exceeded 1 mile in thickness. As the Wisconsin ice began to melt in response to a climatic warming, the clay, sand, and gravel that it had trapped dropped to form ground moraine—a deposit of unsorted sediment that today thinly blankets much of the Massachusetts countryside. Movements of the remaining ice shaped some of the gravel and clay into large mounds, called drumlins, which are elongated in the direction the ice traveled. The main hills of the World's End Reservation are drumlins, as are portions of most of the Boston Harbor islands visible from World's End.

World's End Reservation is a property of the Trustees of Reservations, a nonprofit organization that manages and preserves more than 20,000 acres of land in Massachusetts. In 1967 the Trustees purchased the 251-acre estate that is now World's End. At that time, citizens of the surrounding communities, principally Hingham, raised half a million dollars to save World's End from the ravages of development. Ironically, much of the charm of World's End is derived from landscaping, according to a plan designed in 1890 by Frederick Law Olmsted, in anticipation of subdivision and development. Fortunately for us, the then owner, John R. Brewer, carried the plan only as far

Planters Hill from World's End

as building the roads and planting the trees to line them.

From the traffic circle on MA 3A (Otis Street) in Hingham (1.3 miles west of the junction of MA 3A and MA 228), drive northwest on Summer Street 0.5 mile to a traffic light. Turn left (north) at the light onto Martins Lane, which ends in 0.7 mile at the entrance to World's End. From a small tollhouse at the gate, a warden collects entrance fees from visitors who are not members of the Trustees of Reservations. Parking can be found inside the gate along a road to the right. The reservation is open daily until sunset year-round, but be sure to ask the warden when he will leave and close the gate.

The route described here is a counterclockwise circuit around the entire reservation. Of course, shorter hikes are possible, and you should not hesitate to choose your own route. Because World's End is surrounded by water, it is difficult to get lost here. In particular, if the boardwalks along

the marsh are rebuilt, be sure to take the time to explore them. A detailed trail map is posted near the parking area and may be purchased from the warden. Be forewarned, however, that poison ivy festoons the trails and is omnipresent on the grassy slopes of the reservation. Do not venture off the pathways without learning to recognize this three-leaved peril!

Begin your walk at the end of the last parking area by continuing northeast along the dirt entrance road, closed to cars by granite pillars and a chain. White pine, maple, hickory, and oak trees shade the bracken fern and sassafras seedlings beside this broad path. Partially hidden in the woods on either side are numerous rounded rock outcrops—like large sleeping dinosaurs from mound to knoll in size—of Dedham granodiorite, a 630-million-year-old intrusive igneous rock. Pink and white rectangular feldspar crystals are visible in this lichen-covered, glacially smoothed rock.

After crossing a small causeway with a view across the Weir River, turn right onto another cart path at the line of stately sugar maples. Keep to the right at all forks from here to Planters Hill, which you will climb just before the end of the hike. In about 0.3 mile, the road shrinks to a footpath, which will take you to the rocky shore of the Weir River estuary. Outcrops along the shore consist of a mixture of angular pieces of various volcanic rocks embedded in a fine-grained host rock; the texture looks somewhat like that of chunky peanut butter. The angular chunks are also chunky, however, with white feldspar crystals visible in a very fine olive-to-lavender matrix. Volcanic rocks with textures such as this generally mean that previously erupted and cooled lavas have been reworked into the products of later eruptions or mud flows. Similar rocks can be found on the flanks of Mount Saint Helens in Washington. Here the result is further complicated by crosscutting, buff-colored dikes, which were formed when molten rock was injected along fractures. The best display of rock types here, as well as a good view of the World's End drumlins, is adjacent to a small clearing on the north end of this rocky neck.

Black huckleberries flourish along the trail for seasonal snacking, but keep away from the extremely sharp thorns of the common greenbrier vines that climb the berry bushes. After passing more outcrops of volcanics, you will round a cove to exposures of even-textured granodiorite, like those near the parking area. The grain size of the granodiorite indicates slow cooling and crystallization a few miles below the earth's surface. The finer grain size of the volcanics indicates a more rapid cooling and crystallization at the earth's surface. A contact between the two units, therefore, requires some explanation. Careful mapping and study of these and other outcrops suggest that the 600-mil-

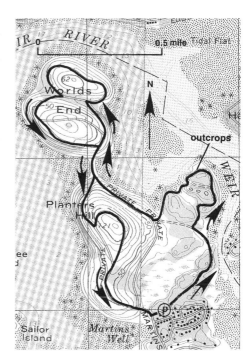

lion-year-old volcanics were deposited on the older granodiorite after removal of two to four miles of overlying rock by erosion.

Eventually the footpath leads you downhill to the maple-lined road once again. Turn right and follow the road along the east side of the Planters Hill drumlin. Drop and cross a man-made connection to World's End proper. (A left turn just before the causeway will shorten the hike by 1.5 miles.) Regular mowing keeps the hills of World's End in open fields, but does not discourage the poison ivy. A great variety of trees, planted according to the Olmsted plan, lines the cart paths. Common maples, oaks, and hickories are interspersed with less common species such as horse chestnut and tulip trees. Turning right at each junction will allow you to circumnavigate the outer pair of drumlins and return to the causeway.

If you would like to peek inside one of the drumlins to see the underlying glacial drift, take a side trail steeply down to the north shore of the northernmost World's End hill. Pick your way left (northwest) along the rock-strewn beach to a small, bare cliff being undercut by storm waves that are not stopped by the riprap of boulders that have been placed along the shore. In the cliff you can see an unsorted and unlayered assemblage of silt, sand, gravel, and boulders that is typical of glacial till throughout New England. A similar cliff is developing along the northwest end of Planters Hill.

Views of Boston Harbor and the skyline are partially obscured by the drumlin hills of Bumkin Island, the town of Hull, and Peddocks Island until you climb Planters Hill, where the skyline, at least, is clearly visible. From the causeway, turn right along the west side of Planters Hill and then, near the crest, left on the road that loops over the top. Views of the Boston skyline, the drumlin-dotted harbor, Graves' Light, and the North Shore beyond it reward you for the detour. Several large glacial erratics rest on the surface of this drumlin and display rock types varying from conglomerate to granite. From the top of Planters Hill, a 0.4-mile downhill walk separates you from the entrance gate. Turn left at the gate following the road you drove earlier to arrive at your car.

45

Whitney and Thayer Woods

Total distance: 3.4 miles (5.5 km)

Hiking time: 2 hours

Maximum elevation: 125 feet (38 meters)

Vertical rise: 290 feet (88 meters)

Map: USGS Weymouth (7½' x 15')

Trailhead: 42°14'02" N, 70°49'29" W

Giant rhododendron bushes, ancient white pines, rocky knolls, open fields, and lush wetlands—these are just a few of the many reasons to visit Whitney and Thayer Woods, located in the town of Cohasset. A network of trails and old woods roads, the latter wide for easy walking and cross-country skiing, provide ready access to this large park.

To find the unmarked entrance to Whitney and Thayer Woods from the junction of MA 228 and MA 3A in Hingham, drive 2.1 miles east and southeast on MA 3A. Opposite the blinking light to Sohier Road, which leads left to Cohasset Village, turn right onto a gravel driveway to a boulder-lined parking area. A small green sign identifies the property as belonging to the Trustees of Reservations and confirms your arrival. A map of the reservation is posted at the parking area and may be purchased at the gas station across the street from the entrance or from the warden at the entrance to nearby World's End Reservation (Hike 44).

From the parking area, walk southeast past a red cedar on a well-used gravel road, which leads to a residence. You will pass a grove of very tall white pines strung with vines of poison ivy and a variety of shrubs, including mapleleaf viburnum, fire cherry, common spicebush, arrowwood, and witch hazel. Hardwoods, however, are the order of the day, and you soon meet varieties of ash, hickory, maple, birch, and beech—all easily distinguished with a field guide. Take the first woods road to the right, labeled Boulder Lane on the USGS map and blocked by a heavy metal gate. Sarsaparilla makes an attractive ground cover along the path,

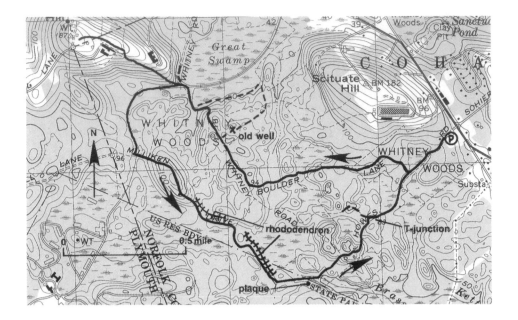

aided by patches of poison ivy, hay-scented fern, and white whirled asters. Look for sassafras trees; they are rarely very large and have three types of leaves—one mitten-shaped—and fragrant, tea-flavoring roots.

The boulders of Boulder Lane are large glacial erratics, inanimate travelers stranded by the melting of the last continental ice sheet some 14,000 years ago. The first of the really large granite boulders is perched on the glacially polished surface of an outcrop of a similar igneous rock, Dedham granodiorite. Both rocks have easily visible crystals of white-weathering feldspar, occasionally stained brown, and gray quartz, signifying crystallization from a magma several miles below the earth's surface. All of Whitney and Thayer Woods is underlain by a foundation of granodiorite bedrock. In most places, however, the rock is hidden by deposits of clay, sand, and gravel, which were also left by the melting ice sheet.

You may notice a white-blazed trail that crosses Boulder Lane twice, the second

time near a large continuous outcropping of granodiorite. Next you cross two low areas, separated by a rocky hill, that keep the path soggy and sport thickets of pepperbush, whose white flowers perfume the air in August. When you come to a T-junction, turn right onto Whitney Road, another woods road, carpeted by needles from old white pines. (If you wish to lengthen the hike, watch for the first road to the right off Whitney Road. Do not take the road, but turn right 25 yards after it to follow Howe Trail on a 0.7-mile ramble past an old stone-walled well and cellar hole, over some rugged country, and along a swamp. This trail eventually crosses a woods road, follows a stone wall over a rocky knob, drops down into the darkness of hemlock trees, and bears left along wetland.) Following Whitney Road, you will join a road covered with crushed stone at the next junction, turning right to begin a downhill stretch. Stay with the crushed-stone trail past a road on the right and past an unlabeled crossing of the Howe

A large erratic

Trail. (If you took the Howe Trail earlier, you rejoin the route here turning right.)

After crossing some old railroad tracks, bear left at a fork with coarse gravel onto Turkey Hill Lane, which leads to the 182-foot summit of Turkey Hill. Here you will find open meadows crisscrossed by mown paths, goldenrod, milkweed, monarch butterflies, and rabbits. Although you must share the summit with radio towers, on a clear day you will have fine views of Boston Bay, Boston Light, and islands such as World's End (Hike 44). The hill itself, like the islands, is a drumlin—a pile of gravel, sand, and clay shaped by the last continental glacier into an elongated hill. The hilltop, a former military radar tracking site, was purchased in 1997 by the Trustees and by the towns of Cohasset and Hingham, preserving its wonderful vistas for the public.

After recharging your solar batteries in the meadow, retrace your steps down the gravel road to the woods. At the bottom of the hill, turn right onto the railroad bed and follow it in a gentle counterclockwise arc. The tracks have been removed or are covered, so the walking is easy. A small stream follows the bed, nourishing touch-me-not plants until it is swallowed by a culvert. Turn left off the railroad bed when it is crossed by a gravel road (Milliken Drive on the USGS map). There is abundant evidence that these paths are also followed by horses, although you will probably meet neither horses nor people on your visit. Cross over a small hill amid black birch, red and white oak, white ash, red maple, and American beech trees. Near the bottom of the hill on the southeast, you will find set on a granite boulder a plaque dedicated to Mabel Minott Milliken in 1927. Keep to the right at the plaque where a road enters from the north.

The plaque marks the beginning of a section of unusual vegetation, some of it planted, including mountain laurel, rhododendron, fetterbush, and North American holly. All but the holly are abundant over the next 0.5 mile of trail. Especially prominent are the rhododendron bushes, which form tunnels for the trail. Visit these woods in late spring if possible for a splendid floral display. But if you come then, it may be wise to wear rubber boots to help you through some wet, muddy spots. Tall, arching fronds of cinnamon fern, growing in clusters, do well in the moist ground. A few hemlocks and white pine add variety to the hardwoods.

When you come to a junction where a road enters on the right, keep to the left. The road to the right leads through a broken fence to Wompatuck State Park. Another plaque to Mabel Milliken marks this junction and, perhaps, the end of Milliken Drive. From this junction the path winds up and down some low rocky hills, past two crossings of the Bancroft Trail, and finally comes to a T-junction. Turn right onto a grassy, seemingly less used woods road. You will soon reach a chain barrier, then a residence, and a gravel road that will lead you back to your car.

46

Great Island

Total distance: 7.5 miles (12.1 km)

Hiking time: 4 hours

Maximum elevation: 80 feet (24 meters)

Vertical rise: 230 feet (70 meters)

Map: USGS Wellfleet (7½' x 7½')

Trailhead: 41°56'00" N, 70°04'13" W

Breathe deeply of the smells of the pines and the nearby sea, and hold them in the reservoir of your mind against the indoor days. Revel in the deep blue of the endless sky framed by the dark green of pitch pine boughs. Delight in the glimpses of warm, yellow sand lapped by the sparkling sea. You are descending Great Beach Hill on your long hike of the Great Island Trail in an almost forgotten corner of Cape Cod. As you discover this marvelous coast for yourself, you will encounter salt marshes, wonderful pitch pine forests, magnificent sandy beaches, and, always, the sea.

To reach Great Island, turn onto Main Street at the traffic lights on US 6 in Wellfleet and in 0.3 mile go left at the fork onto East Commercial Street. Continue past Mayo Beach and onto Cheqnesset Neck Road; in 3.2 miles cross Herring River, and in another 0.4 mile turn left into the Great Island parking lot.

The Great Island Trail starts from the east side of the parking area, where rest rooms are available. The path winds down through the first of several fine pitch pine forests you will traverse today. This species grows in many parts of Cape Cod and can be distinguished from other pines by its cluster of three twisted needles. At the first junction, turn right onto a wide trail, which skirts an upper salt marsh. From here you can see a pattern of landscape features that recurs two more times in your hike. About 0.8 mile south, the wooded slopes of Great Island rise above the intervening bay. The hill that you just descended, Great Island, and Great Beach Hill (farther south and from this vantage point hidden behind Great Island) all have the same geologic origin. During the last ice age, some 20,000 years ago, an ice sheet lay east of Cape Cod, and streams of meltwater carried sand, pebbles, and boulders westward away from the ice. These hills are just three of the many remnants of this glacial outwash plain that also forms much of the higher ground of Cape Cod. When the great ice sheets finally melted and the meltwaters drained back into the ocean, the sea level rose and surrounded Great Island and Great Beach Hill, making them islands. But the work of the sea was not finished; marine currents moving along the coast picked up sand from the glacial sediments of the islands and carried it southward. Eventually this process created sandbars that linked the islands in a long chain. Winds moved the bar sands around to make dunes, and salt marshes became established in the shallow waters on the sheltered side of the dunes.

As you walk, examine the salt marsh on your left. Notice how the *Spartina* grass changes to a coarser species along the edge of tidal creeks (see Wellfleet Bay, Hike 47, for more on salt-marsh grasses). Watch the busy fiddler crabs scurrying amid the sessile mussels and popping down their small burrows in the muddy patches. The pebbly sands exposed on the lower slopes of the hill to the right were deposited by the meltwater streams. As the pebbles rolled along the bottom of stream channels, multiple collisions wore away their corners and edges to produce the rounded shapes you see now. Ahead of you the long, narrow line of dunes, known as The Gut, connects the mainland and Great Island.

The trail takes you to The Gut and there turns left (south) along it to follow the boundary between the salt marsh and the sand dunes. Just before it reaches a promi-

nent knoll of glacial sediments, the trail bends sharply left and continues eastward along the edge of the marsh, with signs to the Great Island tavern and other localities to guide you. In about 0.3 mile, stay left at a trail junction where the more prominent trail heads uphill toward Great Beach Hill and Jeremy Point; your route to the Great Island tavern site continues along the marsh edge. You need to keep a sharp lookout for a small trail that branches right from the path that continues alongside the marsh. This rather obscure junction lies some 600 feet beyond the last trail sign, at the first place where trees reach almost down to the marsh edge and about halfway along the shore of the small bay. The trail, somewhat overgrown in spots, begins to rise steadily through pitch pine, black oak, and bayberry, but it soon levels off and then drops gently to an opening where you can enjoy views over the water toward the town of Wellfleet. Here you will find a small exhibit at a trail fork where the left path goes down to the beach and the right trail continues on to the site of the former tavern. After looking at the exhibit photographs of an excavation at the tavern site and some of the many artifacts found there, take the right fork toward the former tavern site. After about 250 yards you will reach the site, which is marked by a sign and the bouldery remnants of the tavern foundations. Although you can enjoy the tavern beverages only in imagination, you can take a spur trail south to the edge of a sea cliff, where the views are spectacular along the coast to Great Beach Hill and out over Wellfleet Bay to the mainland of Cape Cod.

Return to the tavern site and follow the trail west through the wonderful pitch pine forest. A very strong wind, perhaps a hurricane, blew through here a few decades ago and flattened the pines that you now see lying on the forest floor. The present forest has grown since that catastrophic event. The trail continues easily for 0.5 mile before skirting a wide depression filled with a tangle of blown-down trees. Just beyond, you reach an intersection with a wide trail. Turning right here will take you directly back to your starting point about 1.4 miles away. To continue your hike, turn left toward Great Island and Jeremy Point. Soon you will pass an old well field on the left. You can see many of the pipes that were used to draw water still sticking up out of the ground. Some beautiful thickets of sheep laurel grow in this wetter area. The trail rises out of the depression, passes a granite monument to Priscilla Alden Bartlett, who lived hereabouts until 1962, crosses a hill through pine woods, and then descends toward opening views of salt marshes and Great Beach Hill.

Great Island and Great Beach Hill are connected by a line of sand dunes bounded to the east by salt marshes—landscape features that are very similar to those you passed earlier. The trail takes you along the marsh edge and then south adjacent to the dunes. Climb to the crest of a low point in the dunes just before the rise to Great Beach Hill. You may be tempted to rest here, and it does make a great lunch spot, with good views north and south along a magnificent sandy beach. At low tide, exposed, wide sand flats provide meeting places for hundreds of gulls and terns. The shallow, protected waters warm up quickly to provide good swimming along this beach. Looking farther afield, Provincetown and its famous monument stand out prominently to the northwest, and the low hills of mainland Massachusetts appear hazily on the western horizon.

You will be glad of your rest when you return to the trail and turn right to slog up Great Beach Hill on a soft, sandy path to a forest of low pitch pine. Stay on the promi-

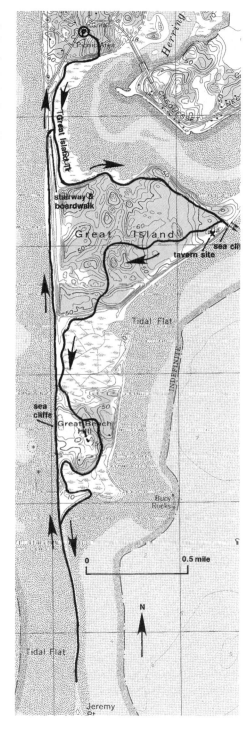

A flock of terns on the shore

nent trail where any small paths branch off, and head downslope through taller pitch pines and some substantial black oaks. Soon views of beaches and the sea appear among the pines. For the third time on your hike, the trail descends to the edge of a marsh. The trail goes westerly along the marsh edge, turns southerly for a while, then wends easterly before swinging southerly once again around low, grass-covered dunes. As you continue to the south, the dunes dwindle to a point where a sign tells you that you have reached Jeremy Point Overlook and warns you that Jeremy Point is cut off at high tide. You cross over to the Cape Cod Bay side of a narrow, sandy peninsula and continue south past low, incipient sand dunes, gravel patches, sand flats, and sandy beaches. This is an important shorebird and tern nesting area, and these birds may be very numerous alongside your route. Currents carry sand southward here to build the long, narrow extension of the peninsula. Rapid changes occur in this dynamic environ-

ment, and in some years an inlet breaches the spit south of the warning sign, turning the southern end of the spit into an island, not accessible on foot. In 1998, however, the shifting sands had sealed the break and one could walk the sand all the way to Jeremy Point. No doubt such breaks and subsequent healings will continue and the potential southern extent of your hike will remain an unpredictable variable.

In any case, you eventually will want to retrace your steps north along the fine, sandy beach to the Jeremy Point warning sign. Here you may return by your outward route, or take the shorter route directly back over Great Beach Hill, or walk back along the magnificent beaches fronting Cape Cod Bay.

In the sea cliffs of Great Beach Hill, you can find fine exposures of sediments deposited by glaciers and meltwater streams. Gray clays with scattered pebbles and boulders form the lower part of the cliff. These sediments, called till, were deposited by a glacier, and they contain fossil wood 42,000 years old. Above the till lie thick deposits of sand, with some gravel, which were carried here by meltwater streams flowing from the edge of an ice sheet. You now have a long, but enjoyable, beach hike ahead of you, as you continue northward past Great Beach Hill and Great Island, where more cliffs of glacial sediment are exposed.

After a long stretch of low dune cliffs bordering the beach, the cliffs begin to gain height; the remnants of a wooden stairway will take you to a boardwalk over the dunes. This brings you to your outward route about midway along The Gut, which connects Great Island, and to your left the last hill that you must climb on the way back to the parking lot.

47

Wellfleet Bay Wildlife Sanctuary

Total distance: 3.0 miles (4.8 km)

Hiking time: 1½ hours

Maximum elevation: 40 feet (12 meters)

Vertical rise: 150 feet (46 meters)

Map: USGS Wellfleet (7½' x 7½')

Trailhead: 41°52'55" N, 69°59'46" W

Sitting in the warm sunshine on a carpet of bearberry, you look out from a clearing in a pine forest over salt marshes busy with a rising tide and feeding birds. This boundary between land and sea creates a complex edge community of plants and animals. The easy, well-defined trails of Wellfleet Bay Wildlife Sanctuary are perfect for exploring the subtleties of habitat variation that characterize so much of Cape Cod's natural landscape.

To reach this Massachusetts Audubon Society sanctuary, follow US 6 for 0.3 mile north from the Eastham-Wellfleet town line to an unnamed road on the left (sanctuary signs are on the corner). The sanctuary parking area is 0.4 mile down the road. Admission is free to members of the Massachusetts Audubon Society, otherwise $3 for adults and $2 for children and seniors. The sanctuary gate is open daily from 8 AM to 8 PM (in summer) AND 8 AM to dark in winter. A trail map (free) and a guide to the Goose Pond Trail ($2.50) are available from the Nature Center. The guide will greatly enhance your understanding and enjoyment of the natural wonders that you will see on your hike. Also at the Nature Center you will find rest rooms and interesting exhibits. The hike described here consists of two loops, Goose Pond Trail and Bay View Trail, both of which begin near the building. You can, of course, hike just one if you are short of time.

Follow the sign as Goose Pond Trail heads westerly from just southwest of the Nature Center. The yucca plants growing just beyond the trail sign may remind you of the desert Southwest, but some varieties are also native to sandy habitats along the

The mouth of Hatches Creek

East Coast. The wide, shrub-lined path winds down toward woodland before crossing the dam on Silver Spring Brook; to the right Try Island, one of the distinctive features on this loop, projects out of the salt marshes. The trail rises easily through a small stand of coniferous trees, planted to stabilize this sandy hill. Here you can practice identification of several species of pine. Non-scaly bark and needles in clusters of five characterize white pine; while clusters of three twisted needles identify pitch pine, very numerous on Cape Cod. Three more pine species grow here, all with paired needles. The native red pine has reddish bark and needles up to 8 inches long; Scotch pine, introduced from Europe, and black pine, imported from Japan, have shorter needles. A bright orange upper trunk and branches provide ready identifi-cation of Scotch pine, while short thorns on the numerous cones distinguish the Japanese black pine.

Leaving the shade of the pines, the trail and boardwalk turn sharply right and cross a causeway that separates the freshwater habitats of Goose Pond from the salt marshes. Invasive phragmites fringe the pond, squeezing out native cattails, and you may see waders, herons, and ducks, which visit to feed and rest. Sand swept over the causeway by storm tides helps to fill the pond and hasten its natural evolution to dry land. Beyond Goose Pond the trail rises a little into a shrubby, partly wooded area, where you can find much shadbush, green-brier, and poison ivy. At a prominent junction, continue straight ahead on a sandy trail past scattered red cedars. Soon you will reach an observation platform that affords

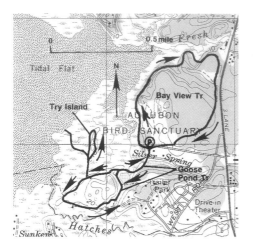

splendid views over the salt marshes, Try Island, Wellfleet Bay, and beyond to Great Island (Hike 46). The large patch of creeping evergreen shrub that begins near the lookout is bearberry. Bearberry thrives in exposed sandy areas and helps to stop the winds from blowing the sand around. Farther along you will pass many struggling sassafras trees, tangled in places with wild grape, poison ivy, Virginia creeper, and beach plum. When you reach a junction near a cabin partly hidden in the trees to your left, turn right toward Try Island, a small, low hill in the midst of the salt marsh.

Walk along the edge of the salt marsh and at the first fork go right along Try Island Trail between another salt marsh, to the right, and a grassy, shrubby, low ridge. You'll soon enter a woods dominated by white oak but interspersed with some pignut hickory and sassafras, which survive here out of reach of destructive fires. A shaded trailside bench invites you to rest and contemplate the salt marsh and its inhabitants. You soon leave the woods, though, and climb a slight rise that affords a good view of the marshes, Cape Cod Bay, and, to the northwest, Great Island. At the next junction, bear left (south) and uphill to return along Try Island's small

ridge crest. Views south encompass more salt marshes, Hatches Creek, a beach, and the sea. Be alert for poison ivy, which lurks amid the trailside honeysuckle and wild grape. Notice how the trees on your left do not grow much higher than the top of this ridge, which protects them from strong, salty northwest winds. A sandy trail descends the grassy slope of Try Island to an intersection where a right turn will take you on a spur trail to the edge of Wellfleet Bay.

This spur provides a good opportunity to explore a salt marsh. Look in the mud for the holes of the small fiddler crab, and if you are quiet, you may see these busy crustaceans scurrying over the mud. Two plants dominate salt marshes: Salt-meadow cordgrass *(Spartina patens)* grows in the higher areas where flooding occurs only during storms or exceptionally high tides; salt-marsh cordgrass *(S. alterniflora)* grows where flooding occurs each tidal cycle. The distribution zones of the two salt-marsh grasses show up very clearly along the tidal creeks.

Boardwalks take you over the wet salt marshes and scattered sand patches to the water's edge, where you can enjoy views out over the mouth of Hatches Creek, sandy beaches, and small islands covered with *Spartina alterniflora*. This provides a good spot to look for birds: Shorebirds, gulls, terns, ducks, herons, and sometimes raptors frequent this coastal sanctuary.

When you feel rested and refreshed by the sea breezes, walk back along the boardwalks and paths to the junction where you left the main trail to begin the Try Island loop. Turn right on the wide, sandy Goose Pond Trail and head southwest between a low dune to the left and the salt marshes. Notice the prettily colored beach lavender that lines this part of your hiking trail. Just beyond another cabin in the nearby dunes, a trail sign directs you left. Follow this wide path through a stand of black locust trees to the edge of an inlet in the salt marsh. Walking along an old road, you pass a clump of cedar trees to the right and then follow the path as it flirts with the edge of the salt marsh to the right. In 350 feet, a smaller trail leaves to the left from the former road. Guided by a sign pointing to the Nature Center, take the path as it winds up a sandy hill capped by a grove of oaks overgrown with black cherry, roses, greenbrier, honeysuckle, Virginia creeper, and poison ivy. Beyond this jungle, the trail winds gently uphill past bayberry bushes and carpets of bearberry, through mixed woods of pitch pine and oak, and past a different view of Goose Pond, eventually to rejoin the main trail. Turn right here and retrace your steps to the trailhead near the Nature Center.

A sign shows you the start of the 1.5-mile Bay View Trail loop. Bearing right, the trail descends easily to the edge of the marsh. The trail hugs the marsh for a short distance, with views to the right through pitch pine woods to the Nature Center. Then your path turns right to head uphill through the pine woods, but soon turns left at a trail junction and descends once more through the woodland to the fringe of the salt marsh.

You should note along here the abrupt changes in plant species between the salt marsh and the slightly higher ground adjacent to it. The marsh has few different plants, being covered mainly by *Spartina* grasses, but the nearby slopes sport a great variety of plant life, including pines, cedar, black cherry, black locust, roses, bayberry, bearberry, and Virginia creeper. Here, you are almost at the high-tide line; only a very narrow supratidal zone separates the high-tide level from ground above the tidal reach.

The Bay View Trail continues through pitch pine woods, where the thick carpet of bearberry invites you to sit for a while, enjoy the view, and think about the subtleties of habitat variations. As high tide approaches, you can watch the slow, persistent creep of the rising water as it reaches almost to the base of the slope on which you are resting. Out in the marsh you may see waders, ducks, green herons, and snowy egrets busily feeding or just pausing between flights. Beyond the marsh on the open water there may be fishing boats, which on hot, hazy summer days appear to hover, ghost-like, in the mist. The trees around you are stunted by exposure to fierce northwest winds that blow in the wake of coastal storms. While you sit, you may see warblers, kingbirds, and robins, and hear bobwhites, which monotonously call their name all through long summer days.

Although you may be tempted to linger in this delightful spot, eventually you will want to continue along the trail through the edge of the pine woods, where there are yet more views over marsh and bay. The trail gradually swings east into an area more protected from winds, where trees can attain greater heights. The trail crosses a small inlet of the highest supratidal marsh before reaching an intersection, where you turn left onto the Fresh Brook Trail. A few oaks mixed in with the pitch pines represent an early stage in a succession that later will lead to an oak forest if it is not interrupted by fire. The trail cuts through a narrow band of trees to an easterly overlook of the meandering stream channel of Fresh Brook. In the tidal lower reaches of this stream, saltwater mixes with the fresh. This valley once extended farther west when sea level was lower during the last ice age and streams drained from the edge of an ice sheet that lay to the east of Cape Cod. As the water from melting ice sheets again became ocean, raising its level, the lower reaches of the stream valleys were flooded by seawater.

The trail continues on a hillside overlooking Fresh Brook and passes through woodlands where oak becomes progressively the more dominant species. After dropping to marsh level and then climbing back up into the forest, the trail reaches a wooden bench and bends right into the woods. At the next intersection, turn left toward the Nature Center on a wide level trail through grass-carpeted pine woods. Alongside the trail you may see rattlesnake weed, which has purple-veined basal leaves and small yellow flowers. In a few minutes you will reach a road in the sanctuary campground. Stay straight ahead, passing the campground rest rooms on your right, and follow the trail that descends gradually across a meadow to the now visible Nature Center.

48

Marconi Beach

Total distance: 5.9 miles (9.5 km)

Hiking time: 3 hours

Maximum elevation: 55 feet (17 meters)

Vertical rise: 140 feet (43 meters)

Map: USGS Wellfleet (7½' x 7½')

Trailhead: 41°53'25" N, 69°57'56" W

Imagine surf breaking on mile after mile of white sand beach sandwiched between expansive blue ocean and a 50-foot-high sea cliff. Marconi Beach on the Cape Cod National Seashore easily matches the grandeur of this image. Limited access over the sea cliff preserves the raw beauty of the beach for those willing to walk for it. Your route combines a 2.3-mile walk along the restless ocean with one through dense oak and pitch pine forests and one to the middle of an eerie white cedar swamp.

Begin your outing with a stop at the Salt Pond Visitor Center, operated by the National Park Service and prominently located on US 6 in Eastham near Coast Guard Beach. The visitors center is open daily year-round and offers a variety of interpretive displays that can enrich your appreciation of the terrain you are about to traverse. From the visitors center, travel 4.9 miles north on US 6 to a road marked with signs for Marconi Beach. Turn right onto the entrance road and right again in a few yards for a 1.7-mile drive to a large parking area. A fee is collected by the Park Service during summer months. The beach is open dawn to dusk year-round.

Lock your car and follow a fenced walkway past the bathhouse to wooden steps that breach the sea cliff and descend to the beach. Walk north along the shore, in summer away from the crowds of sunbathers and swimmers near the lifeguard stands. You may choose your own path, but you will quickly learn that the damp, packed sand near the water's edge is least demanding. As you walk, watch how the waves approach

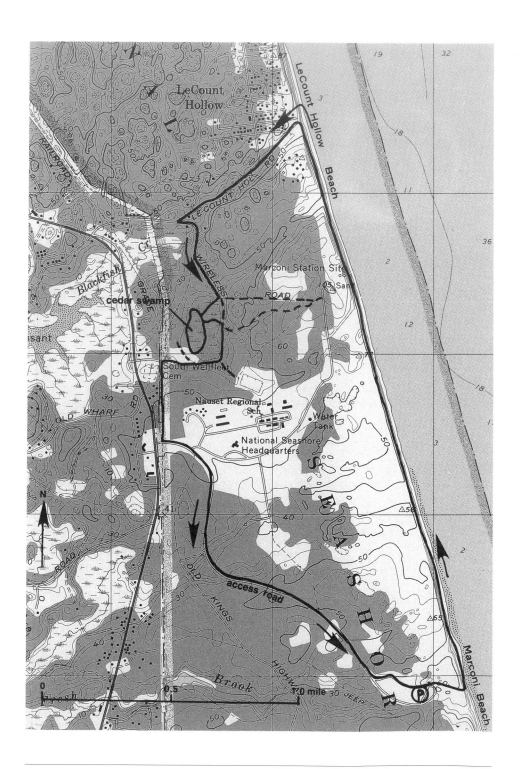

the beach. The direction the waves move depends on weather patterns, but waves seldom crest exactly parallel to the shoreline. Nevertheless, because each portion of the wave decelerates as it nears land, each wave crest swings around so that it almost parallels the shore for its last splash. "Almost" means that as each wave washes on and drains off the beach, it carries sand grains in a zigzag pattern along the shore, making the beach a slow-moving conveyor belt for sand.

Whether the sea is calm or spawning a crashing surf, your imagination will need no additional stimulus to set sail for far-flung adventures. However, if you wish to travel through time to before the dawn of recorded history, pay attention to the cliffs on your left that rise some 50 feet above the water. Exactly what you see will depend on when the last major storm struck the coast. Erosion, which occurs principally during storms, is rapidly eating away at these cliffs, causing their faces to retreat at the staggering rate of more than 1 foot each year. One advantage of this erosion is a periodic freshening of the exposures of sediment in the cliff face. Watch for a place where horizontal layering is clearly visible to approach for a closer view.

Like the cliffs at Great Island (Hike 46), the cliffs along Marconi Beach are built with weakly cemented sediment: clay, sand, and gravel. During the last ice age, when sea level was 400 feet lower, streams flowed westward from a melting ice sheet situated to the east of present-day Cape Cod and deposited the sediment you see today. Details of individual layers record features of these streams. For example, lens-shaped gravel pockets are cross-sectional views of former stream channels. Layers at a slight angle to the generally horizontal bedding reflect the movement of former currents.

If you brought a magnifying glass with you, look more closely at the sand and pebbles, both in the cliffs and on the beach. Most of the sand consists of clear, gray-to-pink crystals of quartz. White- to rust-colored feldspar grains are more abundant in the cliff sediment than in the beach sand. Feldspar is more susceptible to chemical attack than quartz and cannot survive the rigors of a beach environment as long as quartz can. Most other minerals are even less resistant to weathering than quartz and feldspar. A few exceptions stand out in the beach sand, such as the black magnetite crystals, which will adhere to a magnet. Pebbles in the cliffs provide clues to the original source areas for the glacial outwash. Coarsely crystalline granite pebbles and finely layered volcanic pebbles are common. Both could have come from the vicinity of Boston.

Where sediment layers in the cliff are hidden by slumped and windblown sand, you can discover the meaning of the phrase "angle of repose." Dry sand can sustain a slope of up to about 30 degrees; steeper slopes are unstable and will slump spontaneously. A footstep on a slope at its angle of repose will oversteepen the slope locally and cause a lobe-shaped slide of sand—a form of rapid erosion. Beach grass, with its tangle of long roots, retards erosion, as do other coastal plants such as dusty miller and beach heather. Trampling can easily kill these fragile sand-tolerant species, so travel is prohibited in many areas of the National Seashore. Where vegetation is lacking, cheesecloth has been stretched across some of the cliff faces to impede their inevitable retreat.

After walking for about an hour, you will see above the cliff a pavilion and overlooks that mark the site of Marconi Station. Here, Guglielmo Marconi erected an antenna and buildings for the first transatlantic radio

Sedimentary layers in the eroding sea cliff

transmission on January 19, 1903, a message from President Theodore Roosevelt to King Edward VII of Great Britain. Much of the original site has been lost to the sea by cliff retreat since that historic date. Your exit over the cliffs lies about 0.5 mile beyond Marconi Station to the north at LeCount Hollow Beach, which belongs to the town of Wellfleet. If swimmers and a lifeguard stand are not present to indicate where you should turn, you can nonetheless recognize the exit by a wide and well-trampled stretch of rust-colored sand. Stay to the left on the inclined path (to limit your erosional impact). Walk up to the paved parking area and follow the paved entrance road to the southwest.

Watch how rapidly the vegetation changes as you move away from the beach. Beach grass gives way to bayberry (smell the fragrant leaves), which gives way to pitch pine with an understory of bearberry. Bearberry has evergreen leaves, red berries, and red-stemmed runners. Scrubby bear oak, taller black oak, and an occasional white oak overtake but do not eliminate the pitch pine. You will pass Ocean Drive on the right and a private road on the left. Avoid the poison ivy that lies in wait beside the pavement. Beyond the private road, take the first road left, a 135-degree turn. Continue past two houses and a wire barrier proclaiming FIRE ROAD onto sandy Wireless Road. Amid more oaks, sweet fern grows, ready to perfume your fingers as you crush a leaf; bristly locust sports pink fur on its branches and lovely pink blossoms; patches of broom crowberry, which looks like a club moss, raise tiny green spires; and black huckleberry waves its yellow resin–spotted leaves

in the breeze. Stay with the main track, bearing slightly left at the first junction. At the next (five-way) junction, turn 90 degrees right onto a path that brings you to a boardwalk in 60 yards. (For an informative side trip to Marconi Station—and its rest rooms—bear slightly left and walk 0.4 mile due east on Wireless Road.)

When the boardwalk forks, turn right for a counterclockwise circuit of a cedar swamp. Because swamps are generally inaccessible, they can evoke a mystical feeling, much as if they were enchanted forests. Although this swamp is dark even on the brightest of days, sunlight peeking through moss-covered white cedars and red maples delightfully dapples the sweet pepperbush, inkberry, sheep laurel, and ferns that can survive the wet ground. At the next junction, turn right and follow the boardwalk past a bench and out to another sand road. Turn right, and at the fork in a few yards, keep right. At the next junction, turn right again, still on an old road.

At the first opportunity, turn left onto a less used path leading due west and slightly uphill to some power lines parallel to US 6. Turn left and follow the power-line sand road to the paved Marconi Beach access road, on which you drove earlier. Turn left and then right at the fork for a 1.5-mile walk on the pavement back to your car. Although this road can be busy on summer days, you may find the hard surface a relief after walking in so much sand. To foster dune stabilization, none of the paths through the dunes to the beach parking area is open to hikers. In summer, relief in the form of a brisk swim can be obtained near your car.

49

Felix Neck Wildlife Sanctuary

Total distance: 1.9 miles (3.1 km)

Hiking time: 1 hour

Maximum elevation: 22 feet (7 meters)

Vertical rise: 30 feet (9 meters)

Map: USGS Edgartown (7½' x 7½')

Trailhead: 41°27'26" N, 70°28'51" W

A trip to Martha's Vineyard makes you feel special. You're not just going to the beach, but to an island sanctuary somewhere truly away from the cares of the world. These feelings may be traced to the rite of passage by ferry and the thought that one cannot come or go at a moment's notice, or perhaps to the shortage of housing or parking at the beach. For a geologist, the feelings are compounded by the knowledge that Martha's Vineyard will have only a fleeting existence in geologic terms. The island owes its origin to a long pause in the advance of the Wisconsin ice sheet. While melting in this warm "southern" climate, flowing ice dropped its cargo of rocks, sand, and mud to form a moraine that gives the Vineyard its backbone. Unfortunately, this unconsolidated pile of rocks is no match for the erosional power of Atlantic storms and will wash away completely within the next 100,000 years. Nevertheless, there is still plenty of time for you to visit.

Felix Neck Wildlife Sanctuary of the Massachusetts Audubon Society is a special place on the special island. The sanctuary's 350 acres of shore, salt marsh, fields, and woods—preserved for wildlife and education—are yours for the walking. To get to the sanctuary from Vineyard Haven, travel 4.4 miles southeast on Edgartown Road toward Edgartown. The entrance, marked by a granite pillar, is on the left at the top of a rise. (If you're coming from Edgartown, travel 2.1 miles northwest from the Edgartown Beach fork on Vineyard Haven Road. The entrance is on the right at the top of a rise.) Turn left onto a narrow, sandy track

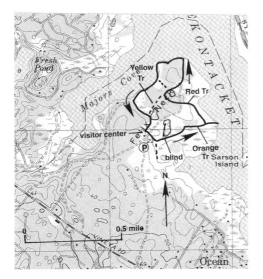

not go farther without learning its appearance. Poison ivy is a master of disguise, but the three slightly notched, waxy leaves growing on a separate stalk attached to a woody runner give it away in most cases. The other principal perils at Felix Neck are the insects, especially mosquitoes and ticks, and you should dress to prevent their making a meal of you.

As you walk along the path, you will see several varieties of oak, pitch pine, and cedar. Rabbits may share the trail grass with you here during twilight hours. A wooden blind has been erected near an enlarged pond to help you see the waterfowl. Like the other rocks on Martha's Vineyard, those lining the pond were brought from the mainland, although these were carried by boat rather than ice. At the appropriate times of the year, you may see Canada geese and mallard, pintail, or black ducks from this blind. Follow the orange-blazed trail to the right of the blind and across a small footbridge, keeping a watchful eye for the poison ivy growing high in the foliage along the path. Look for herons in the marsh to your right through thickets of marsh elder and pepperbush. As you proceed, pitch pine needles will soften your footfalls through a stand of trees that also includes scarlet oak.

With the salt marsh again in view on the right, you will arrive at a junction with the Red Trail. Your path is left on the Red Trail, but you may wish to follow the Orange Trail a short distance to its end at the shore of Sengekontacket Pond for a view of the winged inhabitants of Sarson Island, a tern nesting area. Binoculars will make this stop more interesting. Across Sengekontacket Pond on an arcuate spit of sand are Joseph Sylva State Beach Park and Edgartown Beach, which separate this tidal pond from Nantucket Sound. Sand and gravel moved by longshore currents from the eroding

covered by an oak forest that leads to a large parking area in 0.6 mile. Drive slowly and watch for birds, especially as you emerge from the trees into an open area where osprey poles have been erected. Full grown, these fish-eating birds have an impressive 5- to 6-foot wingspan. Even larger, at least in body, are the wild turkeys that occasionally forage in the same field.

Although information is posted near the parking area, you should walk about 100 yards northeast to the visitors center to find out more about the sanctuary. A small fee is collected from guests who are not members of the Massachusetts Audubon Society. Several trails marked with colored blazes originate at a pole on the right as you approach the center. The route described here begins with a walk southeast on the Orange Trail, across a dirt road and along a wide mown path. After crossing an open meadow decorated in August with orange butterfly-weed flowers, turn left at a junction to follow the orange blazes. Near this junction you will encounter the first of many verdant thickets of poison ivy. This dangerous plant is ubiquitous at Felix Neck and you should

On the shore of Sengekontacket Pond

promontories at Oak Bluffs and Edgartown built and maintain this barrier. The pond is filling with sediment and being transformed: The salt marshes at Felix Neck and elsewhere around the pond are the next stage in this process. Return to the junction with the Red Trail and turn right to follow the coast northward.

Eventually, the Red Trail leaves the coast, enters an oak wood, crosses an unmarked wide path called Old Road, rambles over a small hill, and descends to a junction that is the end of the Red Trail. Turn right onto the Yellow Trail, pausing for a short side trip right to view tiny Elizabeth's Pond. Keep to the right at the junction with Beach Trail. Keep to the left as you walk around a small, cedar-shingled building and across a clearing, following the yellow blazes. We saw a white-tailed deer here at midday in 1998. Note that the trees get smaller as you approach the water once again, a possible

consequence of the more severe microclimate near the shore. Turn left at the end of the Yellow Trail to walk the quartz-sand and pebble beach westward. A tremendous variety of rock types can be found among the pebbles, from granite to schist to siliceous volcanic rocks, a glacial sampling of resistant mainland rocks. Beach grasses are advancing over the sand and beach heather forms miniature, lavender-blossomed forests. Horseshoe crabs or their molted exoskeletons may be present, along with the remains of other crabs and mussel shells. Look for deer tracks in the sand.

A sandy beach with a roped swimming area signals the unmarked Beach Trail leading into the woods. Walk about 150 yards past the beach along a small marsh bordered by marsh elder, and turn left into the woods at a small point of land, the first opportunity. Unmarked Shad Trail is a bit hard to see until you get into the woods, where it is quite clear. Shad Trail will lead you to the Yellow Trail at Turtle Pond, where you should turn right. Sassafras trees grow along the pond at the junction. A boardwalk helps you across a stream that drains the pond into the salt marsh. Soon the Visitor Center will come into view, marking the end of your hike.

50

Caratunk Wildlife Refuge

Total distance: 2.0 miles (3.2 km)

Hiking time: 1½ hours

Maximum elevation: 165 feet (50 meters)

Vertical rise: 140 feet (43 meters)

*Maps: USGS Attleboro, MA (7½' x 15'),
USGS Providence, RI (7½' x 15')*

Trailhead: 41°52'26" N, 71°19'20" W

Birds and birders are notoriously heedless of state borders. Therefore, it should not be too surprising that Caratunk Wildlife Refuge in Seekonk, Massachusetts, is actually owned and operated by the Audubon Society of Rhode Island. Indeed, proximity to Providence ensures a strong Rhode Island showing at Caratunk. Visitors may be greeted by warblers, bobolinks, meadowlarks, kingbirds, woodcocks, pheasant, and grouse—just a few of the many residents of both states that find refuge here. Caratunk offers refuge to people, too, refuge from the cares of urban life while exploring opportunities to enjoy meadows and woods, birds and flowers, bogs and ponds, rocks and solitude.

If you are approaching Caratunk Wildlife Refuge from the north, locate the junction of MA 152 and the Massachusetts end of RI 15 in Seekonk; drive south on MA 152 for 0.6 mile and turn left onto Brown Avenue. From the south, Brown Avenue is on the right 2.3 miles east and then north of the junction of RI 114 and the Rhode Island end of MA 152 in East Providence. Travel 0.7 mile on Brown Avenue to a small parking area and visitors center on the right, just past a golf course. The 195-acre refuge is open daily from dawn to dusk. A small admission fee is charged to all who are not members of the Audubon Society of Rhode Island.

A map of the refuge trail system is posted just east of the parking area and to the right of the white converted barn that contains the Caratunk Education Center. Copies of the map are available in the Education Center. From the information sign, follow the mown path southeast on the edge

An open field near the Education Center

of a large field. Beware of the three-leafed poison ivy that glistens among spotted touch-me-not and various goldenrods along the path. Silky dogwood and red osier dogwood, both with leaf veins that parallel the smooth leaf edges, decorate the trail for a late-spring show. Flowers give way to bluish fruits to match the purple silky twigs of the silky dogwood and to white fruits to contrast with the red twigs of the red osier dogwood. Northern arrowwood, so named because Native Americans once used its shoots for arrows, grows near the dogwood and has similar blue-black berries but dissimilar toothed leaves. Following the first short path to the right will yield overlook views of a wetland and a forest stream, a quiet bench, and a short return to the mown path along the field.

Take the next right turn and descend to a footbridge over a small stream and the remains of a small dam. If you look upstream, you can see a wetland recovering from its inundation by the dam. Crush a leaf of the common spicebush growing next to the steps for a delightful aroma that easily

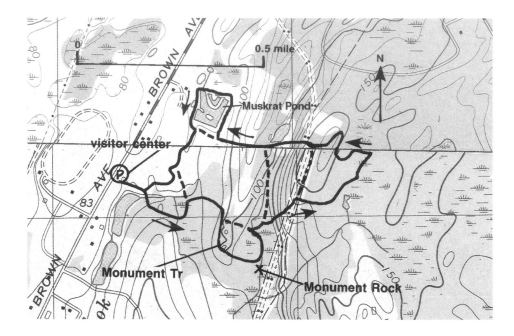

betrays this shrub's identity. Red oak, black birch, yellow birch, and white pine dominate the forest here. Towering old white pines have main trunks deformed into giant umbels by the growth-interrupting appetites of long-dead white pine weevils. The trail curves left as you approach a stone wall beneath the pines. Boulders near the next stream crossing (another small bridge) contain evidence of much more ancient waterways. Sand and gravel carried by 300-million-year-old streams were dropped, buried, lithified, eroded, carved into boulders, and moved a short distance by now melted glaciers. Look closely at these conglomerate boulders and you can see pebbles of granite and schist, along with the usual white quartz. The stream itself carries the orange-brown color and milky foam from vegetable tannins leached from humus upstream. Royal fern, cinnamon fern, and hay-scented fern thrive near the stream.

After the bridge, the trail turns left, passes a small forest of ground cedar, and follows a stone wall draped in greenbrier. A boardwalk helps you over some wet ground. In the middle of the boardwalk, just past a small bench, turn right and walk across some logs and a small bridge on a new trail. Skunk cabbage, sweet pepperbush, and red maple grow in the moist ground here. At the crest of a small ridge, past the corner of a stone wall, turn right, following the yellow blazes along the ridge. With layers (bedding) tilted to the southeast, low outcrops of the pebble-bearing sandstone, seen as boulders earlier, form the backbone of the ridge. Red cedar, bracken fern, ground cedar, running pine, and various mosses decorate the trail. Your route turns left to follow a stone wall and yellow blazes to Monument Rock. The monument is a large slab of the now familiar conglomerate, tilted on end and seemingly held up by a white ash tree that has grown against it.

Turn left (north) at Monument Rock, still following the yellow blazes. At the next junction, make a hard right turn and walk through an obstacle course of large, angular erratic boulders up to 10 feet in diameter, distributed from a nearby source by glacial movements. When you approach a small brook, turn right to cross it on a small wooden bridge and follow a blue-blazed trail uphill to a power line cut. If you haven't yet had a good look at the coarse sandstone and conglomerate, take time to examine the great outcrops along your climb to the power-line. The trail follows a stone wall as it parallels the power lines and then bends 45 degrees to the right, crossing beneath the wires through sun-loving sweet fern, huckleberries, and greenbrier. Turn left on the far side of the power line in the more open area over a gas pipeline. Walk about 100 yards, then turn right into the woods on the first obvious path. Continue straight into the woods following faint blue blazes downhill, then left along a stone wall. The path takes a sinuous route for no apparent reason. Keep to the left of an unusual V-shaped stone wall corner, cross a stone wall that blocks the path, and make a 180-degree turn with the trail as you near the border of the refuge and houses appear ahead.

You are now on a grassy road that leads west, back under the power lines and down into a small valley between two parallel ridges underlain and shaped by the layers of sandstone and conglomerate. More easily eroded rocks (siltstone?) must form the layers between the two ridges. You will cross a granite-post bridge next to the once dammed Ice Pond in the bottom of the valley, climb over the second ridge, pass a fencerow of silver maples adjacent to a field, and approach a large pond hidden in places by dogwood and autumn olive. Muskrat Pond is appropriately named, as you can see if you come at dusk and look carefully for the wakes of these quiet-swimming mammals. To get more views of the pond, turn right to make a counterclockwise loop around it with a white-blazed trail. Here we saw mallard ducks camped on a small island in the pond, scared several rabbits off the trail, and flushed a white-tailed deer. When you reach a large field, jog left past a graceful willow tree and follow a wide mown path on the left of the field. A trail enters from your left. Bend right with the path to follow a curving, high stone wall. Cross the stone wall at an opening and head for the white barn visible ahead next to your car.

Index